ENGLISH WORKSHOP

COMPLETE COURSE

HOLT, RINEHART AND **WINSTON**

Harcourt Brace & Company

Austin • New York • Orlando • Chicago • Atlanta
San Francisco • Boston • Dallas • Toronto • London

T   4 5 6   1 4 0 9   1 0   0 9

TABLE OF CONTENTS

GRAMMAR, USAGE, AND MECHANICS

PREWRITING: FINDING IDEAS

The first step in the writing process is finding an idea worth writing about. The second step is gathering the information needed to put that idea across. Writers use many different methods to discover and to explore ideas. The following prewriting techniques may work for you.

WRITER'S JOURNAL

A *writer's journal* is a daily record of your thoughts, feelings, and experiences. It can be kept in almost any form: a notebook, three-ring binder, folder, or computer. You don't have to worry about spelling, grammar, mechanics, or neatness in your journal. Your journal is just for you, to use in any way you wish. Try to write in your journal every day. Date your entries so that you can know, later, when the experiences recorded in the journal occurred. Here are some ideas for keeping a writer's journal.

- Jot down questions, opinions, feelings, conversations, and images— your own or other people's. Then reflect on your ideas.
- Record dreams, quotations, and interesting events.
- Describe your impressions of events and people.
- Create possible ideas for future essays from stories, poems, or songs.

EXERCISE 1   Planning Your Journal

On the lines provided below, describe your ideal journal. Would the paper be lined or unlined? Would the pages be bound in a book or loose-leaf in a binder or folder? Would the cover have pictures of your favorite person or would it be decorated with images of you and your interests?

_____

_____

_____

_____

_____

_____

EXERCISE 2   Journal Writing

Try keeping a journal for a week. Each day, write the date at the top of the page. Then make notes about whatever you have seen, heard, or thought that is important to you. You might write about an event, a line from a song, a news story, or something a friend said. Include your own ideas and opinions about what you have recorded.

FREEWRITING

Freewriting means writing whatever comes into your mind without worrying about style or correctness. Freewriting allows you to relax about writing and lets ideas emerge naturally. Follow these steps when you freewrite.

- Begin with any word or topic that is important to you. Then for three to five minutes, just write whatever pops into your mind when you think about that topic.
- Write down ideas, images, details, or associations that come into your head.
- Don't stop to think about spelling, grammar, mechanics, or proper manuscript form.
- If you get "stuck," just copy the same word or topic until an idea occurs to you. Or, write questions to yourself about why you're temporarily out of ideas.
- As a variation, try *focused freewriting,* or *looping.* Select one word or phrase from your freewriting and use it as a starting point to "loop" to more writing.

EXERCISE 3 Freewriting

Look through your journal and select one topic, word, or phrase. Freewrite about your idea for three to five minutes on the lines below.

_____

_____

_____

_____

_____

_____

_____

_____

PREWRITING: BRAINSTORMING AND CLUSTERING

BRAINSTORMING

When you *brainstorm*, you think of as many ideas as you can about a topic or problem in a set amount of time. Brainstorming can be done alone or with other people. To brainstorm, follow these steps.

- Set a specific amount of time for the brainstorming session. Five to ten minutes will usually be enough.
- Write the subject on a piece of paper or on a chalkboard.
- Write down every idea that occurs to you. If you're brainstorming in a group, one person should record the ideas.
- Work quickly, and don't stop to judge what's listed. Just keep going until the time is up.

Subject: shoes

Ideas:

1. new fashions for the coming year

2. how technology has changed athletic shoes

3. are expensive shoes really worth the price

4. buying shoes: is it better to buy from a specialty store that will help you make the right choice or from an outlet or discount store where you may save money

5. does advertising have a strong effect on people when deciding what brand of shoes to buy

6. what are the characteristics of a well-designed shoe

7. shoes in the twenty-first century: what changes may we expect

8. your favorite shoe of all-time and why

EXERCISE 4 Brainstorming

Working with a partner, choose a topic from the list below or choose one of your own. On the lines provided, brainstorm a list of possible essay ideas based on the topic.

soccer	Latin America	contemporary music
hurricanes	men and women	friendship
virtual reality	careers in the future	professional football

_____

_____

_____

_____

_____

_____

_____

_____

_____

_____

_____

_____

_____

_____

_____

CLUSTERING

Clustering, sometimes called *mapping* or *webbing*, is a visual kind of brainstorming. Follow these steps to create a cluster chart.

- Write your subject in the center of a piece of paper or in the middle of a chalkboard and circle it.
- In the area around the subject, write related ideas that you think of. Circle these ideas and draw lines showing connections between the words or phrases.
- Keep going. Write new ideas, circle them, and draw lines to show connections.

Below is a cluster diagram on the subject of music.

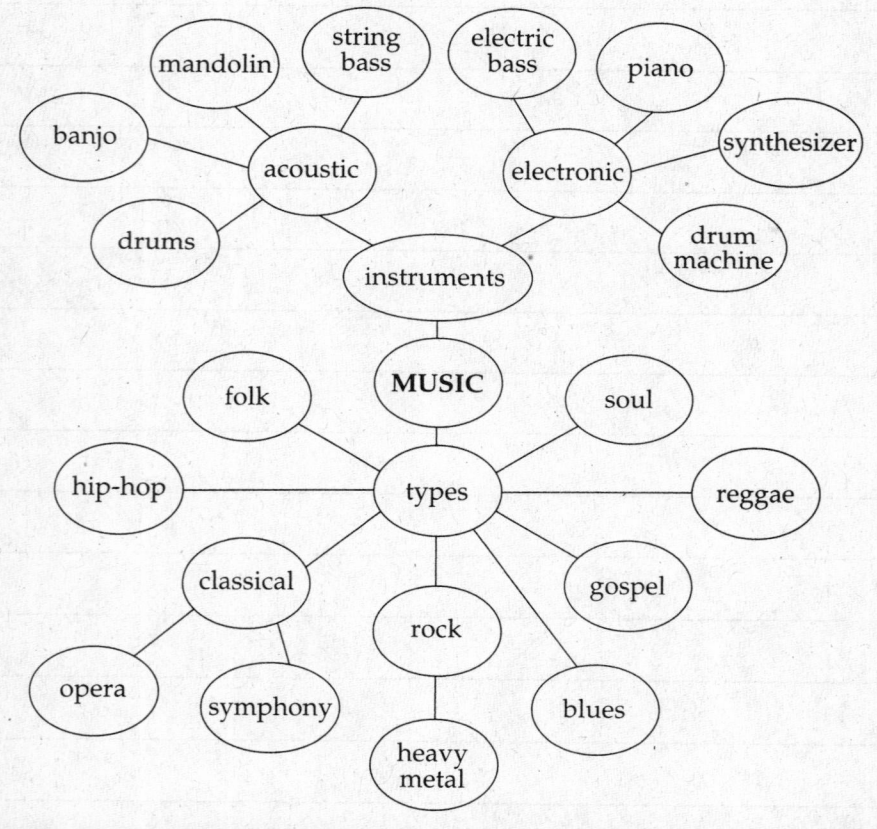

EXERCISE 5 Clustering

Choose another topic from the list for Exercise 4 on page 5, and make a cluster chart in the space provided below.

PREWRITING: ASKING QUESTIONS

ASKING THE 5W-HOW? QUESTIONS

In journalism, reporters are taught to ask the **5W-How? questions** to gather information for news articles. You can use this technique as you prewrite by asking *Who? What? When? Where? Why?* and *How?* about your topic. Consider the following list of questions about the creature *Sasquatch.*

- *Who?*   Who has seen *Sasquatch*?
- *What?*   What does *Sasquatch* look like?
- *Where?*   Where has this creature been seen?
- *When?*   When was the creature seen?
- *Why?*   Why is *Sasquatch* seen by only some people?
- *How?*   How do I find information about this creature?

EXERCISE 6 Using the 5W-How? Questions

Suppose you are going to visit a grandparent or an elderly friend. That person has lived through a historic event that interests you, and you want to find out as much about it as you can. Name the event. Then, on the lines below, write *5W-How?* questions about the event.

_____

_____

_____

_____

_____

_____

_____

_____

_____

OBSERVING

As a writer you need to *observe* the world around you with all five senses. Your writing will be much more effective if you can give sensory details about your subjects. Practice concentrating on and remembering what you experience with your senses—what you see, touch, taste, hear, and smell. Your powers of observation can be developed and strengthened with practice. Here are some notes that give sensory details about an autumn walk in the park.

- *Sight:*   red, orange, gold, and brown leaves, all clinging, falling, and fallen from trees; vast blue openings to the sky through bare tree branches; jacketed and sweatered people walking or jogging
- *Touch:*   tap of dry leaves on face; cool brush of fall breeze; soft flannel jacket on skin
- *Taste:*   tangy, sweet apple cider; salty, yeasty bit of a soft pretzel
- *Sound:*   rustle of dry leaves; scuffing sound of shoes pushing leaves; whisper of breeze in the branches; laughter of children rolling in leaves
- *Smell:*   sharp, toasty odor of burning leaves; hot apple cider smell from snack bar; rich aroma of toasted chestnuts

IMAGINING

The question *What if?* is another version of an expression that you probably used in childhood: *Let's pretend.* Pretending or imagining helps you think of creative writing ideas. Consider the following possibilities.

- Before writing the tragedy *Macbeth*, Shakespeare may have asked himself, "What if the Macbeth of my play did not have as peaceful and successful a reign as the historical Macbeth had?"

- Ray Bradbury, before writing "All Summer in a Day," may have asked himself, "What if it rained for seven years, and then a group of children saw the sun for the first time?"

EXERCISE 7   Observing and Imagining

Choose one of the following four subjects to observe: an animal, a room, some place outside, or a party. First, on your own paper, describe your subject using sensory details. Then meet with a partner who has chosen the same subject. Work with your partner, so that you each write four "What if" questions about the subject.

PREWRITING: ARRANGING IDEAS

Once you gather your ideas for writing, you can start to think of the best way to arrange the ideas to suit your purpose and audience. Here are four common ways of organizing ideas in writing.

ARRANGING IDEAS		
Type of Order	**Definition**	**Examples**
Chronological	Narration: order that presents events as they happen in time	Story, narrative poem, explanation of a process, drama, history, biography
Spatial	Description: order that describes objects according to location	Description (near to far, outside to inside, left to right, top to bottom)
Importance	Evaluation: order that gives details from least to most important or the reverse	Persuasion, description, explanation (main idea and supporting details), evaluation
Logical	Classification: order that relates items and groups	Definition, classification, comparison and contrast

EXERCISE 8 Arranging Ideas

Walk through a room that has special significance for you. Walk slowly, without speaking. Try to gather as many sensory details and ideas as you can about the room. Next, on your own paper, make a list of details and ideas. Arrange the details so that you can describe the room to someone who has never seen it. Then rearrange the details to describe the characteristics of the room that have special meaning for you. Finally, tell what type of order you used for each approach.

WRITING A FIRST DRAFT

A *first draft* is an attempt to get your prewriting ideas down on paper in a sensible order. You will probably write several drafts of an important piece of writing before you are satisfied. You will add and rearrange ideas, add supporting details, and remove unimportant or unrelated details. Here are some tips for drafting.

- Keep your prewriting plan in mind.
- Don't hesitate to change your approach or to add new ideas.
- Write freely, but clearly.
- Don't worry about grammar, spelling, or punctuation.

Here is a draft of a short paper on the advantages and disadvantages of life without automobiles. Notice that the writer has included notes and questions as reminders for later drafts.

Since cars became generally available (how many?) in the early 1900s, people have grown to think of their cars as family members, as friends, and even as romantic partners. Cars allow communities to expand by hundreds of miles. Without their cars, people would either travel more often on public transportation or spend more time in their own communities.

There would be many disadvantages to life without regular automobile travel between communities. Without regular exposure to other communities, people might become more suspicious and limited in their understanding of people from other places. Communities could become insular (isolated?). If a town had no Italian restaurants, the residents might never taste Italian food. If the school in a town had no music program, the people might not be able to study music. Job opportunities might be fewer as well, (Why?).

There would be advantages too, however. Air quality could be dramatically improved (give specific example). There would be fewer deaths and disabilities caused by auto accidents on America's roads and highways. People might walk more and be healthier. People would probably get to know their neighbors better than they do today. Life would slow down, and people might enjoy life more and feel less stress.

EXERCISE 9   Writing a First Draft

Using one of the sets of details that you gathered and arranged in Exercise 7, write a first draft on your own paper.

EVALUATING AND REVISING

EVALUATING

When you finish a draft, you will want to read it and begin to *evaluate* it. When you evaluate a piece of writing, you assess its strengths and weaknesses. You decide what changes should be made to improve it. You might use the criteria below as you evaluate your writing.

- The writing holds your reader's attention.
- The main ideas are clear, and details support them.
- The writing achieves your purpose.
- The ideas flow naturally and logically.
- Connections between ideas are clear.
- Unfamiliar terms are explained or defined. No unrelated details distract your reader.

Sometimes you will evaluate your own work; other times you and a classmate will evaluate each other's work. The following charts contain suggestions for evaluating work.

TIPS FOR SELF-EVALUATION
1. Gain some distance from your writing by setting it aside for awhile and going back to it later. This will help you see it more objectively.
2. Read your draft several times, with a different purpose in mind each time. Read first for content (what is said), then for organization (arrangement of ideas), and finally for style (the way you use words and sentences).
3. Read your paper aloud, listening for confusing statements and awkward wording. Besides forcing you to slow down and pay attention to each word, reading aloud gives you a good sense of your paper's flow—its movement from sentence to sentence and from idea to idea.

PEER EVALUATION GUIDELINES	
Guidelines for the Writer	**Guidelines for the Evaluator**
1. Tell your evaluator your concerns. Where do you think you need the most help? 2. Accept the evaluator's comments gracefully, without becoming defensive or argumentative.	1. Point out strengths as well as weaknesses. 2. Offer specific, positive solutions to the problems you identify. A criticism without a suggestion for a remedy may leave the writer feeling lost. 3. Be sensitive to the writer's feelings. It's true that it's not *what* you say as much as *how* you say it. 4. Focus your comments on content, organization, and style. Because proofreading comes later, ignore mechanical errors, such as spelling and punctuation, unless they interfere with your understanding.

EXERCISE 10   Evaluating

A.   Work with a partner to evaluate the following paragraph, using the three criteria below.

1. Is it interesting?
2. Are there unrelated ideas or details that distract the reader?
3. Are the ideas and details arranged in the best possible order?

> There are as many native people in Guatemala today as there were before the Spanish conquistadors arrived in the fifteenth century. Christopher Columbus may not have been the first European to discover this continent. Many of these people live in the Petén. In the 1960s, population in the Petén was 20,000; today it is 450,000 and expected to be 1.5 million by 2014. Native people make up almost 60 percent of the population in Guatemala.

B.   Write an evaluation of the paragraph above, using the Peer Evaluation Guidelines. Write on your own paper.

REVISING

Revising is acting to correct the problems you raised in your evaluation. The following guidelines may help you.

GUIDELINES FOR EVALUATING AND REVISING	
Evaluation Guide	**Revision Technique**
Content	
1. Is the writing interesting?	**Add** examples, anecdotes, dialogue, or additional details. **Cut** or **replace** repetitious or boring details.
2. Does the writing achieve the writer's purpose?	**Add** explanations, descriptive details, arguments, or narrative details.
3. Are ideas given enough support?	**Add** more details, facts, and examples to support your topic.
4. Are all ideas or details related to the topic or main idea?	**Cut** unrelated or distracting information.
5. Are unfamiliar terms explained or defined?	**Add** definitions or other explanations of unfamiliar terms. **Replace** unfamiliar terms with familiar ones.
Organization	
6. Are ideas and details arranged in the most effective order?	**Reorder** ideas and details to make the meaning clear.
7. Are connections between ideas and sentences logical and clear?	**Add** transition words or phrases (such as *therefore*, *for example*, *because*) or sentences to link ideas.
Style	
8. Is the meaning clear?	**Replace** vague or unclear wording with precise words and phrases.
9. Is the language appropriate for the audience and purpose?	**Replace** formal words with colloquial language and contractions to create an informal tone. Or, to create a formal tone, **replace** colloquial language, slang, and contractions with more formal wording.

Here is an example of a draft that has been revised, following the guidelines on the previous page.

> The ~~last~~ *nineteenth* century was a time of firsts in African American   **replace**
>
> journalism. ~~The first major African American poet was Phillis~~   **cut**
>
> ~~Wheatley, who published her Poems on Various Subjects,~~
>
> ~~Religious and Moral, in 1773.~~ The first African American   **add**
>
> newspaper, called Freedom's Journal, was *originally* published in New
>
> York City in *March of* 1827. The first African American daily newspaper,
>
> the New Orleans Tribune, appeared in 1864. The 1830s and   **tr**
>
> '40s saw the beginnings of two African American magazines,
>
> the Mirror of Liberty and the African Methodist Episcopal   **reorder**
>
> Church Magazine.

EXERCISE 11   Evaluating and Revising Your Writing

Reread the paragraph you wrote for Exercise 9. Using the guidelines in the chart on page 14, evaluate and revise your draft. Finally, rewrite your revised paragraph.

Hi & Lois reprinted with special permission of King Features Syndicate, Inc.

PROOFREADING AND PUBLISHING

PROOFREADING

Proofreading is a final check of your writing for errors in grammar, usage, spelling, and punctuation. Here are some useful techniques you can use as you proofread.

- Put your paper aside for a while. When you come back to it, you'll be able to see your mistakes more clearly.
- Focus on one line at a time by using a sheet of paper to cover all the lines below the one you are proofreading. Also, try beginning at the bottom line and working your way to the top.
- Mark changes by using the revising and proofreading symbols on page 17.

The chart below will refresh your memory about the types of errors you should look for.

Guidelines for Proofreading
1. Is every sentence complete?
2. Does every sentence begin with a capital letter and end with a punctuation mark?
3. Are all proper nouns and adjectives capitalized?
4. Are all words spelled correctly?
5. Are verb forms and tenses used correctly?
6. Does every verb agree in number with its subject?
7. Does every pronoun agree with its antecedent in number and gender? Are pronoun references clear?
8. Are subject and object forms of personal pronouns used correctly?
9. Are frequently confused words (such as *fewer* and *less, effect* and *affect*) used correctly?

To help you proofread, use the following symbols.

Symbols for Revising and Proofreading		
Symbol	**Example**	**Meaning**
≡	thailand	Capitalize a letter or word
ℰ	propper punctuation	Delete a word, letter, or punctuation mark
∧	the ⁿᵉʷ gallery	Insert a word, letter, or punctuation mark
	the new car	Change a word.
/	my Mother	Lowercase a letter.
∽	freqeuntly	Change the order of words or letters.
#	lemontree	Add a space.
◠	board walk	Close up a space.
stet	a fast trip	Keep the crossed-out material. (Write *stet* in nearby margin and place a dotted line under material to be kept.)
¶	"Yes," she said.	Begin a new paragraph.
tr	he walked slowly.	Transfer the circled words. (Write *tr* in nearby margin.)
⊙	Call me	Add a period.
⌄	Oh please come back!	Add a comma.

EXERCISE 12   Proofreading

Proofread the paragraph below. To mark the errors, use the symbols given above.

Marny and I built a tree house, for a local Head start center. It is the project I on for most of this year. Neither Marny nor I had ever built anything or done any carpentry. We got some advice from my father, who is a carpenter but we did all the work ourselves. The materials we had we were sturdy treated Pine boards, redwood stain, nails, bolts, and dowels. The tree house took three weeks to build on weekends and in the evening, and it should last for at least ten years.

PUBLISHING

Publishing is sharing your writing with an audience beyond your teacher. Ways to publish your work include

- sending letters to the editor of your local paper
- submitting articles to your school newspaper
- organizing a writer's group where you can share your writing with friends
- entering writing contests

When you are going to submit your work to others, you need to follow manuscript form.

Guidelines for Manuscript Form
1. Use only one side of a sheet of paper.
2. Write in blue or black ink, or type.
3. If you write, do not skip lines. If you type, double-space the lines.
4. Leave margins of about one inch at the top, sides, and bottom of a page.
5. Indent the first line of each paragraph.
6. Number all pages (except the first) in the upper right-hand corner, about one-half inch from the top.
7. All pages should be neat and legible. You may make a few corrections with correction fluid, but they should be barely noticeable.
8. Follow your teacher's instructions for placement of your name, the date, your class, and the title of your paper.

EXERCISE 13   Ideas for Publishing

Brainstorm with two or three classmates about the following three types of writing projects. List as many ways as possible that each project might be published. Have one member of your group record the group's ideas.

1. an essay about Cinco de Mayo, the Mexican holiday
2. a short story about your sister's basketball team
3. a letter of praise for a local woman who runs an annual food drive

USES OF PARAGRAPHS

DEVELOPMENT OF A MAIN IDEA

A paragraph is usually made up of a group of sentences that work together to develop a *main idea*. This idea can be either stated or implied. The rest of the information in the paragraph relates to the main idea.

> Pyramids differed greatly in construction. Egyptian pyramids were built with quarried stone or limestone blocks. Mayan pyramids were built of stone. The pyramids in Peru were constructed of adobe bricks. The early Egyptian pyramids had steps built into their sides, while the later pyramids had smooth, sloping sides.

In many paragraphs, like the one above, the main idea is stated directly in a *topic sentence*. The other sentences in the paragraph present details that support the main idea. In this paragraph, as is often the case, the topic sentence appears at the beginning of the paragraph. However, a topic sentence may come anywhere in the paragraph. Some paragraphs have no topic sentence at all.

OTHER USES OF PARAGRAPHS

In addition to developing a main idea, paragraphs—sometimes just one sentence long—are often used to (1) show a transition from one idea to another, (2) indicate a change in speakers, or (3) create visual appeal and make reading easier. As you read the following short paragraphs that might make up a newspaper story, notice the way the writer used these techniques.

TOT TAKES A SPIN

"I go for ride," said five-year-old Davie Davidson.

Davie's ride, alone in the family car, sent cars and pedestrians scattering out of the way on Maple Street yesterday as he reached speeds of up to 35 miles an hour.

It seems Davie has always wanted to drive a car. When he found the family car keys unattended on the kitchen table, he decided to take his first test drive.

Thomas Aguilar of the Washington Police Department reported that no one was injured. He added that Davie did manage to smash two mailboxes and dent the family car before he finally came to a stop on the sidewalk two blocks from his home.

"He's one lucky little boy," said Aguilar.

"We're just grateful that he's OK and that he did not hurt anyone else," Davie's mother said at the scene.

No charges have been filed against Davie.

EXERCISE 1   Working Cooperatively to Study the Uses of Paragraphs

Work with two or three classmates to examine the many uses of paragraphs you might see in a day. Check newspapers, ads, cereal boxes, bulletins, manuals, and magazine articles. On the lines below, make a list of the different uses, noting where you found each type. Include in your list at least one paragraph with a main idea stated in a topic sentence. Share your results with other groups.

_____

_____

_____

_____

_____

_____

_____

_____

_____

_____

_____

_____

_____

UNITY

A clear and effective paragraph has *unity*. All of the sentences relate to and develop one main idea. Nothing extra is added that might distract the reader. Unity is needed whether the paragraph states a main idea in a topic sentence, implies a main idea, or relates a sequence of events.

All Sentences Relate to a Stated Idea. In the following paragraph, the main idea is stated in the first sentence. The other sentences in the paragraph provide details about improvements that need to be made.

> The type and quality of food in space leave much to be desired. One of the problems is that astronauts don't have a cooking oven or refrigerator on board. The second problem is that there are very few fresh vegetables and fruits. Another problem is that the foods that are available do not provide a balanced diet. Many of the items are high in sodium and low in fiber.

All Sentences Relate to an Implied Main Idea. The following paragraph does not have a topic sentence, but all the sentences provide details about an implied main idea—a lack of understanding between people.

> During the 1991–92 sports seasons, Atlanta Braves baseball fans urged their World Series team on by doing the "tomahawk chop." To root for their team at the Super Bowl, Washington Redskins followers dressed in turkey-feather headdresses. Supporters of these actions described them as merely symbolic. However, American Indians claimed that these actions portrayed native peoples as savages, rather than as human beings with the same hopes and dreams as everyone else.

All Sentences Relate to a Sequence of Events. You won't find a topic sentence in the following paragraph. But the paragraph has unity because each sentence explains a main idea—the series of actions required to make a vegetable stir-fry.

> To make a delicious vegetable stir-fry, you will need assorted vegetables such as bean sprouts, water chestnuts, snow peas, mushrooms, carrots, and broccoli. You will also need fresh ginger root and peanut oil. Chop the vegetables into bite-size pieces and place the ginger root in the freezer. Heat a wok or deep skillet and pour a small amount of peanut oil into it. Begin cooking denser vegetables like carrots and broccoli first. Then add the other vegetables. Keep stirring with a spatula or a large spoon. Remove the ginger root from the freezer and grate it on top of your meal.

EXERCISE 2   Identifying Sentences That Destroy Unity

In each of the paragraphs below, underline the sentence that destroys the unity of the paragraph.

1.   Sweden is a land of great natural beauty. Nearly half the country is covered with dense forests of conifers and birch. The Swedes take particular pride in the ninety thousand lakes that dot the countryside. California is about the size of Sweden. The capital, Stockholm, is surrounded by water canals that weave through the city, leading to its nickname, the "Venice of the North."

2.   There seems to be no limit to the marketing of items with sports logos on them. Shirts, hats, and jackets with team names are everywhere. So are cups, glasses, magnets, watches, key rings, and belt buckles. Then there are clocks, wastebaskets, and lamps. You can even get license plate frames and a compass for your car. Stamp collecting and coin collecting are popular hobbies. Where will it end?

3.   Growing a plant is an emotional experience. There is something soothing about plunging your hand into dirt to plant a seed. Planting a tree can also be rewarding. It's exciting to see that first little bud burst out of the earth. One can't help but be thrilled to think that the plant will soon be full-grown. It's sad when a plant dies. It's almost like losing an old friend.

4.   The road runner, a member of the cuckoo family, lives in the southwestern area of the United States and in Mexico. The road runner is about two feet long, with more than half of that its tail feathers. Famous for its speed, the road runner has long, powerful legs that allow it to cover ground at a clip of up to 15 miles per hour. Another bird that moves fast is the ostrich.

5.   Each year, sometime in April, hundreds of thousands of female olive ridley turtles come to the beach along Costa Rica's Pacific coast. Each female digs a hole in the sand with her flippers and then lays more than one hundred eggs. Some of the first nests of eggs are destroyed as more females crowd the beach, digging holes for new nests. The waters off this western shore are usually warm. Scientists call the gathering of olive ridley turtles *la arribada* which means "the arrival" in Spanish. But scientists cannot explain *las arribadas* of these endangered sea turtles.

COHERENCE: ORDER OF IDEAS

A strong paragraph has *coherence*. In a coherent paragraph, the ideas are arranged in an order that makes sense, and the relationship between the ideas is clear. Two things help make paragraphs coherent: (1) the order you use to arrange ideas and (2) the connections you make between ideas.

ORDER OF IDEAS

There are four basic ways of arranging ideas to make their relationships clear.

Chronological Order. When you use *chronological order*, you arrange events in the order in which they happened. Chronological ordering works well when you are explaining a process or telling a story.

> Someone sneezes, releasing thousands of organisms, so small you cannot see them, into the air. You breathe in the organisms. One of these, a cold virus, enters a cell in your body where it produces many more viruses. The host cell stops manufacturing cell proteins. Instead, it builds viral proteins. These proteins then manufacture new viruses, which are eventually released from the first cell to enter a new cell and begin the process all over again. Soon, you have thousands of virus cells in your body. You have a cold.

Spatial Order. When you use *spatial order*, you arrange details according to location—near to far, left to right, clockwise, or any other reasonable arrangement. You use this order to help a reader "see" a place or an object.

> My room is my life. The bed backs up to the center of the east wall, between two windows. My nightstand and lamp are on the left side of my bed. Against the north wall is my dresser. I haven't seen the top of it in years. Directly across from the bed are bookshelves, which hold everything from my books to my trophies, and occasionally an article of clothing. The south wall is plastered with posters of my favorite actor.

Order of Importance. You can also arrange your ideas or details in *order of importance*. This can be from most important to least important, or vice versa.

> After seven decades of communist rule, the people of Mongolia are struggling to adjust to a democratic way of life. Today, the government no longer tells the nomads how many animals to raise or the farmers how many crops to grow. But it also no longer guarantees them an income. Gone, too, are the free health-care and retirement benefits. The people of Mongolia have traded security for freedom.

Logical Order. With *logical order*, ideas or details are arranged into *categories*, or related groups. In the following paragraph, details about two types of sculpture are grouped separately.

There are two types of sculpture: sculpture in the round and relief sculpture. You can usually view sculpture in the round from all sides. It can vary from small pieces that can be picked up and viewed to large designs intended to stand in parks, gardens, or other open areas. Relief sculpture is carved into a supporting surface, and can be viewed only from the front and sides. It is divided into two forms, low relief (bas-relief) and high relief, depending upon how far the relief projects from its background.

EXERCISE 3   Creating Order in Paragraphs

In the paragraphs below, each sentence is numbered. For each paragraph, rearrange the sentences in a sensible order by listing their numbers in sequence. Write the numbers on the line below the paragraph, and name the type of order you've used.

1. [1] The players walked onto the court, each knowing this was the most important game she would ever play. [2] Janell won. [3] The crowd held its breath during the final minutes. [4] Katie's first serve was an ace that sailed right past Janell. [5] Halfway into the second set, Janell was down two games, and she knew her only chance was to work the net and throw Katie off balance. [6] Katie took the first set six to three. [7] Janell's strategy worked. [8] Janell took the second set. [9] The third set went into tie-breaker. [10] Then, with a solid backhand shot to Katie's left corner, the game was over.

_____

2. [1] Your résumé gives a short but complete picture of your education and business experience. [2] Writing a résumé and preparing for an interview are two of the most important steps in the job search. [3] The interview gives you a chance to meet your potential employer and to ask questions about the position. [4] It also states your objective in the job search. [5] It also allows you to visit the company and see the actual working conditions.

_____

COHERENCE: CONNECTIONS BETWEEN IDEAS

In addition to ordering ideas, you can also create coherence by using direct references and transitional expressions.

Direct References. A *direct reference* refers to an idea presented earlier in the paragraph. Direct references can be made in three ways: (1) by using a noun or pronoun that refers to a noun or pronoun used earlier, (2) by repeating a word used earlier, or (3) by using a word or phrase that means the same as one used earlier. In the following paragraph, the direct references are in italics. The superscript numbers indicate the type of direct reference.

> A stalactite begins when rainwater clings to the roof of a cave. When the *rainwater*[2] *begins*[2] to drip, one drop hangs. As *it*[1] *hangs*[2], some of the *rainwater*[2] evaporates, leaving a small patch of calcium carbonate on the *roof*[2]. As time passes and more *drops*[2] occur in the same *spot*[3], a stony *bump*[3] and then a *point*[3] form. A *stalactite*[2] is also called a *dripstone*.[3]

Transitional Expressions. *Transitional expressions* are words and phrases that show connections between ideas. The following chart lists some frequently used transitional expressions.

Comparing Ideas	also, and, another, furthermore, just, like, likewise, moreover, similarly, too
Contrasting Ideas	although, but, however, in spite of, instead, nevertheless, on the other hand, still, yet
Showing Cause and Effect	accordingly, as a result, because, by, consequently, for, since, so, so that, therefore
Showing Time	after, at last, at once, before, early, eventually, finally, first, immediately, lately, later, meanwhile, next, often, then, thereafter, until, when, while
Showing Place	above, across, around, before, behind, below, beside, between, beyond, down, here, in, inside, into, next, on, over, there, under, up
Showing Importance	finally, first, foremost, last, mainly, more importantly, then, to begin with, ultimately

The following paragraph shows how transitional expressions are used to connect ideas. Transitional words and phrases are underlined.

> Dog lovers believe their animals make the better pets. Owners of cats, <u>however</u>, strongly disagree. <u>To begin with</u>, argue cat lovers, cats are cleaner <u>and</u> easier to live with, <u>and</u> they don't have to be taken for a walk. <u>Nevertheless</u>, say dog owners, dogs love to be <u>beside</u> their owners <u>when</u> they come home <u>because</u> dogs are affectionate. <u>So</u> are cats, say their owners. The two sides will never agree.

EXERCISE 4   Identifying Direct References and Transitions

On your own paper, make one list of the direct references and a second list of the transitional words and phrases in the following paragraph.

[1] The first president to serve a full four-year term in the White House was Thomas Jefferson. [2] When he lived there, however, it was called the President's House. [3] Although Jefferson was a creative and organized writer, he was disorganized when handling administrative details. [4] The table that served as his desk held important papers. [5] It also held his garden tools. [6] The shelves on his office wall had books, charts and maps mixed in with flowers and plants. [7] When Jefferson was alone in his office, he let his mockingbird out of the cage and allowed it to fly around. [8] He was just as disorganized when he entertained guests. [9] There seemed to be no planning ahead for dinner parties. [10] Nevertheless, Jefferson had such a productive mind that he could operate anywhere.

USING DESCRIPTION

Because paragraphs are written for different purposes, they call for different strategies of development. One strategy for developing a paragraph is *description*. In a descriptive paragraph, **sensory details**—hearing, sight, smell, taste, and touch—are used to create a verbal picture of someone or something. Spatial order is often used to organize descriptive details.

> Layers of grimy, black dirt on the windows kept out the light, giving the house a cold and ghostly sense of loneliness. A pungent, musty odor tickled my nose, and a clammy dampness settled on my skin. Each of my steps across the old wooden floors brought screams of protest from the rotting boards. Rats squealed and scattered across the floor. I shined my flashlight around the room. An old oak rocking chair stood in one corner. Beside it was a small, wooden baby crib. I felt a tear on my cheek as I realized why this abandoned house felt so lonely. This was once someone's home.

EXERCISE 5 Using Description as a Strategy

Choose two of the subjects below. On your own paper, draw two clusters like the one below to collect details for each topic. Focus on sensory details—details of sight, hearing, taste, touch, and smell. On your own paper, arrange each group of details in spatial order.

your favorite vacation   your best friend

a mountain   a concert

a store in your neighborhood   a swimming pool or hole

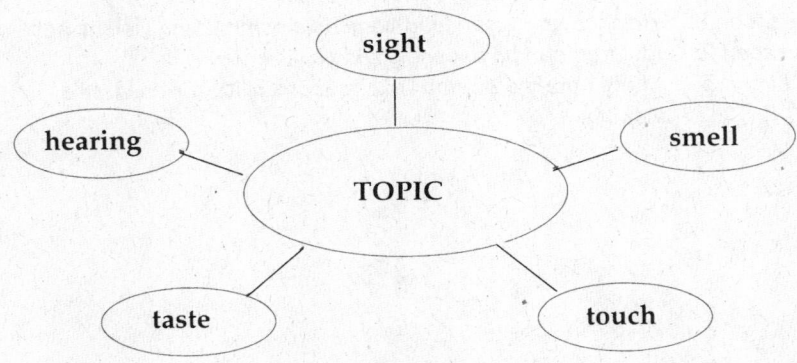

USING EVALUATION

Use the strategy of *evaluation* in a paragraph when you want to share your judgment or opinion with others. An effective evaluation is always supported by clearly stated, relevant reasons. Order of importance is frequently used to arrange these reasons.

> Many people believe that the United States should be less involved in the affairs of the world. This idea is not only short-sighted, but also unrealistic. First of all, the U.S. is still the richest, strongest nation in the world, and, as such, is obligated to assume a position of leadership. Second, the world is moving ever closer to a world market economy. The strength of the U.S. market affects every corner of the world and makes the U.S. a pivotal player in the world economy. Most importantly, the people of the U.S. enjoy an enviable way of life compared to that of people in much of the rest of the world. To ignore those who need our help would be nothing short of inhumane.

EXERCISE 6 Using Evaluation as a Strategy

For each of the three topics below, write a sentence on your own paper expressing your opinion on the topic. Then give two or three reasons to support each opinion.

1. a movie you have recently seen
2. a law requiring all eligible voters to vote
3. guaranteed free college education for everyone

EX.   Topic: Violence on Television
      Evaluation: Networks should restrict violence.
        Reason 1:   Violence on TV can lead to people committing violent acts.
        Reason 2:   Children can be desensitized to violence.
        Reason 3:   Many parents do not take responsibility for children's viewing.

USING NARRATION

The strategy of *narration* is used when you want to explain changes over a period of time. There are three ways to use narration: (1) to tell a story (my first formal dance), (2) to explain a process (how to grow tomatoes), and (3) to explain causes and effects (viruses in computer software). Chronological order, the order in which events occur, is often used to arrange details in narrative paragraphs.

Telling a Story. When you tell a story, whether it is fiction or nonfiction, you are telling readers about events that take place over a period of time. In the following paragraph, the writer uses narration to tell a story about meeting a new sister.

> The first time I saw my little sister, she was just one of about a dozen babies in a hospital nursery. She was three days old when she came home. Actually, I had looked forward to having a little sister, but after about six weeks I changed my mind. All she did was cry, eat, and dirty more diapers than I could count. I pretty much ignored her. Then, one day when she was just a little more than a year old, she looked at me, smiled, and said my name. My heart melted. We have been friends ever since.

Explaining a Process. When you explain how something works or how to do something, you are explaining a process. Just like the events or actions in a story, the steps or events in a process change over time. In the following paragraph, the writer uses the strategy of narration to explain how to make a good cup of tea.

> A pot of tea can be made with either loose tea or tea bags. Begin with a spotlessly clean teapot of glass, china, or earthenware. Use a kettle to heat water until it reaches a full boil. Heat the teapot by filling it with boiling water. Let it stand a few minutes, then pour out the water. Add the tea or bags to the warm teapot, allowing one teaspoon of loose tea or one tea bag for each cup of tea. Pour the boiling water over the tea. Let it stand for three to five minutes. Stir once, then strain the tea or remove the tea bags. Serve the tea with sugar and milk or with lemon.

Explaining Cause and Effect. When you explain causes and effects in a narrative paragraph, you once again tell the way things happened over a period of time. To make the cause-and-effect connections clear, chronological order is often used, with cause coming before effect. In the following paragraph, the writer explains the effects of actions taken by King George III.

In 1775, the American colonies had been fighting battles with the English. In August of that year, the colonists offered King George III the Olive Branch petition, which was an attempt to make peace. But the king refused to accept the petition and declared that the colonies must obey him. Because of this action, the American Congress resisted further British control. As a result, Congress eventually approved the Declaration of Independence on July 4, 1776.

EXERCISE 7   Using Narration as a Strategy

Follow the instructions for using narration to develop the lists below. Write your lists on your own paper.

1. Remember the first time you stood on a stage. List at least four events or actions (real or imagined) that happened.

2. You are teaching a group of eighth-graders about babysitting. Write out at least four of the basic steps of being a good babysitter.

3. Write down at least three causes that made you decide what you will do after you graduate. Then list at least three effects you expect as a result of your decision.

4. Your spending money is low. List three causes that explain why you have such little money. Then list three effects (or results) of having so little cash.

5. Have you ever taken driver education? List four events (real or imagined) that occurred.

USING CLASSIFICATION

When you use *classification* in a paragraph, you look at a subject as it relates to other subjects in a group. There are three ways to classify: (1) divide a subject into parts, (2) define a subject, or (3) compare and contrast the subject with something else. Logical order is usually used to classify material.

Dividing. One way to explain a subject is to *divide* it into parts. For example, the following paragraph explains poetry by describing the different types of poetry.

> Poets use different forms of poetry to write about many different subjects. Narrative poetry, for example, is used to tell a story. Homer used narrative poetry when he wrote *The Iliad*. Another kind of poetry is dramatic poetry, such as some of Shakespeare's writings. Lyric poetry, which is usually shorter than narrative and dramatic poems, may be written in the form of songs, odes, elegies, or sonnets. Blank verse, such as Robert Frost's "Mending Wall," is made up of unrhymed lines in regular meter with five stresses to a line. Free verse, on the other hand, is written without rhyme and with no regular rhythmic pattern. A famous poem written in free verse is Whitman's elegy on Lincoln, "When Lilacs Last in the Dooryard Bloom'd."

Defining. When you *define* a subject, you first identify it as a part of a larger group or class. Then you identify features that make it different from all the others in that class. In the following paragraph, the first sentence identifies the group to which "smell" belongs, the five senses. The rest of the sentences give details about the sense of smell that tell how it is different from the other senses.

> Of all our five senses, the sense of smell is the most valuable when it comes to the subject of food. Sometimes, smell is a warning system about food, such as when a questionable odor tells us not to eat something. Sometimes, smell arouses feelings of nostalgia that remind us of another time, such as when we smell spaghetti sauce or baking bread. And sometimes, the sense of smell is a clock that reminds us to eat even when we don't even know we are hungry. Yes, the smell of food can be more important than its taste.

Comparing and Contrasting. You also use the strategy of classification when *comparing* subjects (telling how they're alike), *contrasting* them (telling how they're different), or when both comparing and contrasting. The following paragraph contrasts apartments and houses.

Whether you prefer an apartment or a house depends on your lifestyle and your pocketbook. Apartments and houses come in many sizes. But you rent apartments and you usually buy a house. In an apartment, however, you don't have to worry about repairing things or mowing the lawn. When you live in an apartment, it's easy to make friends because you have so many other people close by. On the other hand, owning a home gives you more privacy, but it also gives you full responsibility for maintenance and repair.

EXERCISE 8   Working Cooperatively to Use Classification as a Strategy

Work in a group with two other students. Have each person in the group take responsibility for classifying one of the following subjects. After you've finished, share your results and discuss the strategies. Did the strategy work well? What difficulties did you have? Try to answer each other's questions.

1. Divide the category of sports by listing three different types of sports within the group. (What are three kinds of sports that use a stick and a ball? that are team sports? that have targets?) Give examples of sports in each category and then tell their characteristics in each category.

2. What is your favorite sport? Define it by describing its individual features and by telling how it is different from other sports.

3. How do you think sports of the future may be different from the sports of today? How might they be similar? Compare and contrast sports of today with sports seventy-five years from now.

THE THESIS STATEMENT

As you know, one topic may lend itself to many types of writing. As you focus on a topic and determine exactly what you want to say about it, you will be developing your *thesis,* or main idea. When you express your topic's main idea in one or two sentences, you will be creating a *thesis statement.* Consider these two thesis statements.

> **Thesis statement:** Stepping into the Palace Theater is like stepping into a golden fairyland.
>
> **Thesis statement:** The Palace Theater, a significant example of late nineteenth-century theater architecture and design, deserves to be restored and preserved.

A thesis statement serves two functions: it introduces the topic and it states a main idea about that topic. Both thesis statements have the same topic: the Palace Theater. However, the first thesis statement promises to inform readers about the theater's appearance, while the second attempts to persuade readers that the theater needs to be preserved.

Guidelines for Writing a Thesis Statement

1. **Use your prewriting notes.** Your thesis statement develops from what you already know about your topic and what you want to say about it. Think about your aim, or purpose, in writing. Look over the facts and details you've gathered. Is there an overall idea that ties them all together? What idea seems most important?

2. **Clearly identify both your topic and your main idea.** Your reader should not have to guess about either of these. Vague statements such as "I am writing about the Palace Theater" or "Old buildings should be preserved" are not as useful as the examples above. Such statements fail to give necessary information either about the main idea or about the topic.

3. **Revise your thesis statement as necessary.** Nothing is set in stone. As you find additional or new information and develop your ideas, you may wish to modify your thesis statement to reflect your new insights.

The thesis statement, which usually appears in the introduction, serves as an important guide for both the writer and the readers. Later, as you create a plan for your prewriting notes and write your first draft, your thesis statement will help you decide which details and ideas to include and which to leave out.

EXERCISE 1   Analyzing and Revising Thesis Statements

Both thesis statements below are too vague. On the lines provided, rewrite each thesis statement so that it clearly states the topic and presents a main idea about that topic.

1. This paper is about violence on television.

_____

_____

_____

2. This experience has taught me self-reliance and self-confidence.

_____

_____

_____

EXERCISE 2   Writing a Thesis Statement

For the topic and information given below, create a thesis statement that clearly expresses the topic and main idea. Write your thesis statement on your own paper.

Topic: Treating the common cold

Common advice given to cold sufferers:
"Take extra vitamin C."
"Get plenty of rest, and drink lots of fluids."
"Eat chicken soup."

Details

There is some proof that vitamin C can lessen a cold's severity and length. Of thirty studies concerning the effect of vitamin C on colds, just over half concluded that vitamin C reduced the cold's length. The remaining studies showed no effect.

Not getting enough rest during a cold may leave the body too weak to fight off secondary bacterial infections.

Liquids help sore throats and also help the body fight infection.

PLANNING A COMPOSITION

Your prewriting notes provide ideas and details for a composition. A *plan* helps you to organize these ideas and details for presentation to others. Writers use two types of plans—*early plans* and *formal outlines*.

EARLY PLANS

An *early plan,* sometimes called a *rough* or *informal outline,* gives you a rough idea of the kinds of information you want to include. To make an early plan, first group related ideas and then put them in a reasonable order.

GROUPING. Look through all your ideas and details. Group together ideas and details related to each other. Give each group a label that describes what its members have in common. Set aside details that do not fit in any group, but save them in case you revise your thesis later.

ORDERING. Ordering ideas and details involves two steps. First, order the information within each group. Then, order the groups themselves. Common methods for ordering ideas and details include chronological order, spatial order, logical order, and order of importance. Often, writers use more than one method of ordering information within a composition.

 REFERENCE NOTE: For more information on ordering details, see pages 23–24.

FORMAL OUTLINES

A *formal outline* uses letters, numbers, and Roman numerals to organize ideas and details. You may create a *topic outline*, which uses single words or short phrases, or a *sentence outline*, which uses all complete sentences. Although a formal outline is not necessary for every composition, it does provide a clear, visual way for you to check for sound relationships among your ideas. The formal topic outline below was created for a paper about job prospects for the twenty-first century.

> Title: Careers for 2000 and Beyond
>
> Thesis statement: The areas of health care, information processing, and high technology all promise new jobs for the next century.
>
> I. Reasons for growth
>   A. Health care
>   1. Aging population
>   2. New equipment and procedures

B. Information processing
   1. Rise of service sector
   2. Increased amounts of information
C. High technology
   1. Global competition
   2. Need for increased productivity
II. Areas of job growth
  A. Health-care jobs
    1. Home health aides and nurses
    2. Radiological technologists
  B. Information-processing jobs
    1. Information systems managers
    2. Equipment technicians
  C. High technology jobs
    1. CAD/CAM engineers
    2. Robotics engineers

EXERCISE 3   Working Cooperatively to Create an Early Plan

Listed below are notes for a composition on ways to help the homeless. Use these entries to write an early plan on your own paper. Work with a partner to arrange the notes into two or more separate groups. Label each group you create. Then order the entries within each group.

Teens can tutor homeless children in shelters with established programs.

After collecting used books and toys from their homes, from friends, and from neighbors, groups can donate them to shelters.

School and church groups can organize food or clothing drives.

Lawyers can provide free legal assistance to people in homeless shelters.

Teens and adults can teach reading skills to homeless adults at a shelter.

Tradespeople can offer their services to projects such as Habitat for Humanity.

School and scouting groups can raise money for local shelters by holding bake sales and service auctions.

EXERCISE 4   Creating a Formal Plan

Use the early plan you developed for Exercise 3 to create a formal outline on your own piece of paper. You may use either a topic or sentence outline format. Include a title and a thesis statement.

WRITING INTRODUCTIONS

An effective *introduction* serves three purposes.

1. It catches your readers' attention so that they will continue reading.

2. It sets the tone and signals your attitude toward the topic (friendly, critical, humorous, and so on).

3. It states your *thesis*, the main point you are trying to get across. A *thesis statement* is a single sentence that states this point. Often, but not always, your thesis statement will come at the end of your introduction.

WAYS TO WRITE INTRODUCTIONS

Writers use a variety of methods to create interesting introductions. Your choice of methods may be influenced by the topic, the aim, or the tone. Here are eight options that writers often use. You may use them individually or combine them to create your own unique first impression.

- **Open with a question.** Ask a question, perhaps one that your readers already have on their minds or one that might never have occurred to them. Your audience will keep reading to find the answers.

> What does the twentieth-century film *Star Wars* have in common with the ancient epic *Beowulf*? Separated by centuries, continents, and cultures, these two works may not at first glance appear to have much in common, but they do. Both works present mythological heroes who share many common traits.

- **Open with an anecdote or example.** Immediately involve your readers with your topic in a personal way by opening with either an anecdote, a brief story, or an extended example.

> In 1969, African American painter Frederick Brown heard Chicago blues artists Earl Hooker and Magic Sam play at a music festival in Denmark. When he spoke with them afterwards, he commented that they were more popular in Europe than in the United States. In reply, Magic Sam predicted that both he and Hooker would be forgotten soon after their deaths. However, even though both blues men died shortly after this conversation, Brown's series of portraits honoring blues musicians ensures that Earl Hooker, Magic Sam, and others like them will *not* be forgotten.

- **Open with a startling or unusual fact, idea, or opinion.** A new or unusual fact will raise your readers' curiosity and prompt them to continue reading in order to find out more.

> During their lifetimes, today's average U.S. teenagers will pay $100,000 in taxes just to cover the interest on the national debt. Currently, the national debt increases at the rate of $11,000 a second. Facts like these make the national debt every American's concern. The national deficit not only weakens our current economy but also hurts our long-term economic future.

- **Open by directly addressing the reader.** A direct appeal to your readers draws them into the topic and makes them feel involved. It also sets an informal, friendly tone.

> If you think your family received more pieces of junk mail than personal letters in the mail last week, you are probably right. The U.S. Postal Service estimates that the average American home gets 1.5 personal letters and 10.8 bulk mail pieces per week. If the amount of junk and catalog mail your family receives concerns you, you can take specific steps to reduce the quantity.

- **Open with a simple statement of your topic or thesis.** Sometimes the direct approach works best. A clear, direct statement can signal a serious tone and a desire to get started.

> Information from my interviews with women athletes supports findings reported by the Women's Sports Foundation. Participation in sports increases women's self-esteem levels and their academic focus.

- **Open with a description of a person, place, or object.** A vividly drawn word picture can make your readers feel that they are part of the action. It can also increase their knowledge of an unfamiliar subject.

> The box's lacquer finish, as smooth as glass, protects the intricately painted scene showing Russian peasant life as it was almost two hundred years ago. The paint's soft, refined colors work together, yet they remain distinct. This painted lacquer box is more than a memento, however. It is my only keepsake from my Russian grandmother. Its qualities remind me of her. Nonna was a loving, even-tempered woman who blended into a new culture while honoring her distinct heritage.

- **Open with interesting, specific details.** Details that appeal to your readers' senses—sight, touch, taste, smell, and hearing—help your readers to experience a subject more directly.

> The dew on the pickerelweed's lavender blue petals twinkled in the early morning sunshine. I knelt on the marsh path to examine more closely the two yellow spots near the flower's opening. Unfortunately, I was not the only one attracted to the pickerelweed's bright color that morning. The angry, buzzing bee that greeted me was only the beginning of the day's misadventures.

- **Open with your stand on an issue.** When you are writing a persuasive essay, a direct statement on the issue tells readers your opinion right away.

> Central High School should expand its intramural sports program. An expanded intramural program would allow more students to participate in organized sports, would offer students opportunities to learn "lifetime sports," and would increase students' physical and mental well-being.

EXERCISE 5 Identifying Types of Introductions

Identify the technique or combination of techniques used to catch the readers' attention in the following introductions. Write your answer on the line below each paragraph.

1.   Is the American dream dead? Tuan Huynh would answer, "No." After fleeing Vietnam with his family, Huynh came to the United States from a refugee camp in Indonesia. Ten years later, Huynh owned his own apparel-manufacturing business with annual sales of about $30 million. Huynh's story is not unique. Many recent U.S. immigrants are becoming successful entrepreneurs through a combination of ingenuity, sacrifice, and hard work.

_____

2.   Carved between 1,200 and 900 B.C. in Mesoamerica, the largest of the Olmec heads stands eleven feet high and weighs several tons. Along with fifteen other colossal head carvings, it serves as a testament not only to the Olmecs' artistry but also to their engineering and managerial skills.

_____

3.   You have a story to tell. To get others to take notice and listen to it, follow the strategies of professional storytellers.

_____

4.   Although proposals to widen the downtown streets currently seem popular, voters should not support them. Wider roads would create several problems in addition to those we already have.

_____

EXERCISE 6   Working Cooperatively to Write an Introduction

Work with a partner to write an introduction for a composition based on the formal outline you created in Exercise 4. Use at least one of the techniques for writing introductions presented on pages 37–39. Write the introduction on the lines provided below.

_____
_____
_____
_____
_____
_____
_____
_____
_____
_____
_____
_____
_____
_____
_____
_____
_____

WRITING CONCLUSIONS

If the introduction is your first place to make an impression, the conclusion is your last. The *conclusion* of your composition should leave your readers with a final thought and a clear feeling that the composition is complete. A variety of techniques can help you reinforce your main point as well as tell your reader that you have completed what you were going to say.

WAYS TO WRITE CONCLUSIONS

- **Restate your thesis.** An important idea is worth repeating. Use different wording to create a fresh impact, but keep the message the same.

  > For these recent immigrants, who are willing to contribute time, talent, and effort and to give up short-term gains for long-term goals, the American dream is alive and well.

- **Summarize your main points.** This technique provides readers with a final checklist of your important ideas.

  > You can reduce junk and catalog mail by registering your name with the Mail Preference Service. You can also ask that direct-mail merchandisers whose catalogs you do receive not "share" your name with others. A little time and a few sheets of paper can save both trees and landfill space.

- **Predict consequences or future directions for your topic.** Compositions that explore problems and solutions or essays that aim to persuade often end effectively with predictions, suggestions, or warnings.

  > For the present, following these home remedies and bits of popular wisdom may be your best hope for coping with a cold. Don't, however, give up on science. Recent research involving receptor blocking, immune system enablers, and new drugs offers exciting promise. We may yet cure the common cold!

- **Call your readers to action.** Calling readers to action in the conclusion empowers and involves them just as addressing them directly in the introduction does.

> Don't use the excuse that one teenager cannot solve the national debt. Study the issues. Decide where you stand on them and write your elected officials, expressing your opinions. Let members of Congress know that they have your support in making the hard choices. Remember, it is your money and your future, so it is your problem.

• **End with an appropriate quotation.** A striking quotation or one that echoes your thesis offers a strong finish. A quotation can lend authority to your ideas and let readers know that others share your thoughts.

> To those who favor wider streets downtown, Representative Tracey Wilson has the ultimate answer. "We have enough cars now," he contends. "Wider roads will choke our city." Wilson's comment highlights the fact that wider roads are unnecessary.

• **Refer to the introduction.** In your conclusion, a reference to something in your introduction ties the two "ends" of your composition together. It gives readers a signal that you're finishing what you began.

> Magic Sam probably thought his offhand remark unimportant. He thought that he and his music would be forgotten. But Fredrick Brown heard *and* remembered. Now, thanks to Brown's artistry, we can remember, too.

EXERCISE 7   Identifying Conclusion Techniques

Identify the conclusion technique or combination of techniques used in the following paragraphs. Write your answers on the lines below each conclusion.

1.   As I gaze at my box, it is really my grandmother that I see. I see a woman whose calm manner led her family safely through a crisis, a woman equally at ease with Russian fairy tales and the Muppets. I see my Nonna.

   _____

2.   The next time you encounter homeless persons on the street, don't be satisfied by offering them your pocket change. There are real actions that you and others can take to make a lasting difference.

   _____

3.   By shaping your story, using effective timing and gestures, and creating

a mood, you'll not only have your audience listening to your tales, you'll have them begging for more!

---

4.   Many think that the Olmec heads are tributes to individual leaders, but the heads also stand as tributes to an ancient culture capable of solving complex problems and designing activities in order to achieve a common goal.

EXERCISE 8   Writing a Conclusion

Write a conclusion for the following composition, "Careers for the 21st Century." Use one or more of the techniques mentioned in this lesson. Write your paragraph on the lines following the composition. After you've finished, share your conclusion with your classmates. What different techniques were used in your classmates' conclusions? Which seem particularly effective?

Careers for the 21st Century

What will be some of the best jobs in the future? Without a crystal ball, no one can answer that question with absolute certainty. However, based on current trends, experts suggest that the fields of health care, information processing, and high technology will provide growing career opportunities well into the next century.

Several obvious trends make these areas "hot" prospects for growth. First, an aging population, as well as new advances in medicine, science, and technology, indicates growth in the health-care field. Second, the U.S. economy in the 1990s continued to shift from producing goods to producing services. A major product of this service-sector economy will be information. More workers will be receiving information for daily work assignments on personal computers and will be using related hardware. This situation will require people who can manage information and people who can repair and maintain information equipment. A third trend is an increasingly competitive global economy. As a result of this competition, manufacturers will need highly trained engineers who can use sophisticated technologies to increase productivity.

Although most health-care jobs will grow in the next decade, job growth in some jobs will be astonishing. For instance, according to the U.S. Department of Labor, the need for home health aides increased ninety-two percent between 1990 and 2005. These aides, along with traveling nurses, care for patients who are able to recover in their own homes because sophisticated monitoring devices can link them to hospitals. The Department of Labor also predicts that the demand for radiological technologists will rise seventy percent in the early 2000s. These technologists use computer-enhanced radiation equipment to both produce images and treat disease.

As the service sector of the economy needs and produces more information, new positions will emerge. Information systems managers will be needed to choose and manage computer systems and design procedures for large companies and offices. They will be responsible for networking computer stations so that workers in many locations can share information. Of course, more computers, printers, disk drives, tape readers, fax machines, and duplicating machines in the workplace will require more training for workers and more repairs. Equipment technicians will be needed to handle these duties.

According to career specialist Carol Kleiman, engineers will lead the list of professionals most in demand in the early 2000s. Demand for computer-aided design (CAD) and computer-aided manufacturing (CAM) engineers will be especially high. These engineers will use computers to automate the design and manufacture of new products. Robotics engineers will also be increasingly in demand. They will further develop the sophisticated integration of computers and machines.

_____

_____

_____

_____

_____

_____

_____

_____

_____

_____

_____

_____

_____

_____

_____

_____

A HIGH SCHOOL REFLECTION

Your high school years are coming to a close. This is a major passage, a time when you not only look forward but also look back. It's natural to *reflect* on—to think about—such a significant four years. What memories stand out for you? What experiences changed you and how you view yourself, others, or the world around you? Writing about a significant experience in a *personal essay* is not only a way to recapture it. It's a way to understand it. In the following essay, a high school senior remembers a freshman experience and explores its meaning now.

The Music Lesson

Leland Sterne

I like football, but I'll have to admit that the band—not the team—has been the biggest attraction ever since I was a kid. The first marching band I saw was in a downtown homecoming parade. I was on my uncle's shoulders when they struck up a fight song about half a block away. Kids started clapping along, the whole crowd got excited, and when the blue and gold uniforms came into view, I was hooked. I probably started whining for a horn that day.

Of course, when I actually saw a half-time show, I got even more obsessed. To be able to play that great music and wear a uniform and make complicated patterns and get cheered—well, you get the picture. By that time, I'd chosen the trumpet and was making progress. Some kids I knew were in music lessons by force, but lessons and practice were never a chore for me. Music is just fun.

So, naturally, when I got to high school, I joined the band. Playing in the music room was terrific, with so many good musicians. We rattled the windows! Drilling on the field, though, was something else. I stumbled along all right at first, just learning commands and some simple patterns. But then we had to play. From the bleachers, blowing a trumpet while marching seemed natural: left, right, stop, turn, whatever—in rhythm. Ha! I didn't feel like I had two left feet; I had three or four. I just couldn't stay in step. I couldn't even play very well because my music was bobbing up and down. It was cold, too, and frozen fingers didn't help.

It also didn't help that the other three freshman got the hang of it fast. Every day they looked a little better, and every day I was the same. Near the end of one practice, I got so nervous I turned completely opposite to direction and slammed into a senior. She dropped her trumpet, stopped cold, and shouted, "What is the matter with you? Wake up!" That's still the most embarrassing moment I can think of. Every single person was looking at me, and my face felt like fire.

I came back only one more day. Two weeks: that was my whole marching band career. I said it really didn't matter; I could still play my horn. I even pretended that being in band wasn't so cool. But the truth is, I regret quitting to this day. I know people who made their best friends in band. They all had fun together, especially on bus trips. When they played at Mardi Gras, I sure couldn't say band wasn't cool.

It's not only what I missed, though. It's that I didn't have to miss it. Since then I've seen that most people have to struggle with something. Who's perfect at everything from the start? Besides that, you can ask for help. I've done it since then, from learning skateboarding to my summer job, building decks. I'm never going to be a master carpenter, but with hard work and help from the crew, I found out I could earn my wage and do decent work.

I could have asked the other freshmen band members for help. I could have talked to the bandmaster. I could have simply kept at it. And maybe I would never have been perfect at drill—but still good enough for the band. Now I'll never know. What I do know is this: When a good opportunity goes marching by, you should get in step and stay there long enough to see what you can do.

Thinking About The Model

The model essay was written to recreate one person's particular experience and to express his thoughts and feelings. How does the writer do this? How does he tell a good story, as well as explore meaning? Answer the following questions to take a closer look at the reflection.

1. Does the beginning of the model essay draw you in—capture your interest? If so, why?

   _____

   _____

2. The essay's beginning also provides background information. Why are the first two paragraphs a good preparation for the writer's high school experience?

_____

_____

3. Specific, sensory details make an experience much more real to readers. List three words or phrases in the model that involve your senses. What does the writer make you see, hear, or feel?

_____

_____

4. Expressive writing lets the writer's voice come through. The writer speaks as "I" and can use a personal style. Choose one phrase or sentence that shows the model writer's informal wording. Write it on the line.

_____

5. Throughout the model, the writer lets you in on his thoughts and feelings. What were his emotions while learning to march? After he quit?

_____

6. The writer chose the band experience because it was important to him. In your own words, why? What did he learn?

_____

_____

ASSIGNMENT: WRITING A HIGH SCHOOL REFLECTION

Write about one experience that made a difference to you while you were in high school. Bring the experience to life for your readers, and be sure to make clear why it was important.

Prewriting

What high school experience has special significance for you? It doesn't have to be as dramatic or unusual as winning a competition. It could be simple or everyday—like a class that helped you overcome a problem. The following steps will help you choose an experience and develop it.

Step 1:   You may know immediately what you want to write about: Some life-changing events are hard to miss. But if not, you can start from general areas like these below and see what they call up from your high school years:

- **people:** friends, enemies, teachers, coaches, family
- **emotions:** fear, disappointment, pride, surprise, insecurity, frustration, triumph
- **places:** classrooms, playing fields, laboratories, offices, computer lab, the gymnasium, the auditorium
- **values:** maturity, responsibility, honesty, friendship, loyalty, sacrifice, skill, leadership

On the following lines, brainstorm specific experiences from your own life, taking off from the suggestions above. List every idea that comes to mind now, even if it seems small or if you don't know why you've thought of it. Don't edit yourself; just jot notes until you're out of ideas.

_____

_____

_____

_____

_____

_____

_____

_____

_____

_____

_____

_____

_____

Step 2:   Choose one experience from your list to write about. Here are three "test questions" to help you decide whether an experience will make a good reflection paper:

- Do you feel comfortable sharing the experience?
- Can you remember the experience in detail: Is it vivid in your memory?
- Does the experience have personal, important meaning for you?

Choose an experience that gets a "yes" to each question. (Brainstorm more experiences if necessary.) Write your final topic here.

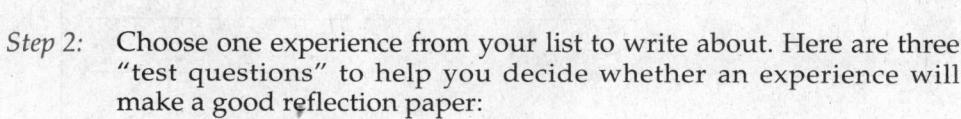

Step 3:   Now start gathering details by replaying the experience in your memory. You want to give readers clear, sharp details about

- **what happened** (the events, or stages, of the experience, in order)
- any important **people** involved (who are they? what do they look, act, sound like?)
- any significant **settings** (what did the place look like—or even smell like?)
- your own **thoughts, feelings, and reactions**

Use the chart on page 50 to record details. Your particular experience will determine whether you have a lot of details about people, for example, or just a few. But make details specific and distinct: touch readers' senses. When you've finished, write one phrase or sentence that explains why the experience was important: how you changed, what you learned, or any insight you gained.

WHO OR WHAT?	DETAILS
Events	

Thoughts and feelings

During the experience: _____

After the experience: _____

The importance of the experience

Writing

A first draft is simply a way to get your thoughts down on paper. Use the information from your prewriting chart to draft your essay, but don't hesitate to include additional thoughts or details that occur to you. This plan will help guide your writing.

Beginning	• Stir readers' attention: make them want to read on • Give any background information that readers need to understand the experience

Middle	• Present events in the order in which they happened. Use transitional words such as *then, when, the next day, later* so that readers can easily follow the experience. • Use vivid details that appeal to the senses. • Weave your thoughts and feelings into your narration and descriptions.

Ending	• Draw a final conclusion about what the experience meant to you. Go beyond flat statements like "I learned what maturity really meant." Add a final example, a quotation, a look to the future: a fresh and satisfying close.

Evaluating and Revising

Unfortunately, you can't relive experiences. You can't repeat a great high school moment—so that you would enjoy it even more. You can't repeat a bad one either—so that you would make it turn out differently. You *can*, however, shape, change, and improve your draft essay until it's just as you want it. You *evaluate* its strengths and weaknesses and *revise* until no weaknesses are left. You'll use the following **Questions for Evaluation** to revise a classmate's and your own essay.

Questions for Evaluation

1. Does the beginning grab the reader's attention? Does it introduce the experience and give background information if necessary? If not, what can be added or changed?

    _____

    _____

2. Does the essay reflect on one experience? Does it clearly present what happened? If not, what unnecessary details can be cut? What details can be added or reordered to clarify events?

    _____

    _____

3. Are vivid sensory details used to describe events, people, and places? If not, what details can be replaced or added?

    _____

    _____

4. Are the writer's thoughts and feelings included? If not, where can they be added?

    _____

    _____

5. Does the essay close in a satisfying way? Is the importance of the experience clear? If not, what details or observations can show how the writer changed or what the writer learned?

    _____

    _____

Peer Evaluation

Exchange rough drafts with a classmate, and follow these steps.

Step 1:   Read the draft carefully. Don't focus only on the writer's feelings. That is, pay attention to *how well* as well as to *what* the writer has written. At this point, though, don't worry about mechanical mistakes.

Step 2:   Offer specific, positive solutions to the problems you identify.

Step 3:   Answer the **Questions for Evaluation** in writing.

Self-Evaluation

Use these steps to evaluate your own rough draft.

Step 1:   Read your classmate's evaluation of your paper. Mark any comments you want to use or think about. You may want to have a discussion with the reviewer, too.

Step 2:   Read your draft twice, with a different purpose in mind each time. Read first for what is said and a second time for how your ideas are arranged.

Step 3:   Because the subject of the essay is you, objectivity is hard. But try to read as someone who has *not* lived the experience. Answer the **Questions for Evaluation** for your own draft.

Now use both your and your classmate's evaluations to revise your paper. Don't hesitate to make major changes or to go back to prewriting steps. Keep revising until you answer all the **Questions for Evaluation** with "yes."

 # Proofreading and Publishing

Step 1:   Check your paper for spelling errors, and correct them. Reading backwards from the end of the paper or from right to left of each line makes each word stand out clearly. If a spelling even looks suspicious, check a dictionary. For help with spelling problems, see Chapter 24.

Step 2:   Check for and correct errors in grammar, mechanics, and usage. Refer to the **Guidelines for Proofreading** on page 16.

Step 3:   Make a clean copy of your revised and proofread essay.

Step 4:   Publish your reflection in some way. Even if, because it's personal, you don't want to share it with a wide audience, you can share it selectively. Here are possible ideas.

A. Show the reflection to someone who played an important role in the experience you wrote about.

B. Make a class collection of high school reflections, and share it with first-year students. Each writer could have the option of being "anonymous" by covering his or her name.

C. Make a book of the essays written by your special friends in class, and duplicate it so that each person has a copy. Create a cover that identifies your graduating class. You may want to reread the memories at each high school reunion.

FOR YOUR PORTFOLIO

Put your responses to these questions in your portfolio with your reflective essay.

1. What did you know at the end of writing this essay that you didn't know when you started?

2. For this assignment, you identified a special experience of your high school years. What if you had to choose an object or a place rather than an experience? What would it be, and why is it significant?

Shoe, by Jeff MacNelly, reprinted by permission: Tribune Media Services.

A TELEVISION SCRIPT

When you're watching your favorite TV series, you're probably not thinking about written words: you're watching and listening. Yet every situation comedy, action series, or drama starts with a written story, in the special form of a *television script,* or *screenplay.*

Just from watching TV, you probably know more than you think about writing stories for television. In this chapter, you'll combine that knowledge with special scriptwriting skills. As you write the opening of a television program, you'll not only exercise your creativity but also gain insight into how the shows you watch are made.

For example, a situation comedy usually runs twenty minutes (allowing ten minutes for commercials). The first three to five minutes set up a *central conflict,* or problem, faced by the main character or characters. The next ten minutes build this conflict to a high point, or *climax.* The remaining time *resolves,* or ends, the conflict. Here is a student's script for the first segment of a situation comedy. (As you read, don't worry about unfamiliar technical terms or abbreviations. They'll be explained later, and you can follow what's happening without them.)

Dog Tired

by

Corinna Russell

SFX DOGS AND CATS

C-U OF POSTER READING "PLEASANT VALLEY HUMANE SOCIETY: ADOPT A PURR-FECT COMPANION TODAY"

PULL BACK TO INT. FRONT OFFICE OF AN ANIMAL SHELTER

SFX DOORBELL CHIMES

A RED-FACED MR. MARKOWITZ ENTERS, LEADING A TAME-LOOKING, ADORABLE ENGLISH SPRINGER SPANIEL ON A LEASH. MARKOWITZ IS WEARING A SUIT WITH A TORN JACKET AND PANTS LEG. SANDRA, THE HUMANE SOCIETY CLERK, GETS UP FROM HER DESK AND MEETS MARKOWITZ AT THE DOOR. SANDRA IS YOUNG, CHATTY, BRIGHTLY DRESSED.

SANDRA Gee, Mr. Markowitz. I didn't expect to see you back. Is something wrong?

MARKOWITZ (OBVIOUSLY UPSET) Wrong? No. I put all my clothes through a food processor before wearing them. Look at this suit. It cost three hundred dollars. You see anything wrong with it?

SANDRA Well, I don't know how to say this tactfully, but it's not really your color. I mean, forest green's a fall color. You're more of a winter. You know, with your dark hair and pale skin. You'd probably look better in blue or gray. Yeah, gray. Gray's good for a pale face.

MARKOWITZ *(POINTING TO HIS FACE)* Look at this face. This is not a pale face. This is a red face, a crimson face. It is a face the color of a radish. And do you know why my face has this particular color?

SANDRA *(LOOKS WITH CLOSER ATTENTION)* Oh, you're right. Now, Mr. Markowitz *(SHAKING HER FINGER AT HIM)*, you can't just stop being a winter with one visit to a tanning booth. You're burned!

MARKOWITZ *(EXPLODES)* You bet I am! This dog destroyed my suit and tried to destroy the rest of my life. It is a vicious, uncontrollable beast, and I'm bringing it back.

C-U OF SPRINGER SPANIEL, LYING PEACEFULLY WITH HEAD RESTING ON PAWS

CUT TO SANDRA, LOOKING DOWN AT DOG

SANDRA Certainly looks like a killer.

PULL BACK TO BOTH CHARACTERS

MARKOWITZ He's acting.

SANDRA Acting?

MARKOWITZ Yes. He's pretending to be a mild-mannered English Springer Spaniel, but really he's Godzilla with floppy ears.

SANDRA What exactly did the dog do, Mr. Markowitz? *(TRACK AS SHE GOES TO DESK AND SITS)* If you're going to return him, I'll have to fill out a report.

MARKOWITZ *(FOLLOWING HER)* He chewed up my three-hundred-dollar suit. *(HELPLESSLY)* Why would a dog chew up a three-hundred-dollar suit?

SANDRA Well, he's a dog. I mean, you can't expect him to understand about prices and things. *(TAKING PEN AND PAPER)* When did this happen?

MARKOWITZ Yesterday afternoon. After the paint.

SANDRA *(STOPS WRITING)* What paint?

MARKOWITZ I had these painters in, redoing the kitchen. He knocked over a paint can and he stepped in the paint. Then he tracked the paint all over the living room. *(SITS DOWN IN CHAIR NEXT TO DESK, HEAD IN HANDS)* My living room carpet is now pink with a white paw-print motif.

ANGLE ON SANDRA

SANDRA Sounds kinda nice. Too bad it wasn't a little girl's room or something. (*PAUSE*) Pink and white are spring colors, you know. Cheerful.

MARKOWITZ LEANS IN CLOSE TO SANDRA, STARTLING HER.

MARKOWITZ Well, here's something cheerful for you. I'm going to spring a bill on you for the carpet cleaning. And the suit. And the eighteen roses he dug up in the garden. And for the psychiatrist.

SANDRA Psychiatrist?

MARKOWITZ My neighbor, Mrs. Peabody. She says that the dog drove her cat Sprinkles crazy. And now she's got to take the cat to one of those pet shrinks over in Beverly Hills.

PULL BACK TO SHOW WHOLE OFFICE

SANDRA That's sweet. (*SHE RISES, WALKS TO SPANIEL, PETS IT AFFECTIONATELY*) You know, we like to see people take care of their animals' emotional needs. (*TAKES LEASH*) Get up, boy. (*DOG RISES OBEDIENTLY*)

CUT TO MARKOWITZ, WHO BOLTS OUT OF CHAIR AND GETS BEHIND IT. PULL BACK.

SANDRA It's okay, Mr. Markowitz. I'll hold the beast while you leave.

CUT TO INT. BREAKFAST TABLE. FATHER, MOTHER, AND TWO CHILDREN EATING CEREAL.

FATHER No. I will not have a dog in this house. They smell. (*PUTS NEWSPAPER IN FRONT OF FACE AND READS*)

MOTHER Not if you bathe them, dear. You would smell too if you didn't take a bath.

CHILDREN START TO LAUGH. MOTHER GIVES WARNING HEAD SHAKE.

FATHER (*LOOKS OVER PAPER*) And they slobber. And they bark. And you have to walk them and feed them and use those awful scoopers.

CHILDREN (*IN UNISON*) Please. We'll take care of him. You won't have to do a thing.

MOTHER Honey, I promised. Suppose we get a really quiet, gentle, easy-going dog that doesn't require a lot of work.

FATHER Great idea. A stuffed dog would be perfect. You know, with the little buttons for eyes.

CHILDREN But Daddy . . .

FATHER (*GIVING UP THE FIGHT*) Okay. But if there are any problems—any problems at all—the dog goes. You understand me?

CHILDREN (*JUMPING UP TO HUG FATHER*) Thank you, Daddy!

CUT TO INT. ANIMAL SHELTER OFFICE. MOTHER IS TALKING TO A DIFFERENT CLERK, JOEY.

SFX DOGS AND CATS

JOEY Let's see. Quiet. Easy-going. No trouble. You know, I think I've got just the dog for you. (*GOES THROUGH DOOR INTO SHELTER AND LEADS OUT MARKOWITZ'S EX-DOG*) What do you think? He's even had all his shots.

C-U OF DOG, LYING PEACEFULLY WITH HEAD RESTING ON PAWS

MOTHER He's perfect!

FADE OUT ON DOG

Thinking About the Model

This model is the opening of a comedy script. The writer created several characters and two settings (an animal shelter and a breakfast table). While your script may be very different—perhaps shorter, more action-oriented, or limited to one location—the model script gives helpful examples of scriptwriting *elements.* Answer the questions below to see how the writer created a script for a story.

1. *Dialogue* in a script, the words spoken by characters or a narrator, is not enclosed in quotation marks. In the model, how does the writer indicate dialogue for different characters?

   _____

2. Dialogue is crucial to television storytelling for several reasons. For example, background information may be given in dialogue rather than in a visual scene. Give one example of Mr. Markowitz's dialogue that tells you what the spaniel has done.

   _____

   Dialogue also shows characters' personalities, because people have different speaking styles. In the model, give one example of Sandra's very casual, informal language.

   _____

Dialogue also shows emotions or mood. Give one example from Sandra's dialogue of her sarcastic (and humorous) attitude toward Mr. Markowitz.

_____

3. Besides dialogue, a script contains writing called *stage directions*, or *set directions*. The directions give information to the director, actors, camera operators, crew, and set designers. How are the set directions typed in the model script to show that they are not dialogue?

_____

4. Set directions supply many different kinds of information. Find one example in the model script of each type of information that follows. Copy the direction on the line below.

   A setting (location): _____

   A character's costume: _____

   A character's emotion or reaction: _____

   An object a character uses: _____

   How or where a character should move: _____

   A change in camera position: _____

5. The model script's set directions use the special *jargon,* or technical language, of television writing, as well as standard abbreviations. A *CUT*, for example, means "a quick change from one scene or camera shot to another." *INT.* stands for "interior" (an indoor scene). *SFX* stands for "sound effect." *C-U* stands for "close-up," a camera shot in very close range of the subject. Find one example in the model for each jargon word or abbreviation below, and copy it on the line provided.

   CUT: _____

   INT.: _____

   SFX: _____

   C-U: _____

6. The first part of a television comedy or drama sets up a *conflict,* or problem, to be developed in the second part. What conflict do you expect will be developed in the second part of the model screenplay?

_____

_____

ASSIGNMENT: WRITING A TELEVISION SCRIPT

Write an introductory scene for a television program of your choice: situation comedy, drama, science fiction, or action. You'll use basic storytelling elements of character, dialogue, and conflict. You'll also write set directions that describe sounds, setting, characters, and camera work. As you write, think about your *viewers* and *listeners:* your audience. Set up a problem—in dialogue, action, and visual pictures—that will really hook viewers into staying tuned.

Prewriting

To get ideas for your script, think of the television programs you enjoy. Do you like comedies with offbeat characters? outdoor adventures? detective or police stories? or dramas about high school students? Use these steps to stimulate your ideas.

Step 1:   Television programs are often developed around particular places or a person with a particular occupation. For example, a program might be set in a television newsroom or a space station. The main character may be a model or a football coach. *Brainstorm* with a classmate to come up with possibilities, and write them below. Some starting ideas are given.

Places	**Occupations**
A car rental shop that rents "junkers"	An airline pilot or steward
A fast-food restaurant	A summer camp counselor
A top-secret experimental laboratory on the ocean floor	A girls' basketball coach
_____	_____
_____	_____
_____	_____

Step 2:   Choose the one idea you'll write about. Remember that you need both a *main character* (or *characters*) and a *central conflict.* Starting with your ideas in Step 1, brainstorm both elements on your own paper. If your starting idea is a place, what problem might occur there, and who would be involved? If your starting point is a person or people in a job, what trouble do they get into? Who (or what) causes it? To brainstorm, just keep asking yourself "What if . . . ? Write your final story idea on the lines provided on the next page.

Main character(s): _____

_____

Problem: _____

_____

Step 3: Now use *freewriting* to unlock ideas about *characters*, *setting*, and *events*—each element on a separate sheet of paper. Read the hints below before you begin. Then just let your mind and pencil go. Write whatever comes into your head.

Characters: What are your main characters' names? How old are they? What do they look, dress, talk, and act like? What are their best and worst traits?

Setting: What place or places will viewers see? What is the time: the year, time of day, season? Is weather important? What furniture or artwork is in a room? What buildings, trees, equipment do you want in a landscape? Are any props ("properties"), such as a briefcase or a hat, important to the action? [Hint: Sketch an outdoor scene or a floor plan of a room.]

Events: What do characters *say* and *do* to bring about the conflict? Are all actors on the screen all the time? Do some come in and out? Do you need to shift scenes from one setting to another, or forward or backward in time?

Step 4: Next review your creative notes and make an outline. Put the most important details into the story map on page 62. You may not use every part of the printed map, or you may need more room. If so, continue the map on your own paper.

Step 5: Dialogue is so important in a television script that you should think about it before you begin your draft. Your characters' language needs to match their personalities—whether a smart-alecky, brainy brat or a grandmother who recently arrived from Italy. For example, in the model Sandra's informal language, like "Gee" and "Yeah," matches her age and her easygoing manner. From your story map, choose an event, and write some possible dialogue for one or more of the characters involved. Identify each speaker in capital letters, as did the model.

_____

_____

_____

_____

_____

STORY MAP

MAIN CHARACTER(S)

- Name: _____

  Descriptive details: _____

  _____

- Name: _____

  Descriptive details: _____

  _____

- Other characters (list): _____

  _____

SETTING

- Place and time: _____

  Descriptive details: _____

  _____

- Place and time: _____

  Descriptive details: _____

  _____

PLOT

- Central conflict: _____

  _____

Events in order (indicate scene shifts, if any):

- _____

- _____

- _____

- _____

- _____

- _____

- _____

- _____

 **Writing**

Write a draft of your script, using your story map and the guidelines and technical terms that follow it. Be sure to reread the model television script on pages 55–58 before you start writing.

1.   **Think visually.** Remember that your audience is made up of *viewers*, not *readers*. Give set directions to move your characters around and to keep action interesting. Also use the great storytelling possibilities of cameras, which can take viewers from the inside of a tiny cabin to an icy mountaintop, from a group scene to one character's face. You can *show* someone sneaking in a window—a plot event—without any words at all. *Use the list of terms and techniques on page 64 to get visual ideas.*

2.   **Use your ears.** Remember to indicate sounds that occur or music that will set a mood.

3.   **Get inside your characters.** Or let them get inside of you. Read the descriptive details in your story map, close your eyes, imagine you're the character in the situation, and watch to see what you do. Use people you know or have seen as models for mannerisms and personality.

4.   **Make dialogue sound natural.** Remember that no two people talk alike. Also, in conversation people rarely speak with perfect grammar or even in complete sentences. Informal English, dialect, and slang are expected in dialogue if they fit a character.

5.   **Help your "other audience": the actors and crew.** Television viewers don't see your script. They see the finished product. What you write is actually read by the actors, director, costumers, camera operators, and other technicians. Keep them in mind as you write set directions. Are you making the visual picture in *your* mind clear to *them*?

6.   **End strongly.** Remember: You're writing a scene right up to the point of a commercial. You don't want viewers changing channels! End your scene with a "hook" that puts a question or expectation in your viewers' minds.

7.   **Follow scriptwriting format.** Don't worry about getting the script format perfect now, but do keep format in mind. Look back at the model, and follow these basics in your first draft: Write set directions in capital letters; label each speaker; start a new paragraph for each speaker.

TECHNICAL TERMS AND ABBREVIATIONS

C-U: Close-up; camera shot taken at very close range.

Cut: A quick change from one scene or camera shot to another.

Ext.: Exterior; an outdoor scene.

Fade in, fade out: A gradual appearing or disappearing of a scene or sound.

Int.: Interior; an indoor scene.

Long shot: A camera shot taken from a considerable distance.

Pan: Moving the camera across a scene or landscape. (Also see **tracking shot**.)

POV shot: Point-of-view shot; a camera shot taken as if through a character's eyes.

Pull back: Pull the camera back to increase the amount of scene the viewer sees.

SFX: Sound effect.

Tracking shot: A shot in which the camera follows a person or an object that is in motion.

V.O.: Voice over; a voice of someone unseen, commenting or narrating "over" the scene appearing on the screen. A voice-over speaker may be a narrator who is not a character, or a major character who sometimes speaks as a narrator.

Zoom in, zoom out: Move the camera rapidly toward or away from the subject.

Evaluating and Revising

A television pilot, as you probably know, is a trial for a new program. Viewers are the evaluators who decide its fate. Yet even before a pilot gets on the air, its script has gone through extensive *evaluation* and *revision*, usually at the hands of many collaborators: writer, director, producer, perhaps actors and sponsors. They decide where the script is strong or weak and how to fix the weaknesses. Now, with a partner as collaborator, you'll do the same for your script, using the **Questions for Evaluation** on the following page.

Questions for Evaluation

1. Are the characters believable and vivid? If not, how can the dialogue be made more realistic for the character? What can be added to the set directions about the characters' clothes, actions, or emotions?

2. Does the script introduce a central conflict to be developed in the rest of the program? If not, what problem could the main characters face? How could events be changed to add tension or suspense? What dialogue could be added?

3. Are set directions used to describe sound effects, music, setting, characters, and camera work? If not, what information could be added or improved?

4. Is the closing strong? If not, what could be added or changed—in dialogue, events, or camera work—to leave viewers with high tension or curiosity?

Peer Evaluation

Exchange rough drafts with a classmate, then follow these directions.

Step 1:   To begin, read the first draft of the script silently. Then read it out loud; as much as possible, act it out. Hearing the dialogue and visualizing action and camera shifts are the best ways to evaluate what is missing—what actors, crew, and audience need.

Step 2:   On your own paper, answer the **Questions for Evaluation**.

Self-Evaluation

To evaluate your own draft, follow these steps.

Step 1:   If possible, work with your peer reviewer and other students. Divide up the roles in your script, and read dialogue aloud. Also read set directions aloud. If you can't do this, read your script aloud by yourself. Imagine you're watching your script unfold on a home TV screen.

Step 2:   Answer the **Questions for Evaluation** for your own script on a separate sheet of paper. Then read your peer reviewer's evaluation of the script. Circle the ideas that you want to use from both evaluations.

Revise your draft screenplay. Don't hesitate to make major changes, cut a section, or begin again. In television, it's much easier to make many script revisions than it is to reshoot whole scenes later!

Proofreading and Publishing

Step 1:   Check your script for proper form. Script formats vary somewhat, but the format of the model is typical.

A. Write **set directions** in capital letters. Underline the names of characters in set directions. When directions occur within dialogue, enclose them in parentheses.

B. For **dialogue,** write the name of the speaker in capital letters, followed by a colon. If you're writing on a computer, make the name boldface. Begin a new paragraph whenever the speaker changes.

Step 2: Find and correct misspelled words, using a dictionary whenever necessary. For help with spelling problems, see pages 325-335.

Step 3: Find and correct any errors in capitalization, punctuation, grammar, or usage—except for nonstandard English used to make dialogue realistic. Refer to the **Guidelines for Proofreading** on page 16.

Step 4: Make a clean copy of your revised and proofread script.

Step 5: Publish your screenplay in one of the following ways, or think of another way to share it with others.

A. Work with other students to present your screenplay as *readers' theater.* In readers' theater, the actors stand before an audience, or sit on chairs or stools, and read the parts. You can designate a narrator to read any necessary set directions.

B. Videotape your screenplay, or present it as a stage play. Decide the role you want to take: director, actor, technician, or simply author/observer.

FOR YOUR PORTFOLIO

Keep your responses to the items below with your script in your portfolio.

1. Finish your screenplay, or make an outline that completes the plot.

2. What famous actors or actresses can you visualize playing the characters you created? Why?

3. In this assignment, did you like thinking visually and then putting your visual ideas into words? Why or why not?

4. Do you think writing this script will affect how you see television programs from now on? Why or why not?

5. Usually a movie or television script is made into a *storyboard* before shooting. A storyboard is a sketch of what the film or video will look like, shot by shot. An artist sketches the camera shots in panels (like a cartoon strip), with brief directions or portions of dialogue below each panel. If you like to draw, create a storyboard for part of your script.

A RÉSUMÉ

Have you ever had to make a good impression quickly? That's what a résumé, written for a potential employer, needs to do. The French word *résumé* means "summary," and your résumé is a clear, brief summary of your experience and qualifications. As you work toward your goals in school or business, you'll often need to submit a résumé. The following example was prepared by a high school senior nearing graduation.

MARIA LOPEZ
123 Middle Street
West Town, CA 94400
(415) 555-7300

JOB DESIRED: A position in advertising, publishing, or journalism that will use both my graphic arts and editing skills

EDUCATION: Sierra High School, West Town, California (graduation May 2007)
Special courses of study: graphic arts (three years), business, and mathematics
Honors: Sierra High recognition award for helping to organize Career Day

WORK EXPERIENCE: September 2005 to present: apprentice, Bright Light Advertising, West Town, California
- Assist design and production staff, including the preparation of presentation boards for clients
- Prepare weekly production memo
- Operate Zircon computer with WordWorld software (currently in training on PageBuilder graphics)

2004 to present: assistant editor, *Sierra Highlights* school newspaper
- Edit copy, write headlines, illustrate stories, design ads, help lay out pages

Summer 2003: courier, Bright Light Advertising

OTHER EXPERIENCE AND SKILLS: 2001–2004: assistant coordinator of food pantry, The Help House

- Kept inventory of donations, solicited contributions

Business skills
- Broad experience with word-processing programs
- Dictaphone, calculating machine experience

Languages
- Fluent Spanish; conversational Italian

REFERENCES:

Miriam Taylor	James Mendoza
President	Graphic Arts Instructor
Bright Light Advertising	Sierra High School
P.O. Box 3016	245 Mission Road
West Town, CA 94400	West Town, CA 94400
(415) 555-1389	(415) 555-6604

Thinking About the Model

A résumé must give the reader essential facts in an easy-to-read format. Take a closer look at the model résumé. What did Maria include? How did she organize the information? To analyze the résumé, answer these questions.

1. After Maria gives her name, address, and phone number, how does she organize the rest of her information? What are the five main headings?

   _____

   _____

2. The job desired, or *career objective*, is a statement about the kind of career or position the person wants. In her résumé, Maria includes several possibilities for work without sounding too vague or general. Explain how she does this.

   _____

   _____

3. Under "Work Experience," Maria gives the dates of her employment and the title of her current job at Bright Light Advertising. But she also lists other information about this job. What kind of information is it?

   _____

   _____

4. A young person entering the job market may not have much salaried work experience. That's why a category like "Other Experience and Skills" is especially important. Under this heading, what community volunteer work does Maria list? what facts about her office abilities?

   _____

   _____

5. Résumés usually end with two or three references. These are people who will give positive evaluations of your skills, work habits, or character. What are the relationships of Miriam Taylor and James Mendoza to Maria?

   _____

   _____

ASSIGNMENT: WRITING A RÉSUMÉ

Write a résumé to give to potential employers. In your résumé, include how you can be contacted, a job or career objective, facts about your education, a work history, other experience and skills, and the names of references. As you plan and write, think about your reader: a busy person who may give your résumé a *quick* review. What facts will be important to an employer? How can you make them stand out clearly?

Prewriting

Step 1:   Write down the facts for the heading of your résumé.

Your legal name: _____

Street address: _____

_____

City, state ZIP Code: _____

_____

Telephone number, with area code: _____

Hint: Make your name stand out on the résumé. You can capitalize it, (as Maria did) underline it, or both. If you're using a word processor, you can make the letters larger or use a special typeface.

Step 2:   Draft a sentence that gives your ***desired job*** as a career objective—a statement that tells an employer you have definite interests and skills. Remember that your job description shouldn't be too general (*a sales position*) or too specific (*a sales position for high-tech home sound systems*). Keep possibilities open but don't be vague. (See the job description in the model.) On your own paper, brainstorm **jobs you would like to get** and **skills you have to offer.** Then use your notes to write a job objective on the following lines.

Note: You can revise and refine this objective later, after writing your entire résumé.

OBJECTIVE: _____

_____

_____

_____

_____

Step 3:   Supply information about your high school education. Give the name of the school, the city, and state. If you have attended more than one school, list them all and supply dates of attendance. List schools in order of most recent attendance, starting with your current school. Indicate the date (month and year) you will graduate. Other information you may include is

- core courses or special areas of study
- honors or club memberships
- grade point average and class ranking

Use the lines below to gather your data.

EDUCATION:

Schools (names, locations, dates of attendance, graduation):

_____

_____

_____

_____

_____

_____

_____

_____

_____

_____

_____

Other education facts (core courses, honors, clubs, grades, etc.):

_____

_____

_____

_____

_____

_____

Step 4: Now list your work experience by filling in the chart below. Again, if you've had more than one job, begin with the most recent and go in reverse chronological order. Here's what you should include:

- dates (period) of work
- name of company or business; city and state
- duties and skills you use on the job

Notice in the model résumé (page 67) that Maria includes an unpaid position—assistant editor of her high school newspaper—under "Work Experience." Her school experience is directly related to the job she wants, so listing it here is a good idea. Under "Work Experience," you can list *any work directly relevant* to the job you are seeking.

WORK EXPERIENCE:

Dates, company, address	Duties or skills

Step 5:   Next, think about your "Other Experience and Skills." In this category, include all other qualifications you'd like an employer to know about. The types of information you might list are:

- volunteer work (may show technical skills, such as operating camera equipment, or social and organizational skills, such as planning a church trip)
- clubs and memberships
- facts about your skills (such as software programs you know, machinery you can operate, languages you speak, etc.)

Think about what you like to do and what you do well. On the lines below, brainstorm *all* your skills or activities that might interest a prospective employer. Later, you can delete those you don't think are important for your résumé.

OTHER EXPERIENCE AND SKILLS:

_____

_____

_____

_____

Step 6:   Finally, list two or three *references*: people who can recommend you. Think of **teachers, employers, principals, advisors, and family friends**. Who will be able to give an employer positive information about your work or your personal qualities? Write the names of possible people below. Remember to ask permission before listing someone on the résumé. Also, be sure you include their correct addresses and phone numbers.

REFERENCES:

_____

_____

_____

_____

_____

_____

Writing

Use your prewriting notes to draft your résumé on your own paper. There is no single correct style of headings and indentations for résumés, but you may want to follow the style shown in the model (page 67). The main headings are also outlined below. Although you're writing a rough draft, don't ignore format. In a résumé, grouping information is a basic element of the writing. Each heading and the information should be precise and brief.

Main Parts of a Résumé
[your name]
[street address]
[city, state ZIP Code]
[area code/telephone number]

JOB DESIRED:
EDUCATION:
WORK EXPERIENCE:
OTHER EXPERIENCE AND SKILLS:
REFERENCES:

Evaluating and Revising

Think of your draft résumé as a rehearsal for an interview. You've tried to put your best foot forward. Now you can go back, look at your sure steps and your false steps, and make the final performance even better. Working with a classmate, you can use these **Questions for Evaluation** to evaluate your draft résumés and then to revise them.

Questions for Evaluation

1. Does the résumé begin with the writer's name, address, and full phone number? If not, what item is missing, or where has the information been placed?

2. Does the résumé include these headings/categories: "Job Desired," "Education," "Work Experience," "Other Experience and Skills," "References"? If not, what category should be added? (Note: These categories are basic, but the wording of the headings is not set in stone. Just be sure the writer includes all important information.)

3. Does the résumé provide details of job duties the writer has performed? If not, what specific descriptions can be added?

---

4. Does the résumé include courses, technical skills, non-work experience, and personal abilities that might be interesting or important to an employer? If not, what details could be added?

5. Does the résumé end with the names, addresses, and phone numbers of at least two references? If not, what information should be added?

Peer Evaluation

Exchange rough drafts with a classmate, and follow these steps.

Step 1: Read primarily for content, but do tell your classmate if the format or styling of the résumé is hard to read. As a reviewer, you're pretending to be an employer. How easily you can take in information makes a difference.

Step 2: Answer all the **Questions for Evaluation** on your own paper. When you're replying to an *If not . . . ?* question, give the writer concrete suggestions. You may, for example, be able to suggest kinds of skills the writer is overlooking.

Self-Evaluation

Now evaluate your own résumé. Follow these steps.

Step 1: Read or listen to your classmate's evaluation of your draft. Circle or make notes of comments you want to use. You can also ask questions to get more detailed ideas.

Step 2: Reread your draft, imagining that you are the employer who has just received it in the mail. (You might actually do this: Put the résumé in an envelope, prop your feet on a desk, take it out of the envelope, and read. In other words, role-play a boss who knows you only as a piece of paper.)

Step 3: Answer the **Questions for Evaluation**, and then review both sets of answers.

Now revise your résumé. If necessary, you can even go back to prewriting to gather more information about experience and skills. Make revisions on the draft, or recopy it with your changes.

Proofreading and Publishing

Clear and consistent form is essential in a résumé, so proofreading is important. You should take as much care with the appearance of a résumé as you would with your personal appearance for an interview. Follow these steps.

Step 1:   Check carefully for spelling errors, using a dictionary if necessary.

Step 2:   Correct errors in grammar, capitalization, usage, and mechanics. (Refer to the proofreading checklist on page 16.) Even though a résumé, as a summary, does not use many complete sentences, all language use must be correct. It must also be consistent. Check the following aspects of your résumé's mechanics, one at a time:

• **Main headings:** Are they all written the same way—full capitals, for instance? Or underlined? Make them consistent.

• **Initial capitals:** If you capitalize the first word of a new line, use this style each time. Check each new line for consistency.

• **Phrases:** If you use phrases rather than full sentences, make the phrases similar in form. For example, "*Prepare* weekly memos" and "*Operate* Zircon computer" both begin with verbs.

• **Indentation and spacing:** Make sure that your indentations and spacing create the correct categories of information. Look at the model résumé (page 67) to see how the writer uses the same indentation and spacing within each section of the résumé.

• **Punctuation:** Are you using colons after headings? Are you using periods at the ends of lines, or omitting them? Whatever punctuation style you choose, do it the same way every time.

Step 3:   After you've made all corrections, prepare a final, clean copy of your résumé on your own paper. For this assignment, you may handwrite it. When you submit a résumé to an employer, you should type it.

Step 4:   Here are two ways to publish your résumé.

A. Use it. Job seekers usually enclose a résumé with an application for a particular job. You can also leave a résumé when you fill out an application form at a job site.

B. At school, you can publish your résumé by creating, with classmates, a display for juniors and seniors. Many students will be looking for a job when school ends, whether part-time or full-time. Also, offer your résumé to school counselors who are advising graduating seniors.

C. You can attach a résumé to an application for school admittance or financial aid.

FOR YOUR PORTFOLIO

Respond to the following items, and keep your responses with your résumé in your portfolio.

1. Now that you've finished your résumé, which part of it do you think is strongest—most impressive to an employer? Weakest? What actions can you take to strengthen the weak parts?

2. Photocopy and quick-print shops specialize in producing résumés for job seekers. They will print your typed résumé on special paper or typeset and print it. Visit a shop to see formats and paper choices, and ask for samples and prices. The formats the shops offer may give you ideas for retyping your own résumé.

FRANK AND ERNEST ®by Bob Thaves

Frank & Ernest reprinted by permission of NEA, Inc.

A LETTER OF APPLICATION

What job attracts you? Do you need a scholarship for further schooling? A persuasive *letter of application* can be an important tool in your life. Often, a letter is the first impression an employer or selection committee has of you. Here's a letter of application from a high school student looking for an important first job.

16 Elm Street
Hawkins, MI 49677
April 20, 2008

Ms. Thea Wilson
Old Town Builders
215 Main Street
Hawkins, MI 49677

Dear Ms. Wilson:

I am writing to apply for an apprentice carpenter position with your company. I learned about the apprentice program through my shop teacher, Mr. Ted Gaither. I believe this program is a wonderful opportunity to use my skills and learn more.

I already own the basic carpentry tools and have some experience doing odd jobs, so I can be useful in your work now. In my high school shop classes, I've taken both beginning and advanced woodworking. I also read blueprints, and I plan to attend a continuing education class to learn to read an architect's plan.

I know that estimating costs and time for a job is an important part of carpentry and the construction business. I do not yet have that kind of experience, but my math skills are good. I help with bookkeeping in my parents' restaurant. With more on-the-job experience, I can quickly learn the business side of carpentry, too.

I know that as an apprentice I will have to work very hard, doing basic tasks under careful guidance. I have learned discipline in my two years on the track team. When I have a goal, I dedicate myself, and I really want to become a professional carpenter.

I will be glad to give you the names of references who can tell you about my qualifications. If you need to telephone me for more information, my number is 555-3792. I am available for part-time work now and for either part-time or full-time work when I graduate in June.

Thank you for considering my application.

Sincerely,

Masako Dai

Thinking About the Model

Would you be persuaded to give Masako Dai a job—or at least an interview? Probably you would. Now that you've read the model letter, look more closely at how the writer tries to convince Ms. Wilson. Answer the following questions.

1. Exactly what position is the writer applying for? Where does he put this information in his letter?

   _____

   _____

2. A job applicant's most persuasive **reasons** for being hired are having the needed skills and experience. Then the applicant supplies **evidence:** facts and examples. In the model letter, what carpentry skills and experience does the writer mention, and what evidence does he give of them?

   _____

   _____

   _____

3. Often, new job seekers don't have a lot of experience. The letter writer admits, for example, that he's inexperienced at estimating labor costs and time of completion. However, he gives evidence that he can learn. What is the evidence?

   _____

   _____

4. Personal qualities and characteristics can make a difference in job success, too. What personal example does the writer use to show he will make a good apprentice?

   _____

   _____

5. What important facts does the writer give the employer at the end of the letter?

   _____

   _____

ASSIGNMENT: WRITING A LETTER OF APPLICATION

Write a letter of application for a job that you would like to have and can do. Think hard about your audience: a possible employer. Your aim is to convince this person that you're a good candidate and should be considered for the job.

Prewriting

For this assignment, write a letter for a *real job*—either one you wish you had, or one advertised in the newspaper. (Look in the classified ads section.) You may not mail the letter (although you can if you're job hunting), but you'll get practice matching your skills to actual job requirements.

Step 1: Think of a job you want, or select a job advertisement you want to respond to. Maybe you'd really like to work in a sporting goods store you often visit. Maybe you see an interesting want ad for a trainee position in a printing shop. List jobs you're interested in on these lines.

_____

_____

Look over the possibilities you've gathered, and ask yourself, "Which jobs can I really *do*?" Choose one you have a good chance of getting. On the lines below, write the individual you'll contact (or a title such as "Personnel Director" or "Store Manager"), the company, and the address.

Name or title: _____

Company: _____

Street: _____

City and ZIP Code: _____

Step 2: Next, outline what the job requires. What are the requirements, the skills you'll need, and any special conditions or requirements (such as a car, night hours, or previous experience)? Read ads closely to get these facts. Also use your personal knowledge, and do research if necessary. You can talk to people who have the job or ask a librarian or guidance counselor for references or resources. Write the job details in the left column of the chart below.

Step 3: Now list your qualifications: the evidence that shows you can do the job. Identify **skills, experience, education** or **training**. Also consider **personal characteristics, awards** or **honors, grades,** and **aptitudes** (gifts or talents). Remember, if you lack a specific qualification, you can use something *related*—like the model writer's bookkeeping experience. You could also explain how you'll overcome the lack. In the chart, write qualifications for each of the job details.

Job skills, tasks, requirements	My qualifications
1.	1.
2.	2.
3.	3.
4.	4.

References, people who can provide positive opinions of your work and qualities, are another type of persuasive evidence. Identify two adults (usually not relatives) who could tell an employer about your character, work record, or schoolwork. You won't give these names in the letter, but you'll offer to supply them. List the names of two possible references here.

Step 4: Now, to focus your energy and attention before writing, write one strong statement explaining **why you want this job** or **why you're the right person for this job**. Review your chart first. Then write quickly, and be bold—convince someone!

Writing

Your letter will use standard business-letter form, but for your first draft, don't worry about correct form. Concentrate first on the body of the letter: the paragraphs after "Dear——." Here are guidelines that will help you write a persuasive letter.

| **Beginning** | • Identify the job you're applying for.
• Tell how you know about it (unless you are applying for an unadvertised job).
• Possibly make an opening statement about your desire for the job or about your qualifications. |

| **Middle** | • Give details of your qualifications for the job: experience, skills, education, personal qualities, honors, aptitudes, etc.
• Show your desire for and interest in the work. |

| **Ending** | • Offer to provide references.
• Supply needed information such as how to contact you and your availability for work.
• Thank the employer for considering you. |

Write your rough draft on your own paper, using these steps:

Step 1:   Draft the body of the letter first, but leave a large space at the top of the paper.

Step 2:   After you draft the body, add the other parts of a business letter: heading, inside address, salutation, closing, and signature. The chart on page 84 explains each part. For examples, look at the model letter on page 77.

 **Evaluating and Revising**

Now take your first draft and make it better. If you've been in a job interview (successful or not), you know that you *always* replay it and think, "I should have said . . . " With a letter, you actually get the chance to polish your persuasiveness. You can *evaluate* your letter's strengths and weaknesses and then *revise* the weaknesses. Use these **Questions for Evaluation** to judge your letter and a classmate's letter.

Questions for Evaluation

1. Does the opening paragraph of the letter clearly identify the job being applied for? Does it tell how the writer knew about the job? If not, what details can be added?

   _____

   _____

2. Does the letter give details of the writer's job qualifications? If not, what facts or examples can be added?

   _____

   _____

3. Does the letter convincingly show the writer's interest? If not, what phrases or sentences could be added to show the work is important to the writer?

   _____

   _____

4. Does the ending offer to provide references? Does it supply any needed information about contacting the writer or about the writer's availability? If not, what can be added or changed?

   _____

   _____

   _____

Peer Evaluation

Exchange rough drafts with a classmate, and follow these steps.

Step 1:   Read your classmate's letter as if you were the employer. Focus on the letter's information and persuasive appeal, not on grammar and mechanics.

Step 2:   Answer each question in the **Questions for Evaluation**, either in writing or in a conference with the writer.

Self-Evaluation

To evaluate your own draft, follow these steps.

Step 1:   Again, pretend you are the employer reading the letter. This is harder to do for your own letter than for your classmate's letter, but it will yield results. Read your letter closely. Would you be persuaded to give this applicant a chance?

Step 2:   Answer the **Questions for Evaluation** on your own paper. Then read, or listen to, your classmate's evaluation of your letter. Pay close attention when you both have similar comments: Those are areas of your letter that definitely need work.

Now use both evaluations to revise your letter. You can revise on the draft, recopy it with changes, or start over completely.

Proofreading and Publishing

How do you dress for a job interview? As neatly and carefully as possible! Your application letter needs the same attention to appearance, because it represents you. Now is the time to make sure the form and mechanics of your letter are as correct as possible.

Step 1:   Check each word for correct spelling, and use a dictionary whenever you suspect a mistake. Also proofread for errors in capitalization, grammar, usage, and mechanics. Use this book as a reference, both to help you spot problems and to correct them.

Step 2:   Be sure you've followed proper business-letter form. Use the chart on page 84 to check the heading and other parts of the letter. Make any necessary changes on your last revision.

Step 3:   Make a final clean copy of your letter. Write it on your own paper.

Step 4:   Use one of the following suggestions to publish your letter.

A. If you are applying for the job, recopy the letter and mail it. If possible, type the letter.

B. Work with the school guidance counselor to make a display of your class's letters, along with other job-hunting tips, for the juniors and seniors at your school.

Parts of a Business Letter	
Heading	Divide the letter in half by drawing an imaginary line vertically down the middle. Begin the heading to the right of the line. On separate lines, write • your address • city, state, and ZIP Code (A comma follows the name of the city.) • date of letter (A comma separates the day of the month from the year.)
Inside Address	Leave a margin at the left of the letter. Begin the inside address at the margin. On separate lines, write • the name or the title of the person you are writing (*Personnel Director*, for example) • the name of the business • street address of the business • city, state, and ZIP Code of the business
Salutation (Greeting)	Begin the salutation at the left margin. Begin the first word and all titles and nouns with a capital letter (*Dear Mr. Jones* or *Dear Sir or Madam*). A colon follows the salutation.
Body	Indent the first line of each paragraph.
Closing and Signature	Line up the closing under the heading. You might write *Sincerely* or *Yours truly*. Capitalize only the first word. A comma follows the closing. Skip four lines, and type or print your legal name. Sign your legal name in the space just below your closing.

[heading] — _____
            _____, ___
            _____, ___

_____
_____
[inside address]
_____
_____, ___

_____ : —[salutation]   ┌[body]

_____
_____
_____
_____
_____
_____
_____
_____
_____
_____
_____
_____
_____
_____
_____

[closing] — _____,
[signature] — _____
[typed or printed name] — _____

FOR YOUR PORTFOLIO

Respond to the two items below and put your responses with your letter in your portfolio.

1. During this assignment, you probably came across jobs you *wished* you could apply for. What job would you like to prepare yourself to get?

2. In the library, with a school counselor, or at the company itself, find out more about the work: what it involves, what education you need, whether it's a growing field.

COORDINATING IDEAS

8a **Equally important ideas in a sentence are called** *coordinate ideas.*

To show that ideas are coordinate, join them with a coordinating conjunction (*and, but, for, nor, or, so, yet*) and/or with appropriate punctuation.

(1) When you use a coordinating conjunction, a semicolon, or a semicolon and a conjunctive adverb to combine two independent clauses, the result is a *compound sentence.*

EXAMPLES   Steven wrote the music for that song, **and** I wrote the lyrics. [comma and coordinating conjunction]
Steven wrote the music; I wrote the lyrics. [semicolon]
Steven and I wrote the song; **accordingly,** our names are on the copyright. [semicolon with conjunctive adverb and comma]

(2) In addition to linking coordinate independent clauses, you can also link coordinate words and phrases in a sentence.

EXAMPLES   **Two whirligigs and four pink flamingos** decorate our neighbor's front lawn. [compound subject]
The bagger **tossed the groceries with his right hand and caught them with his left.** [compound predicate]
Should we give the striped tie **to Dad or to Grandpa Sam?** [coordinate prepositional phrases]
Turning the corner and heading for home plate, the base runner prepared to slide. [coordinate verbal phrases]

NOTE   When you join two independent clauses with a coordinating conjunction, place a comma before the conjunction. However, a comma is not necessary if the clauses are very short and your meaning is clear without the comma.

        COMMA NECESSARY   Marcie cooked a grand meal and presented it magnificently**,** and Jim set the table.
        COMMA UNNECESSARY   Marcie cooked a meal and Jim set the table.

8b **Ideas joined by a coordinating conjunction should be of equal importance. Otherwise, the sentence will contain** *faulty coordination.*

To avoid faulty coordination, place less important ideas in subordinate clauses or phrases.

FAULTY   The day was beautiful, and we went to a water park.
REVISED   **Because the day was beautiful,** we went to a water park.
REVISED   We went to a water park **to enjoy the beautiful day.**

EXERCISE 1   Using Appropriate Coordinating Conjunctions

Complete each sentence below by deciding which connecting word will best fit in the blank. Add the correct punctuation to go with the connective you choose. Write your answers on the line provided.

EX.   1. Jonathan was the best artist in the class _, and_ he became the best runner on the track team.

1. I would love to go _____ I don't have time today.

2. Jorge wants to learn the piano _____ he signed up for lessons.

3. My cousin painted the chair _____ I painted the table.

4. It's snowing _____ the temperature outside isn't as cold as it was this morning.

5. It was a beautiful plant _____ it needed fresh soil.

6. Maxwell is my friend _____ he is my neighbor.

7. My dog is big _____ he is gentle.

8. The car broke down _____ we called a tow truck.

9. Fred loves a vacation _____ it is when he can relax.

10. It is raining _____ the sky is blue.

EXERCISE 2   Combining Sentences by Coordinating Ideas

On the lines provided, combine the sets of sentences below by joining the two sentences. Be sure to choose a connective that expresses the correct relationship between the ideas. [Note: There may be more than one way to revise each sentence.]

EX.   1. Orla wanted to wash her car. She filled a bucket with water.
       Orla wanted to wash her car, so she filled a bucket with water.

1. My friend Otis wanted to be a professional dancer. He teaches school today.

   _____

2. I would like to see the play *Our Town*. I went to see *Cats*. _____

   _____

3. Yukio could give the report. Julia could give the report. _____

   _____

4. Sheena said hello to Roger. He turned around and said, "How are you?"

   _____

5. I wasn't tired yesterday. I took a nap in the afternoon. _____

   _____

SUBORDINATING IDEAS

Ideas that are of less importance in a sentence are called *subordinate* ideas. A subordinate clause adds information about the main idea in an independent clause.

8c You can subordinate an idea in a sentence by placing it in a *subordinate clause*.

(1) A subordinate *adverb clause* modifies a verb, an adjective, or an adverb in a sentence.

A subordinate adverb clause begins with a subordinating conjunction, such as *after, although, because, if, since, when, whenever, where,* or *while.*

The subordinating conjunction you use shows your reader the relationship between the ideas in the adverb clause and the independent clause. Adverb clauses usually express a relationship such as *condition, cause or reason, time or place,* or *purpose or result.*

CONDITION   I can play with the team on Friday **if I do well on my English test Thursday.**

REASON   Wayne Gretzky was known as "The Great Gretzky" **because he was such an outstanding skater and puck-handler.**

TIME   **After she removed the barnacles,** Jo Beth repainted her dinghy.

PURPOSE   Max changed seats **so that Mom and Dad could sit together.**

(2) A subordinate *adjective clause* modifies a noun in a sentence.

A subordinate adjective clause begins with *who, whom, whose, which, that,* or *where.* Before you use an adjective clause in a sentence, decide which idea you want to emphasize and which you want to subordinate.

TWO IDEAS   Trina's basketball is made of leather. It is of regulation size and weight.

COMBINED   Trina's basketball, **which is made of leather,** is of regulation size and weight. [subordinates *of leather*]

Trina's basketball, **which is of regulation size and** is made of leather. [subordinates *of regulation size and weight*]

(3) A subordinate *noun clause* is used as a noun in a sentence.

A subordinate noun clause usually begins with *that, what, whatever, why, whether, how, who, whom, whoever,* or *whomever.*

TWO IDEAS   Luisa bought a shirt. She said she liked it.

COMBINED   Luisa said **that she bought a shirt she liked.** [direct object]

According to **whoever sold Luisa that shirt,** she liked it. [object of a preposition]

EXERCISE 3   Revising Sentences by Using Adverb, Adjective, and Noun Clauses

Combine each pair of sentences below by changing the sentence in italics into a subordinate clause. The hints in parentheses will tell you what words to use at the beginnings of the clauses. You may need to delete some words from the italicized sentence. Write your revised sentences on your own paper.

EX.   1. *The reporter wrote that excellent news story*. The reporter won an award. (Use *who*.)

    1. The reporter who wrote that excellent news story won an award.

1. I *go to San Francisco*. I ride the trolley cars. (Use *whenever*.)

2. *Graduation will be held in the gymnasium*. The principal told me. (Use *that*.)

3. *The meeting ended*. We served refreshments. (Use *after*.)

4. I often write to my aunt. *She lives in Morocco*. (Use *who*.)

5. Blue jays and cardinals are Joel's favorite birds. *Sandra said so*. (Use *that*.)

6. The man at the table is an actor. *I've seen him in two movies*. (Use *whom*.)

7. *This bread contains walnuts and raisins*. My grandmother told me. (Use that.)

8. Sal needs to go to the barber. *His hair is in his eyes*. (Use *because*.)

9. *Monique will be a great president one day*. I am positive. (Use *that*.)

10. I have a neighbor named Ms. Rego. *She feeds my cat when I am away*. (Use *who*.)

11. *The storm ended at midnight*. Branches were scattered in the street. (Use *after*.)

12. Cranberry juice is in the pantry. *My brother told me*. (Use *that*.)

13. I admire that woman. *She is running for mayor*. (Use *who*.)

14. Lynn needs a plaster cast. *She broke her ankle*. (Use *because*.)

15. Mr. Wong is a teacher. *I think he is great*. (Use *whom*.)

16. Gerald will be hired for the job. *He will go to the interview*. (Use *if*.)

17. *I cannot attend this rehearsal*. I should tell you. (Use *why*.)

18. Pam enjoys working for the newspaper. *She is a reporter*. (Use *who*.)

19. We should leave early. *We can arrive on time*. (Use *so that*.)

20. *Harry shopped at the mall*. He didn't find the birthday card he wanted. (Use *although*.)

need to know this

USING PARALLEL STRUCTURE

You can make your writing smoother and clearer by checking your sentences for *parallel structure*.

8d A sentence has *parallel structure* when it uses the same grammatical form to express *parallel*, or equal, ideas.

(1) Use parallel structure when you link coordinate ideas.

FAULTY   Suzu likes baseball and to collect postcards. [noun paired with an infinitive]

PARALLEL   Suzu likes **baseball** and his postcard **collection.** [noun paired with a noun]

(2) Use parallel structure when you compare or contrast ideas.

FAULTY   For a dancer, moving gracefully is as important as to take the right steps. [gerund compared with an infinitive]

PARALLEL   For a dancer, **moving** gracefully is as important as **taking** the right steps. [gerund compared with a gerund]

(3) Use parallel structure when you link ideas with the correlative conjunctions *both...and, either...or, neither...nor,* or *not only...but also.*

FAULTY   I want both to live in Chicago and working in advertising. [infinitive paired with a gerund]

PARALLEL   I want both **to live** in Chicago and **to work** in advertising. [infinitive paired with an infinitive]

Be sure to place correlative conjunctions directly before the parallel terms. Otherwise, your sentence may sound awkward and unclear.

UNCLEAR   They not only wanted to go shopping but also to see a movie.

BETTER   They wanted **not only** to go shopping **but also** to see a movie.

EXERCISE 4   Revising Sentences by Correcting Faulty Parallelism

On the lines provided, revise the following sentences by putting parallel ideas in the same grammatical form. Add, delete, and replace words as necessary. [Note: There may be more than one way to revise each sentence.]

EX.   1. I want to visit Washington, D.C., and seeing all the monuments.
      I want to visit Washington, D.C., and ~~~~ see all the monuments.

1. During our school vacations, I like bicycling, walking, and to swim at the state park. _____

_____

2. Marty believes reading a good book is more rewarding than to watch television. _____

_____

3. Hector hopes either to write his entire mystery novel or at least starting it this summer. _____

_____

4. Ms. Shapiro is recognized for being active in town government and as a baseball coach. _____

_____

_____

5. Bonita enjoys algebra and to study earth science. _____

_____

6. My sister Shanelle would like both to plan the local road races and running in them. _____

_____

7. When completing assignments, doing work accurately and neatly is more important than to be fast. _____

_____

_____

8. Not only is keeping old newspapers around the house messy, but they are also a fire hazard. _____

_____

9. My sister Sienna likes sailing and to paddle in a canoe. _____

_____

10. Neither cleaning the living room nor to sweep the kitchen appeals to Leroy, who is exhausted. _____

_____

_____

SENTENCE FRAGMENTS AND RUN-ON SENTENCES

8e A sentence should express a complete thought. If you punctuate a part of a sentence as if it were a complete sentence, you create a *sentence fragment*.

(1) A *phrase* is a group of related words that does not contain both a verb and its subject. If a phrase gets separated from the sentence it belongs with, it becomes a *phrasal fragment*.

FRAGMENT   The cuckoo laid its egg. In a mockingbird's nest.
SENTENCE   The cuckoo laid its egg **in a mockingbird's nest.**

(2) A *subordinate clause* has a subject and a verb but does not express a complete thought. Unlike an independent clause, a subordinate clause cannot stand on its own as a sentence.

FRAGMENT   I've always appreciated my mother. Who taught me how to
            throw a football.
SENTENCE   I've always appreciated my mother, **who taught me how to
            throw a football.**

8f Each complete thought in your writing should come to a full stop. If you run together two sentences as if they expressed a single thought, you create an error called a *run-on sentence*.

There are two kinds of run-on sentences. A *fused sentence* has no punctuation at all between the two complete thoughts. A *comma splice* has just a comma separating the two thoughts.

            FUSED   Mom carried the stroller onto the bus Billy carried the baby.
COMMA SPLICE   Some children on the bus gave up their seats, they helped us
                carry our belongings, too.

Depending on the relationship you want to show between the two ideas, you can fix a run-on sentence in several ways.

(1) Make two sentences.

EXAMPLE   Some children on the bus gave up their seats**. They** helped us
           carry our belongings, too.

(2) Use a comma and a coordinating conjunction.

EXAMPLE   Mom carried the stroller onto the bus**, and** Billy carried the baby.

(3) Change one of the independent clauses to a subordinate clause.

EXAMPLE   Mom carried the stroller onto the bus**, while Billy carried the baby.**

(4) Use a semicolon.

EXAMPLE   Some children on the bus gave up their seats**;** they helped us carry our belongings, too.

(5) Use a semicolon with a conjunctive adverb followed by a comma.

EXAMPLE   Some children on the bus gave up their seats**; furthermore,** they helped us carry our belongings.

EXERCISE 5   Revising Sentences to Eliminate Fragments and Run-ons

On your own paper, revise each sentence fragment or run-on sentence below. [Note: There may be more than one way to revise each sentence.]

EX.   1. Lynne learned to play the violin then she joined a youth symphony.
        1. *Lynne learned to play the violin. Then she joined a youth symphony.*

1. She is thankful for her friend Pablo. Who told her about the symphony.

2. Pablo plays the cello, he has been in the symphony for two years.

3. The symphony meets every Wednesday night they use the high school music room.

4. The musicians take turns driving. To the evening rehearsals.

5. Last year the symphony traveled to a competition in Canada they played well and had a wonderful time.

6. The symphony took second place. With their performance of Aaron Copland's *Appalachian Spring*.

7. Pablo also played a violin solo, he received a loud round of applause.

8. The symphony gave a concert on the steps of the town hall. When they returned home.

9. The concert drew a large crowd, the audience was quite impressed. By the variety of the music and the skill of the musicians.

10. The concert was a success, it raised a lot of money for a local soup kitchen.

UNNECESSARY SHIFTS

8g Avoid unnecessary *shifts in subject*.

A sentence is much clearer when it has the same subject throughout. Shift subjects in a sentence only when you need to express your meaning.

AWKWARD Students should turn in their portfolios by Monday if you want them back before the holiday.

BETTER **Students** should turn in **their** portfolios by Monday if **they** want them back before the holiday.

8h Avoid unnecessary *shifts in verb tense* and *voice*.

Changing verb tense or voice in mid-sentence can create awkwardness and confusion. Use the tense and voice you start with unless you have a good reason for changing.

AWKWARD When we went to Catalina Island, I see a whale. [shift in tense]
BETTER When we **went** to Catalina Island, I **saw** a whale.
AWKWARD Jasmine combed her cat, but no fleas were found. [shift in voice]
BETTER Jasmine **combed** her cat but **found** no fleas.

Often the best way to correct a shift in voice and tense in a compound sentence is to use a compound verb. Omit the second subject, and use the second verb in the same voice and tense as the first. You may also need to delete a comma when you take out the second subject.

AWKWARD I have always listened to his records, and his concerts are really enjoyable.
BETTER I **have** always **listened** to his records and have enjoyed his concerts.

A shift in voice usually causes a shift in subject, too. Notice that in the uncorrected sentence in the last example, the shift from active to passive voice results in a shift from the subject *I* to the subject *concerts*.

EXERCISE 6 Eliminating Unnecessary Shifts in Sentences

On the lines provided, revise each of the following sentences to eliminate unnecessary shifts. [Note: There may be more than one way to revise each sentence.]

EX. 1. Members should pay their dues if you want to have a spring party.
    Members should pay their dues if they want to have a spring party.

1. I enjoy Uncle Mateo's chili, and his cornbread is really delicious. _____

_____

2. When I went to concerts in the city last summer, I hear great jazz
   musicians. _____

   _____

3. Ana almost completed the entire obstacle course, but was not given
   enough time. _____

   _____

4. Parents should sign permission slips if you want your children to go on
   the field trip. _____

   _____

5. We traveled to the White Mountains, and we admire the forests of birch
   trees. _____

   _____

6. Corky likes the sweaters at Darla's Boutique, and the socks and hats are
   beautiful also. _____

   _____

7. Willis wanted to organize a musical group, but not many musicians could
   be found. _____

   _____

8. As I studied for my biology test, I listen to the howling wind and to the
   pouring rain. _____

   _____

9. All travelers should check their new schedules if you don't want to miss
   your trains. _____

   _____

10. My father grows roses in his garden, and daffodils grow there, too. _____

    _____

REVIEW EXERCISE

A.   Revising Paragraphs for Clarity

On your own paper, revise the paragraphs below to correct faulty coordination, errors in parallel structure, errors in subordination, and unnecessary shifts. [Note: There may be more than one way to revise each sentence.]

EX.   [1] My sister knows a lot about hot-air balloons, and she was asked to judge the Independence Day Balloon Race.

[1] Because my sister knows a lot about hot-air balloons, she was asked to judge the Independence Day Balloon Race.

[1] It was Independence Day, and my town was having a large carnival.

[2] A crowd of people gathered, watching hot-air balloons and to eat hot dogs.

[3] The crowd cheered the balloonists as the balloons filled with heated air and rise into the summer sky.

[4] A person must be a bit of a daredevil if you want to ride in a hot-air balloon. [5] Because I don't like to ride in hot-air balloons myself, they seem dangerous to me. [6] In my opinion, a person has to be crazy if you want to go up in one of those things. [7] However, many people enjoy the experience of sailing slowly through the sky and to wave to people on the ground below.

[8] Fortunately, no accidents occurred at the Independence Day Race, and a good time was had by all the balloonists and spectators. [9] The balloons drifted over the park and landing safely across the river on the enormous courthouse lawn. [10] Mr. Haltom, in his large red-white-and-blue balloon, both won the balloon race and was presented the award as the most skillful balloonist.

B. Revising Paragraphs to Eliminate Fragments and Run-ons

On your own paper, revise the following paragraphs to eliminate the sentence fragments and run-on sentences. [Note: There may be more than one way to revise each sentence.]

EX.   Science fiction is one of the most exciting varieties of literature in science fiction stories and novels, authors present alternate worlds that excite the imagination.

Science fiction is one of the most exciting varieties of literature. In science fiction stories and novels, authors present alternate worlds that excite the imagination.

1   All fiction writing involves leaps of the imagination however, the

2 biggest leaps are usually taken by science fiction writers. Writers of

3 science fiction imagine worlds. That do not yet exist. They take us on

4 incredible journeys. In time and space. Deep into the earth. To distant

5 planets. Back into the distant past or forward into the far-off future.

6   People use the term *science fiction* in different ways, some people use it

7 to refer to any highly unrealistic or improbable story. However, it is

8 probably best to use the term *fantasy*. For those improbable stories that do

9 not contain scientific elements. Most experts would agree that a story

10 needs to involve science. If it is to be considered science fiction.

12   The first outstanding American science fiction writer was Edgar Allan

13 Poe one of his stories, "The Unparalleled Adventures of One Hans Pfaal,"

14 tells about a flight to the moon aboard a hot-air balloon. Poe inspired

15 many imitators. Including Jules Verne. Who predicted the invention of

16 submarines in his novel *Twenty Thousand Leagues Under the Sea*. Other

17 excellent early science fiction writers include H.G. Wells, Edgar Rice

18 Burroughs, and Madeleine L'Engle, some popular, modern-day science

19 fiction writers include Ray Bradbury, Isaac Asimov, and Virginia Hamilton.

COMBINING BY INSERTING WORDS

By using sentence-combining techniques, you can add detail to your sentences and variety and smoothness to your writing style.

8i **You can combine short sentences by taking a key word from one sentence and inserting it in another sentence. You may need to change the word into an adjective or adverb before you can insert it.**

Using the Same Form	
ORIGINAL	Sutki revised the essay. She did it cleverly.
COMBINED	Sutki **cleverly** revised the essay.
ORIGINAL	Greta is a harpsichordist. She is talented.
COMBINED	Greta is a **talented** harpsichordist.
Changing the Form	
ORIGINAL	Eddy pedaled up the hill. His speed was slow.
COMBINED	Eddy pedaled **slowly** up the hill.
ORIGINAL	I stared at the sunrise. Its colors were bright.
COMBINED	I stared at the **brightly colored** sunrise.

EXERCISE 7 Combining by Inserting Single-Word Modifiers

On the lines provided, combine each pair of sentences by inserting an adjective or adverb into the first sentence.

EX.   1.   Manuel knitted mittens for his baby sister. He was careful.
Manuel carefully knitted mittens for his baby sister.

1. I watched my grandparents dance to their favorite song. It made me

happy. _____

_____

2. Jocelyn is a mechanic. She is trustworthy. _____

_____

3. My friend Oscar cleaned all the windows. He was quick. _____

_____

4. June watched her brother dance and sing on the stage. It filled her with pride. _____

_____

5. Pia walked to the podium to get her high school diploma. She walked slowly. _____

_____

6. Al planted shrubbery in his front yard. It was beautiful. _____

_____

7. My father and I had a discussion. It was interesting. _____

_____

8. My friend Martin revised his research paper. He revised his research paper skillfully. _____

_____

9. My new kitten Freckles batted at the rubber ball. Freckles looked playful as she batted the ball. _____

_____

10. Porter began his first day at his new job. He was nervous. _____

_____

11. Stella gave a bag of clothing to charity. The bag was large. _____

_____

12. Maya Angelou spoke at the conference. She is inspiring. _____

_____

13. My friend walked around the cafeteria looking for her lost bracelet. She was sad. _____

_____

14. We waited for the train from Memphis to arrive. We were anxious. _____

_____

15. Max began mowing the lawn. He did it yesterday. _____

_____

COMBINING BY INSERTING PHRASES

A *prepositional phrase* is a group of words consisting of a preposition, a noun or pronoun that serves as the object of the preposition, and any modifiers of that object.

8j **You can sometimes combine two related sentences by taking a prepositional phrase from one sentence and inserting it into the other without any change in form. You can also combine sentences by changing part of a sentence into a prepositional phrase.**

ORGINAL   Addie replaced the spark plugs. She did it after school Monday.
COMBINED   **Afterschool Monday,** Addie replaced the spark plugs.

ORGINAL   We sang and danced. We were enjoying the party.
COMBINED   We sang and danced **at the enjoyable party.**

8k **Sometimes you can combine two sentences by taking a participial phrase directly from one sentence and inserting it into the other. Other times you will need to change a verb into a participle before you can insert the idea into another sentence.**

ORGINAL   I like this tea. It was made in England.
COMBINED   I like this tea **made in England.**

ORGINAL   I was a friend of the groom. I took pictures at the wedding.
COMBINED   **Beinga friend of the groom,** I took pictures at the wedding.

NOTE   Place a participial phrase close to the noun or pronoun it modifies. Otherwise, you may give your sentence the wrong meaning.

MISPLACED   Sitting in their nest, Laura found the birds astonishing.
CORRECT   Laura found the birds **sitting in their nest** astonishing.

8l **You can sometimes combine sentences by placing one of the ideas in an appositive phrase. The appositive phrase should be set off by a comma, or by two commas if you place the phrase in the middle of the sentence.**

ORGINAL   Bill Bradley is now a political speaker. He formerly played basketball at Princeton.
COMBINED   **A former Princeton basketball player,** Bill Bradley is now political speaker.

or

Bill Bradley, **a former Princeton basketball player,** is a political speaker.

EXERCISE 8   Combining by Inserting Phrases

Combine each pair of sentences below by changing the italicized sentence into a phrase and inserting it into the other. You may need to change or delete words. [Note: There may be more than one way to combine each sentence pair.]

EX.   1.   *Vargas got tired of waiting.* She decided to design the cover herself.

   Vargas, tired of waiting, decided to design the cover herself.

1. We worked hard. *We were working on our history project.* _____

   _____

2. Earl is now an English teacher at Wilson High School. *He formerly was a*

   student there. _____

   _____

3. I like the whole-wheat bread. *It was made at the local bakery.* _____

   _____

4. I went to Marcia's house. *I helped Marcia babysit her brothers the other night.*

   _____

5. Jamie went to the library. *He went on Saturday afternoon.* _____

   _____

6. Jillian learned about measuring the mass of gas. *She learned about this in*

   chemistry class. _____

   _____

7. I like those warm woolen sweaters. *They were made in a small town in*

   Ireland. _____

   _____

8. Uncle Ernie did not catch the flu this year. *He is exceptionally healthy.* _____

   _____

9. My friend made low-fat yogurt shakes. *She made them for an after-school*

   snack. _____

   _____

10. Anita painted the outside of the garage. *She is my youngest sister.* _____

   _____

COMBINING BY COORDINATION AND SUBORDINATION

8m **You can combine** *coordinate,* **or equally important, words, phrases, or clauses by using either a coordinating conjunction (***and, but, for, or, nor, so, yet***) or a correlative conjunction (***both...and, either...or, neither...nor***).**

ORIGINAL   Marcia helped with the decorations for the banquet.
              Marcus also helped with the decorations for the banquet.
COMBINED **Both Marcia and Marcus** helped with the decorations for the banquet.[compound subject]

ORIGINAL   We can make phone calls. We can go door-to-door.
COMBINED We can **either** make phone calls **or** go door-to-door.[compound verb]

ORIGINAL   The sink was stopped up. Liona got the plunger.
COMBINED The sink was stopped up, **so** Liona got the plunger.[compound sentence]

 REFERENCE NOTE: For more information on coordinating ideas and punctuating compound sentences, see pages 139 and 181.

EXERCISE 9   Combining by Coordinating Ideas

On your own paper, combine each of these sets of related sentences below by forming a compound subject, compound verb, or compound sentence. [Note: There may be more than one way to combine each sentence pair.]

EX.   1. Otto will be there. Rebeka will be there.
      1. *Both Otto and Rebeka will be there.*

1. We can make a model volcano for science class. We can make a model rain forest.
2. The apartment was noisy. Esther couldn't fall asleep.
3. The living room isn't warm. The kitchen isn't warm.
4. I wanted to prepare dinner. Nobody else was hungry.
5. Everyone wanted a holiday party. Only four people offered to help plan the event.
6. Sampson likes to eat fresh spinach. Sampson likes to eat fresh squash.
7. You can take the bus to South Station. You can take the train to South Station.
8. The car won't start. The old truck won't start.
9. I am looking forward to spring. The flowers will be in full bloom.
10. I believe Avery has enormous potential. I also believe Enrico has enormous potential.

8n   If two sentences are unequal in importance, you can combine them by placing the less important idea in a subordinate clause.

ORIGINAL   Greg Louganis is an Olympic Gold Medalist in diving. He is now pursuing an acting career.

COMBINED   Greg Louganis, **who is an Olympic Gold Medalist in diving,** is now pursuing an acting career. [adjective clause]

ORIGINAL   Spending some time in the sun is good for most people. Sunlight causes the body to produce vitamin D.

COMBINED   Spending some time in the sun is good for most people, **because sunlight causes the body to produce vitamin D.** [adverb clause]

ORIGINAL   Kitty enjoys listening to books on tape. She told me why.

COMBINED   Kitty told me **why she enjoys listening to books on tape.** [noun clause as direct object]

 REFERENCE NOTE: For more about combining sentences with subordinate clauses and the words that introduce subordinate clauses, see pages 175–181.

EXERCISE 10   Combining by Subordinating Ideas

On your own paper, combine each pair of sentences below by changing one of the sentences into a subordinate clause. [Note: There may be more than one way to combine each sentence pair.]

EX.   1.   My father is a great writer. He is now working on a novel.

     1.   *My father, who is a great writer, is now working on a novel.*

1. Ashley and Carter like to watch science fiction movies. They explained to me why.

2. Franz rides his bike for three miles each day. It makes his body feel strong and healthy.

3. My sister is graduating this year. She has decided to become a middle school science teacher.

4. We fed carrots to the baby rabbits. The rabbits love this crunchy vegetable.

5. That building is going to be a post office. I just learned that it will be completed in about two years.

6. The paper explained that the parade would be postponed. It explained why.

7. That doctor is teaching a class about good eating habits. She began teaching it when she finished medical school.

8. My brother is saving his allowance. He wants to go to summer camp.

9. City Hall is the oldest building in town. A neighbor told me that.

10. The Dahlis own one restaurant. They are now building another restaurant on Park Drive.

VARYING SENTENCE BEGINNINGS

8o   You can improve the overall style of your writing by beginning some sentences with introductory words, phrases, or clauses.

When you vary sentence beginnings, you sometimes need to reword the sentences for clarity. Be sure to place phrase modifiers close to the words they modify.

SUBJECT FIRST	We were unsure, so we double-checked our figures.
REVISED	**Unsure,** we double-checked our figures. [single-word modifier]
SUBJECT FIRST	Jana signalled a turn and prepared to enter the expressway.
REVISED	**By signalling a turn,** Jana prepared to enter the expressway. [prepositional phrase]
SUBJECT FIRST	Pilar rushed under the basket, positioning herself for the rebound.
REVISED	**Positioning herself for the rebound,** Pilar rushed under the basket. [verbal phrase]
SUBJECT FIRST	Giorgio was shaving every other day by the time he turned eighteen.
REVISED	**By the time he turned eighteen,** Giorgio was shaving every other day. [adjective clause]

NOTE   Sentence connectives like *and, but,* and *however* can help you make transitions between ideas. Usually you use these connectives to link ideas within a sentence. Sometimes, though— especially in informal writing—you can use one at the beginning of a sentence for variety and emphasis.

EXAMPLE   Jodie played only one solo. **But** what a solo it was!

EXERCISE 11   Varying Sentence Beginnings

On the lines provided, revise the following sentences by varying their beginnings. The hint in parentheses tells you which type of beginning to use.

EX.   1. Nina had written three or four songs by the spring. (*phrase*)
           By the spring, Nina had written three or four songs.

1. The baby suddenly began to cry. (*single-word modifier*) _____

   _____

2. Martina helped me with the project because it was a big job. (*clause*) _____

   _____

3. I saw several flashes of lightning during the night. (*phrase*) _____

    _____

4. I'll need food and medicine to help that stray puppy. (*phrase*) _____

    _____

5. My dad was a painter before he took up sculpting. (*clause*) _____

    _____

6. Gerardo ran into the gymnasium and asked, "Could I be on one of the

    teams?"(*phrase*) _____

    _____

7. It was fortunate that Theo brought a bright flashlight. (*single-word modifier*)

    _____

8. I scatter birdseed on the ground whenever the weather becomes cold. (*clause*)

    _____

9. Diane wanted an old book, so she looked in the telephone directory for

    used bookstores. (*phrase*) _____

    _____

10. I'll need to increase my work hours to earn enough money for that

    telescope. (*phrase*) _____

    _____

11. Kyle gave me a pat on the back when I won the chess tournament. (*clause*)

    _____

12. I was disappointed when that movie theater closed last summer. (*clause*)

    _____

13. Five of us plan to clip those hedges over the weekend. (*phrase*) _____

    _____

14. I was thrilled, and I ran to give everyone the good news. (*single-word modifier*)

    _____

15. I can count on my best friend whenever I'm in a difficult situation. (*clause*)

    _____

VARYING SENTENCE STRUCTURE

8p   When writing, use a variety of sentence structures rather than a string of simple sentences.

You can improve your writing style by using a mix of simple, compound, complex, and compound-complex sentences.

Paragraph with Simple Sentences
Edmond Halley was an English astronomer. He went to the island of St. Helena. He went in 1676. He was just twenty years old. He wanted to make a list of the stars in the Southern Hemisphere. This had never been done before. He later studied comets. Comets are clouds of dust, ice, rock, and gas. They are frozen. Halley saw a comet in 1682. It was interesting. He noticed that its path was similar to the paths of other comets. It resembled a comet seen in 1607. It also resembled a comet seen in 1531. He guessed it would return in 1758. It returned. Halley's Comet keeps reappearing. It reappears every 76 years.

Revised Paragraph with Varied Sentence Structure
Edmond Halley was an English astronomer. In 1676, when he was just twenty years old, he went to the island of St. Helena, and he did something that had never been done before. He made a list of all the stars in the Southern Hemisphere. He later studied comets, which are frozen clouds of dust, ice, rock, and gas. In 1682, Halley saw an interesting comet and he studied it carefully. He noticed that its path was similar to the paths of other comets, one in 1607 and one in 1531. He guessed, correctly, that it would return in 1758. Halley's Comet reappears every 76 years.

 REFERENCE NOTE: For information about the four types of sentence structures, see page 181.

EXERCISE 12   Working Cooperatively to Vary Sentence Structures

Work with a partner to revise the paragraph below. Use sentence-combining techniques to vary the sentence structures. Write your answers on your own paper.

EX.   1. I read about Kabuki theater.

     2. I read a book from the library.

       I read a book from the library about Kabuki theater.

1   Kabuki is an interesting type of theater. It combines song, dance, and

2 mime. People wear elaborate costumes. *Kabuki* is a Japanese word. It

3 means "song," "dance," and "skill." Kabuki was started in the sixteenth

4 century. It was started by a former Japanese priestess. Her name was

5 Okuni. She staged religious dances. She performed for audiences in her

6 hometown. Okuni's dancing became popular. She decided to make her

7 show bigger. She assembled a group of women. They had experience with

8 song and dance. She taught them her performance. Kabuki theater today is

9 similar to the earliest Kabuki theater. It still uses singing and dialogue. It

10 uses a type of audience participation. The audience participation is

11 unique. Actors talk to spectators. Spectators respond with words.

12 Sometimes they respond by clapping to a rhythm. When Kabuki started,

13 most themes were based on religious teachings. Contemporary events

14 appeared in later Kabuki performances.

EXERCISE 13   Writing a Nomination by Using a Variety of
Sentence Structures

Write a short paragraph of at least ten sentences, nominating someone for the Friend of the Year Award. If you want your reader to be convinced that your choice is the best one, you'll need to make your paragraph interesting, vivid, and clear. Capture your reader's attention by using a variety of sentence structures.

EX.   For the Friend of the Year award, let me introduce you to Ingrid Svenson.

REDUCING WORDINESS

8q Avoid wordiness by using only as many words as you need to make your point.

Choose simple, clear words rather than complicated ones. Do not repeat words or ideas unless it is absolutely necessary. Use these steps to revise wordy sentences.

(1) Take out a whole group of unnecessary words.

WORDY   Before calling Mike on the telephone to ask him about working on the drama production, I made a list of possible questions I might ask him with the intention of trying to find out how I could help.

BETTER   Before **telephoning** Mike about working on the drama production, I made a list of questions **about how I could help.**

(2) Replace complicated words and expressions with simple, clear ones.

WORDY   Akio transferred the waste material to the large metallic receptacle.

BETTER   Akio **put** the **garbage** in the **can.**

(3) Reduce a clause to a phrase.

WORDY   Mahala, who was the captain of the team, batted first.

BETTER   Mahala, **the captain of the team,** batted first.

(4) Reduce a clause or a phrase to one word.

WORDY   I painted it with my brush that was made of horsehair.

BETTER   I painted it with my **horsehair** brush.

EXERCISE 14 Revising Sentences to Reduce Wordiness

On the lines provided, revise each of the following sentences to make them less wordy. [Note: There may be more than one way to revise each sentence.]

EX.   1.   Please emit a warning at the precise moment the train is preparing to exit the station.
Please let me know as soon as the train is ready to leave.

1.   Cousin Estrella and I put the sneakers that were damp near the vent that gives off heat. _____

_____

2. Chuck, who was the last person to leave, locked the door and pulled the shades. _____

_____

3. Before building, we sketched pictures of the ideas we intended to use in order to build a nice doghouse. _____

_____

4. I was unable to swiftly complete the mathematical equations upon which my homework was based due to the fact that exhaustion overcame me. _____

_____

5. My knee was scraped after the fall, but I returned to the seat on the bicycle. _____

_____

6. Those are my boots that I use for hiking. _____

_____

7. Kim, who was born in Korea, would love to make a trip to her homeland someday soon. _____

_____

8. Please supply your instructor with a piece of paper which gives a message from your parent in order that your instructor may know why you are late.

_____

_____

9. When Oliver misplaced his wallet the day before today, he found it right away, which was lucky. _____

_____

10. That terrific radio show is on the radio every morning and in the early evening. _____

_____

CHAPTER REVIEW

A. Revising Sentences for Clarity

On your own paper, revise each of the sentences below to eliminate faulty coordination or faulty parallelism.

EX. 1. Hubert likes water better than drinking juice.

    1. Hubert likes water better than juice.

1. The plant dried out, and I forgot to water it.
2. Writing a poem is as creative an activity as to paint a picture.
3. Pauline is not only a great horseback rider, but also she runs.
4. My brother sent his résumé to a company, and they are located downtown.
5. The dog needs grooming and to be vaccinated.
6. Arthur is not only helpful as a lifeguard but also in teaching.
7. I want more recipes and to have more time for preparing meals.
8. Lorna likes basketball better than playing volleyball.
9. Sam works a paper route, and his route is Main Street and Jewett Street.
10. I changed the light bulb, and it burned out.

B. Revising Sentences to Eliminate Fragments and Run-ons

On your own paper, revise each item below to eliminate sentence fragments and run-on sentences. If a sentence is correct, write C.

EX. 1. Charles Lindbergh flew nonstop across the Atlantic in 1927. Which made him an international hero.

    1. Charles Lindbergh flew nonstop across the Atlantic in 1927, which made him an international hero.

1. Other people had flown the Atlantic, he was the first to fly alone.
2. Lindbergh needed a special kind of plane. That could carry him nonstop from New York City to Paris.
3. In a plane called the *Spirit of St. Louis*, Lindbergh took off from Roosevelt Field, New York.
4. The trip took thirty-three hours, it was 3,500 miles long.
5. He landed in Paris, France. To find an excited crowd waiting for him.

C.   Combining Sentences

On your own paper, combine each pair of sentences below. Change one sentence into a phrase or clause and insert it into the other sentence.

EX.   1.   The auditorium was filled. Many people waited to see a great show.

     1.   *The auditorium was filled with people waiting to see a great show.*

1.   My friend Magda works at the variety store in town. It is near the center of town.

2.   Please bring me more of that delicious soup. That's all I want for lunch.

3.   We collected cans and bottles all morning. We were able to take a large load to the recycling center.

4.   It was a breezy day. We brought our new blue box kite to the beach.

5.   Lee ran after the bus. He waved his arms and shouted, "Stop—my book bag!"

D.   Revising Sentences for Variety

On your own paper, revise each of the sentences or pairs of sentences below to vary the style. The hint in parentheses will tell you how to revise.

EX.   1.   The snow stopped. I helped my little brother build a snowman.
       (*Change to a complex sentence.*)
     1.   *When the snow stopped, I helped my little brother build a snowman.*

1.   We refinished the chairs. Uncle Emil liked the chairs very much. We gave them to Uncle Emil for his birthday. (*Change to a compound-complex sentence.*)

2.   I stood on a small ladder as I washed the windows. (*Begin with a phrase.*)

3.   Carmen dressed warmly before the hayride so that she wouldn't get cold. (*Begin with a clause.*)

4.   The guests arrived early for Thanksgiving dinner. We gave them cheese and crackers. (*Change to a complex sentence.*)

5.   The flowers were wilting. I changed the water in the vase. (*Change to a compound sentence.*)

6.   I danced as I listened to my sister's band. (*Begin with a phrase.*)

7.   The tomatoes and cucumbers were ripe. We made a big salad. (*Change to a complex sentence.*)

8.   We were told that the goat at the farm was friendly. We fed him grain. (*Change to a complex sentence.*)

9.   The organization held a press conference so that people would understand the issue. (*Begin with a clause.*)

10. Gabrielle lost her keys in the yard. She found them. (*Change to a compound sentence.*)

THE ORIGINS OF ENGLISH

About seven thousand years ago, speakers of the language now called *Proto-Indo-European* settled along the coast of the North Sea, in what today is northern Germany and Denmark. This group of migrants—composed of the Angle, Saxon, and Jute tribes—was collectively called the *Anglo-Saxons*.

Some Anglo-Saxons left northern Germany to take jobs with the Roman army, working as mercenaries in the British Isles. After the Roman troops pulled out of Britain, many Anglo-Saxons stayed on, and their relatives from the Continent arrived to join them. These Germanic peoples took over the south of Britain and named it after themselves, *Engla land*, "the land of the Angles." Today we know it as England. They also called their language *Englisc*. We call it *Old English*.

Although English has changed over the centuries, many everyday words are quite close to Old English.

Old English	Modern English
finger	finger
fot	foot
brothor	brother
hnutu	nut
tun	town

After the Anglo-Saxons had been converted to Christianity by monks from Rome, they borrowed many words from Latin.

Latin	Modern English
scol	school
butere	butter
vinum	wine
caesus	cheese

From the ninth to the eleventh centuries, large numbers of Northmen, or Norsemen, invaded England and settled among the English. The Norse introduced words from Scandinavian countries into Old English.

Norse	Modern English
vagn	wagon
hros	horse
vindauga	window

MIDDLE ENGLISH

In A.D. 1066, yet another group of Norsemen conquered England and made French and Latin the language of law, administration, and culture. Called the Normans ("northern people"), they had earlier settled in France and learned French. The Norman conquest of England marks the beginning of the *Middle English* period. By the end of this period, thousands of words from the Normans had been taken into English.

Words Borrowed from Norman French
attorney, court, envy, felon, government, honest, jury, literature, mirror, palace, praise, service, trespass, uncle

MODERN ENGLISH

Near the end of the fifteenth century, printing was introduced to England. For the first time, many people could have books to read. The mass production of books and the resulting increase in literacy helped to standardize the English language and to make universal education possible. Although standardized to a large extent, *Modern English* has continued to absorb words as English-speaking peoples have encountered speakers of other languages all over the globe and as new inventions, ideas, and discoveries have created new linguistic needs.

Words Borrowed from Other Languages
alligator, assassin, banana, kimono, luau, patio, sauerkraut, yacht, yam

EXERCISE 1   Identifying Origins of Words

Look up the words below in a dictionary that gives etymologies (word origins). For each word, write all of its earlier forms, and identify the language of each form. Also write the word's original meaning if it is different from the current meaning. Write on your own paper.

EX.   1. goal
    1. *gaelan (OE)—hinder; gol (ME)—boundary*

1. course	6. castle	11. reed	16. bayou
2. anger	7. judo	12. dairy	17. boil (v.)
3. die	8. judge	13. take	18. haunt
4. pork	9. tomato	14. seat	19. courage
5. gentle	10. dish	15. fellow	20. powder

FORMAL AND INFORMAL ENGLISH

LEVELS OF USAGE

Like your clothing, your language can be formal, informal, or somewhere in between. Whether you use formal or informal language usually depends on the situation. *Informal English* is usually spoken English. *Formal English* is usually written English.

WRITING	
Formal	**Informal**
serious essays, official reports, research papers, some literary criticism	personal letters, journal entries, newspaper and magazine articles, and some nonfiction books, novels, short stories, plays

SPEAKING	
Formal	**Informal**
banquets, dedication ceremonies, addresses, presentation ceremonies	everyday conversation at home, school, work, and recreation

INFORMAL USAGE

Colloquialisms and *slang* are two kinds of expressions that give flavor to informal English.

Colloquialisms are the everyday words and phrases of conversational language. Besides their use in casual conversation, colloquialisms also have a place in expressive and creative writing because of their vividness.

EXAMPLES   At home, my cousins like to **kid around.**
When Jessie spilled her tomato juice, Mom **lost her cool**.

Slang consists of new words, or old words used in new ways, that are especially colorful.

EXAMPLES   *chew the fat*: talk it over
chill out: calm down
couch potato: a person who does little but watch television

Slang is considered highly informal and is inappropriate in most kinds of writing. However, like colloquial language, slang has a place. For example, in fictional dialogue, slang can help make your characters sound more like real people.

EXERCISE 2   Classifying Language as Formal or Informal

Identify the level of usage of each sentence below by writing *formal* or *informal* on the line before the sentence.

EX. <u>informal</u> 1. That radio station plays all the hottest new music.

_____ 1. "What are you up to this weekend?" asked Carmen.

_____ 2. The campers are psyched for the summer to begin.

_____ 3. When you recycle, separate glass, aluminum, and plastic.

_____ 4. You'd better hurry up, or we'll miss the beginning of the movie.

_____ 5. After two weeks of negotiation, the union finally reached an agreement.

_____ 6. Marcelo threw himself into his work at the community center.

_____ 7. "Jump in when you recognize the song," the singer invited his audience.

_____ 8. It is a great honor for me to introduce this evening's guest speaker, Ms. Nina Echohawk.

_____ 9. Hana gets up at the crack of dawn to go to swimming practice.

_____ 10. In 1950, Gwendolyn Brooks was awarded the Pulitzer Prize in poetry.

_____ 11. As the archeologist brushed the tablet's surface, the hieroglyphs emerged.

_____ 12. The town threw a big bash to commemorate its centennial.

_____ 13. Linda insisted that her mind was made up.

_____ 14. Rugby football is a popular sport in England, Australia, New Zealand, and France.

_____ 15. Ella Fitzgerald could really belt out a song.

_____ 16. My sister is bummed out about losing her tennis match.

_____ 17. In 1978, the first female astronauts were admitted to the space shuttle program.

_____ 18. Gina watched the hawk soaring above the field.

_____ 19. My friend Chico whipped up a delicious dinner.

_____ 20. That comedian is such a card.

SPECIFIC AND VIVID WORDS

SPECIFIC WORDS

A *general noun* is a word that refers to a broad category of things rather than to any specific thing or kind of thing. A *general verb* is a word that refers to a kind of action rather than to any specific action.

9a **When you are writing, use specific rather than general words.**

Because general words call up only a vague picture in your reader's mind, they are less interesting, and can even produce misunderstandings. The more specific a word is, the more impact it will have on an audience.

GENERAL NOUNS	Jonah petted the **cat**.
	The **car** pulled into the driveway.
SPECIFIC NOUNS	Jonah petted the **Siamese**.
	The **Corvette** pulled into the driveway.
GENERAL VERBS	Nadia **liked** her health instructor, Ms. Swanson.
	Ima **said,** "I have a cold."
SPECIFIC VERBS	Nadia **admired** her health instructor, Ms. Swanson.
	Ima **whispered,** "I have a cold."

VIVID WORDS

Vivid words are specific words that appeal to the senses.

9b **Use vivid words to make a dramatic impression on your readers and to help you get your meaning across accurately.**

When your audience can see, hear, touch, taste, and smell what you are describing, your writing will come alive for them.

DULL	Lani eagerly came to breakfast.
VIVID	Attracted by the aroma of waffles sizzling on the griddle, and the "glug, glug" of orange juice being poured into clear plastic tumblers, Lani rushed across the polished wood floor into the sunlit kitchen.

EXERCISE 3   Revising Sentences for Specific and Vivid Words

On your own paper, revise the italicized words in each of the following sentences, using specific and vivid words. Add as many details as you wish.

EX.   1. Wildflowers *grow* on the hills.
   1. Wildflowers blanket the hills in purple and yellow.

1. The *weather* spoiled the picnic.

2. Toni's dress looks *nice*.

3. The saltwater aquarium contains *fish*.

4. "I'll be in charge of the decorations," Sam *said*.

5. As the *storm* blew harder, the windows *shook*.

6. Tanya and April were *tired* after hiking all day.

7. "Water is rushing into the boat," *said* the captain.

8. The carpenter *took* the *tool* from her workbelt.

9. Suni *closed* the door behind her.

10. Suddenly, a *dog* came around the corner.

11. The tennis player *enjoyed* her victory.

12. I just read an *interesting* article about British colonialism.

13. The New Hampshire woods are *pretty*.

14. You look *sad*.

15. After she *tasted* the *hot food*, Celia's eyes watered.

16. We had a *nice* time at the *party*.

17. The *driver* will be waiting beside *the car*.

18. Each evening, the *dog eats* her food.

19. At the end of a long day at school, their teacher *sat down*.

20. *Many flowers grow* in our backyard.

Drabble reprinted by permission of UFS, Inc.

LEVELS OF MEANING

NONSEXIST LANGUAGE

Nonsexist language is language that applies to people in general, both male and female.

9c   When you are referring to humanity as a whole, gender-specific expressions are inappropriate and misleading.

GENDER-SPECIFIC	man	mankind	fireman	foreman
NONSEXIST	**humanity**	**people**	**firefighter**	**supervisor**

In the past, many skills and occupations largely excluded either men or women. Today, most jobs are held by both men and women, and our language is adjusting to reflect this change.

GENDER-SPECIFIC	housewife	draftsman	mailman	manmade
NONSEXIST	**homemaker**	**drafter**	**letter carrier**	**synthetic**

DENOTATIONS AND CONNOTATIONS

9d   Before you use a word, you need to know both its denotation and its connotations.

A *denotation* is the strict dictionary definition of a word. *Connotations* are the emotions and associations that a word may suggest. Notice the differences among the examples below.

EXAMPLES   Dad **spoke** to us for fifteen minutes.
Dad **lectured** us for fifteen minutes.
Dad **babbled** at us for fifteen minutes.
Dad **yelled** at us for fifteen minutes.
Dad **explained** things to us for fifteen minutes.

Any word may arouse different emotions and associations in different people. But there are some words that have no connotations for most people.

EXAMPLES   listen   glass   table   remember   water

LOADED WORDS

9e   Use loaded words with care.

Words and phrases that have strong connotations, either positive or negative, are called *loaded words*.

EXAMPLES   The Senator called the proposal "ill-considered."
The Senator called the proposal "idiotic."

This riverfront property is now available at a low price.
You can buy this swampland now, cheap.

Because they appeal to emotions, loaded words can create bias. Advertisers, politicians, salespeople, and writers of newspaper editorials all use loaded words to influence their audiences. Writers of narratives use loaded words to get readers emotionally involved with situations and characters. Even writers of informative articles do not always use objective language.

EXERCISE 4   Revising Sentences Containing Sexist or Loaded Language

Underline the sexist or loaded word or words in each sentence below. In the space above, write a more neutral expression.

EX.   1.   My brother <u>smirked</u> as the photographer took our picture.
(smiled)

1.   Carol jabbered to us about her new job.

2.   Ben prefers old-fashioned music.

3.   I like the odor you're wearing. What is it called?

4.   To voice your opinion on public policy, write to your congressman.

5.   The Museum of Contemporary Art exhibits weird paintings.

6.   Rafi gossiped about his science project with his professor.

7.   If you think you can persuade me, you're crazy.

8.   The salesgirl helped me find a gift for Toshio.

9.   Fanatics have been demonstrating outside the courthouse all week.

10.   Would you ask the stewardess when we'll be landing?

11.   Martin approached the stage at a snail's pace.

12.   Many strange crafts are exhibited at the cultural center.

13.   The politician hired a public relations firm to run his propaganda campaign.

14.   My brother and sister are firemen.

15.   According to the invitation, sloppy clothing is acceptable.

16.   Mankind must cooperate if they want to preserve the environment.

17.   Pedro made his decision after cautiously considering his options.

18.   The cancellation of the play was tragic.

19.   The cake recipe calls for fake vanilla flavoring.

20.   A successful journalist needs to be pushy.

UNCLEAR LANGUAGE

9f   Use words that say exactly what you mean.

Many words sound so much alike or seem so close in meaning that they are easily confused with one another.

EXAMPLES
disinterested	famous	imply
uninterested	notorious	infer
irritate	infringe	skeptical
aggravate	intrude	dubious

9g   Avoid tired words and clichés.

A *tired word* is one that has become vague and bland from overuse.

EXAMPLES   fine   great   nice   so   very

A *cliché* is a tired expression. Many clichés are figures of speech—metaphors, similes, or personifications. Others are hyperboles—exaggerations for special effect. In most cases, clichés are trite and stale, and a better word choice is available.

EXAMPLES
lazy as a mule	the calm before the storm	wise as an owl
the bottom line	in this day and age	long arm of the law

9h   Avoid mixed idioms and metaphors.

An *idiom* is an expression that cannot be taken literally. It says one thing but means another. A *metaphor* is a figure of speech that describes one thing by comparing it to another, basically different, thing.

IDIOMS	I lost my head.	That takes the cake!
METAPHORS	the head of the bed	the roof of the mouth

It's important to use idioms and metaphors correctly and consistently. If you mix up idioms or metaphors, you may confuse your readers.

IDIOM   Time flies.

MIXED IDIOM   Time speeds.

METAPHOR   The fog wound slowly through the city streets. [Fog is compared to a river.]

MIXED METAPHOR   The fog wound slowly through the city streets and touched passersby with its cold, damp fingers. [Fog is compared to both a river and a person.]

EXERCISE 5   Choosing Correct Words

For each sentence below, underline the word in parentheses that correctly completes the sentence. Use a dictionary to check the meanings of any words that you are unsure about.

EX.   1.   M. C. Escher was a (*noted*, *notable*) graphic artist.

1. Escher was (*anxious*, *eager*) to create designs from repeated figures.
2. Through an (*intense*, *intensive*) study of geometry, he discovered how to repeat complex, interlocking figures across a surface.
3. Escher advanced this study (*farther*, *further*) than any artist before him.
4. Some of his optical (*allusions*, *illusions*) resemble kaleidoscopes.
5. Many of his designs (*include*, *comprise*) fanciful lizards and fish.
6. Viewers cannot always (*anticipate*, *predict*) how the patterns will repeat.
7. They are (*shocked*, *surprised*) to see how new figures emerge.
8. In one design (*incredible*, *incredulous*) lizards hatch from hexagons.
9. People are still delighted by the visual (*affects*, *effects*) of his designs.
10. Escher was truly a pioneer of (*contemporary*, *modern*) graphic art.

EXERCISE 6   Working Cooperatively to Revise Sentences for Clarity

Working with a partner, rewrite each sentence below to eliminate the italicized misused words, tired words and clichés, and mixed idioms and metaphors. Write the sentences on your own paper.

EX.   1.   The president's speech was *food for thought.*
   1.   The president's speech was thought provoking.

1. Kesha has been *busy as a bee.*
2. Don't leave me *up in the air.*
3. The documentary was *interesting.*
4. You're *getting the bark off the wrong tree.*
5. The police commissioner vowed that the investigators *would leave no stone unturned.*
6. Raymond supported his thesis with *historic* evidence.
7. At daylight saving time, you need to adjust the *fingers* of the clock.
8. Reggie completed the puzzle and said, "That was *a breeze.*"
9. "*There's more to golf than meets the eye*," the instructor stated.
10. Marla is a *good* singer.

CHAPTER REVIEW

A. Questions About the Origins of English

Answer the questions below on the lines provided. Use a dictionary if needed.

1. What language is the earliest ancestor of Modern English? _____

   _____

2. Name two influences on the development of Old English. _____

   _____

3. What is the significance of the Norman Conquest? _____

   _____

4. What languages had influence during the Middle English period? _____

   _____

5. Which period saw the introduction of standardized spelling? _____

   _____

6. What language originally provided the words *master* and *altar*? _____

   _____

7. From what language did English speakers most recently borrow *medicine*
   and *saint*? _____

8. Which is the word origin of *wheel*? _____

   _____

9. What are the Old English and Middle English forms of *priest*? _____

   _____

10. What is the word origin of *etymology*? _____

    _____

B. Revising a Passage to Avoid Sexist, Loaded, and Unclear Language

In the following paragraph, draw a line through the italicized words or
expressions. In the space above, write clear, neutral words and expressions that
have appropriate connotations.

EX. [1] American Indian women create ~~variable~~ (various) forms of art.

[1] Among many Indian nations, the *girls* are the principal artists.

[2] Women *impress* their art in objects, such as blankets, pots, and baskets.

[3] Although the articles are *handy*, they are considered pieces of art as well.

[4] Many Plains Indian women have been *honorable* for their beautifully designed baskets. [5] Baskets given as marriage gifts are not *intentional* for everyday use. [6] Navajo women are also *widely famed* for their blanket weaving. [7] Some of their blankets have *easy*, geometric designs. [8] Others display *confusing* combinations of colors and shapes. [9] To show appreciation for much-needed water, clouds often *dot* the water pots the women make. [10] These women artists *enlighten* other women about these arts from generation to generation.

C. Working Cooperatively to Eliminate Inappropriate and Unclear Language in a Paragraph

Working with a partner, draw a line through any inappropriate, vague, unclear, or tired words and expressions in the paragraph below. Then rewrite the paragraph on your own paper using clear, specific, and fresh language. Some sentences contain no errors.

EX.   [1]   Yoshiko Uchida made a name for herself as a writer.
　　　 1.   Yoshiko Uchida gained recognition as a writer.

　　[1] She enjoyed success as a writer of books for kids and adults. [2] She put out her first collection of stories in 1949. [3] Uchida, the child of first-generation Japanese immigrants, based her writing on Japanese culture. [4] Some of her stories were tales of Japanese folktales. [5] The years she spent in an internment camp during World War II also had a big effect on her writing. [6] Following the bombing of Pearl Harbor, the U.S. government shipped thousands of Japanese Americans to the camps. [7] After five months in one internment camp, the twenty-year-old Uchida and her family were shipped to Topaz, a guarded camp in Utah. [8] She taught elementary school at Topaz until she was released to accept a graduate study position at Smith College in 1943. [9] Her parents were relinquished from the camp later that year. [10] After her mother's death in 1966, Uchida wrote *Journey to Topaz: A Story of the Japanese-American Evacuation*, as a tribute to things her parents had gone through. [11] This book was her first about the Japanese-American things. [12] From that day forward, she has written many interesting stories about Japanese-American culture. [13] In 1982, Uchida wrote a book called *Desert Exile: The Uprooting of a Japanese-American Family*, about her experiences during the internment. [14] Uchida hoped that her writing might give young Japanese Americans a sense of self-centeredness. [15] A multitude of prestigious accolades attest to Uchida's success in producing books that respond to young people's need for identity.

NOUNS

The Eight Parts of Speech			
noun	adjective	pronoun	conjunction
verb	adverb	preposition	interjection

10a A *noun* is a word used to name a person, a place, a thing, or an idea.

PERSONS   janitor, Dorothea Dix, aunt, rock star, friend
PLACES   Dallas, Idaho, station, park, cafeteria, lake
THINGS   orange, modem, illness, orchid, insects
IDEAS   education, ambition, theory, courage, democracy

10b A *common noun* names any one of a group of persons, places, things, or ideas. A *proper noun* names a particular person, place, thing, or idea.

COMMON NOUNS   man, state, event, holiday, language, vehicle, street, building
PROPER NOUNS   Thomas Jefferson, Texas, Winter Olympics, Groundhog Day, Swahili, Isuzu Trooper, Museum of Modern Art, Pennsylvania Avenue

10c A *concrete noun* names an object that can be perceived by the senses (hearing, sight, smell, taste, and touch). An *abstract noun* names a quality, characteristic, or idea.

CONCRETE NOUNS   Mexico City, sidewalk, teakettle, President Lincoln, toucan, wombat, light, chill
ABSTRACT NOUNS   truth, gratefulness, belief, bravery, attitude, fate, democracy, wit

10d A *collective noun* names a group.

EXAMPLES   herd, troop, congress, pack, jury

10e A *compound noun* consists of two or more words used together as a single noun. Some compound nouns are written as one word, some as separate words, and others as hyphenated words.

EXAMPLES   boardwalk, Ferris wheel, editor in chief

EXERCISE 1   Classifying Nouns

On your own paper, classify each of the following nouns. First, write *comm.* for *common* or *prop.* for *proper*. Then, if the noun is *compound*, write *comp.*, and if it is *collective*, write *coll.* Use a semicolon to separate your answers.

EX.   1.   family
       1.   *com.; coll.*

1. happiness
2. ski jump
3. jury
4. meteor
5. Hannah Johnson
6. parking lot
7. doubt
8. Emilio Estevez
9. team
10. psychology
11. blackberry
12. Mount Everest
13. enthusiasm
14. roller coaster
15. Englishman
16. flock
17. fishing rod
18. California
19. sketchbook
20. Tuesday
21. father-in-law
22. cello
23. crowd
24. blue
25. pony express

EXERCISE 2   Classifying Concrete Nouns and Abstract Nouns

On your own paper, classify each of the italicized nouns below. Write *con.* for *concrete* or *abs.* for *abstract*. Use a semicolon to separate your answers.

EX.   1.   *Enrico* never misses his karate *lesson.*
       1.   *con.; abs.*

1. *Yolanda* put on her elbow-length *gloves.*
2. The *sunset* tonight is an amazing *purple.*
3. Jorge has nothing but *impatience* for junk *mail.*
4. *Oprah Winfrey* shows great *talent* as an interviewer.
5. My family eats a great deal of *soup* in the *winter.*
6. The store *motto* is "*satisfaction* guaranteed."
7. We dropped our old *telephone*, and it still worked when *Mom* used it.
8. "Do not trade *justice* for economy," the *speaker* urged.
9. I love the type of *pottery* with the cracked *finish.*
10. She hasn't any *tact*, but she makes up for it with her *humor.*
11. The *confidence* of the *runner* inspired us.
12. *Joel* called his mother after the *game.*
13. At *school* we discussed family *traditions.*
14. My *house* is a historical *landmark.*
15. Many people have great *respect* for Edmonia Lewis's *sculpture.*

PRONOUNS

10f A *pronoun* is a word used in place of a noun or more than one noun.

Personal Pronouns	I, me, my, mine, we, us, our, ours, you, your, yours, he, him, his, she, her, hers, it, its, they, them, their, theirs
Relative Pronouns	that, which, who, whom, whose
Interrogative Pronouns	who, whose, what, whom, which
Demonstrative Pronouns	this, that, these, those
Indefinite Pronouns	all, another, any, anybody, anyone, anything, both, each, either, everybody, everyone, everything, few, many, more, most, much, neither, nobody, none, no one, one, other, several, some, somebody, someone, something, such
Reflexive and Intensive Pronouns	myself, ourselves, yourself, yourselves, himself, herself, itself, themselves

NOTE In this book words such as *my, your, his, her, ours,* and *their* are treated as possessive pronouns rather than as adjectives. Follow your teacher's guidelines when referring to such words.

The word that a pronoun stands for is called its ***antecedent***. A pronoun may appear in the same sentence as its antecedent or in a following sentence. The antecedent may be a noun or another pronoun.

EXAMPLES **Latoya** loves her **cat. She** takes good care of **it.** [*Latoya* is the antecedent of *she. Cat* is the antecedent of *it.*]
We told **her** that **she** could stay with **us.** [*We* is the antecedent of *us. Her* is the antecedent of *she.*]

EXERCISE 3   Identifying Pronouns

Underline the pronouns in the following sentences.

EX.   1. <u>Which</u> of the hats did Alfred choose?

1. Try to be <u>yourself</u> during the interview.

2. <u>Everyone</u> wanted to get tickets to the concert.

127

3. Jake always knocks too hard on our door.

4. Math is the class that follows gym.

5. Clea sang a song nobody else knew.

6. The writer himself couldn't understand the book.

7. Before the hike, Sally and Mia tightened the laces on their boots.

8. Divers collected many of the specimens out near the reef.

9. My sister has always wanted to be in the Olympics.

10. The grocer told Henry those were the last of the apples.

11. Who is available to help move the piano?

12. Aunt Phyllis took me to Guatemala last year.

13. We walked silently up the hill and into the woods.

14. Carlos is the neighbor who helped free the bat from the brambles.

15. These are the mittens made in Norway.

EXERCISE 4   Identifying Pronouns and Their Antecedents

Underline the pronouns in the paragraph below. Circle the antecedent of each pronoun.

EX.   [1] Louis Braille dedicated his life to helping people with visual impairments.

[1] The son of a saddlemaker, Louis Braille blinded himself in an accident at the age of three. [2] At the time, the accident seemed tragic, yet it set in motion an extraordinary life and career. [3] Braille went to Paris to attend a school that taught visually impaired people to read using bent twigs. [4] But, of course, books themselves could not be made of twigs. [5] Then Braille met a visually impaired concert pianist who paid for him to learn to play the church organ. [6] Eventually, Braille earned his reputation as a talented organist, and good fortune followed. [7] But the young man had taken a vow to help visually impaired people, and he never forgot it. [8] Using money that he made playing the organ, Braille worked for years on his ideas to help others like himself. [9] The result was the Braille reading system, into which both numbers and letters can be translated. [10] If Louis Braille had never lost his sight, perhaps most people who are blind would still be unable to read for themselves.

ADJECTIVES

↪ *describe noun*

10g   An *adjective* is a word used to modify a noun or pronoun.

To *modify* means "to describe or to make more definite." Adjectives modify nouns or pronouns by telling *what kind*, *which one*, or *how many (how much)*.

What kind?	helpful librarian, cool breeze
Which one?	that star, **final** exam, **next** day
How many?	**more** work, two steps, **less** time

The most frequently used adjectives are *a, an,* and *the*. These words are called *articles*.

↪ *generalized*

A and *an* are *indefinite articles*. They refer to any one of a general group. *A* is used before words beginning with a consonant sound; *an* is used before words beginning with a vowel sound. *An* is also used before words beginning with the consonant *h* when the *h* is not pronounced.

EXAMPLES   Pressed between the pages of the book was **a** single rose petal.
    We saw **an** interesting film about African history.
    Having dinner with the president is **an** honor.

particular

The is the *definite article*. It refers to a particular person, place, thing, or idea.

EXAMPLE   The last song of the evening was a slow, sad one.

Sometimes nouns are used as adjectives.

EXAMPLES   What caused the **train** wreck? [*Train*, usually a noun, is used as an adjective to modify the noun *wreck*.]
    The **restaurant** manager donates food to a local shelter.
    [*Restaurant*, usually a noun, is used as an adjective to modify the noun *manager*.]

NOTE   Some pairs or groups of nouns are considered compound nouns. By checking a dictionary, you can avoid confusing a noun that is used as an adjective with a noun that is part of a compound noun.

COMPOUND NOUNS   space station, soy sauce, goose egg, Mexico City

EXERCISE 5   Identifying Adjectives in Sentences

Underline the adjectives in each of the sentences on the following page, and circle the word or words each adjective modifies. Do not include *a, an,* or *the*.

129

EX. 1. The Polos set out for China in 1271 A.D. to visit the <u>Mongol</u> (emperor), Kublai Khan.

1. Their long (journey) took them over vast deserts.

2. The Polo brothers, Niccolò and Maffeo, were Venetian merchants, and Marco was Niccolò's son.

3. The Polos were bringing holy oil from Jerusalem to Kublai Khan.

4. They traveled through the Pamir Mountains, which had higher peaks than any other mountains they crossed.

5. At night, they used the stars to tell them the correct direction to head.

6. That trip brought the Polos to wondrous places.

7. The Polos spent a year in Campichu, a grand city full of golden statues.

8. Marco Polo described the Gobi Desert as having sandy hills and valleys and containing no food at all.

9. In 1275 A.D., the Polos arrived at the Khan's summer palace in the eastern city of Shangtu.

10. Their historic journey had taken over three years.

11. Kublai Khan employed Marco Polo as a foreign official of the Asian empire.

12. On one trip Marco went to Yunnan province.

13. As a traveling official, Marco was expected to be a keen and truthful observer.

14. Later, he told incredible tales about mysterious China.

15. A curious writer, Rustichello, made Marco's travels famous in a book, *Description of the World.*

16. The book was the first record of a European's impression of Chinese civilization.

17. Some descriptions were of places that Marco only heard about from other people.

18. Marco's experience inspired European explorers to go to the East.

19. It seems clear that Marco was courageous and resourceful.

20. The Polos returned to Venice twenty-four years after they left it.

VERBS

10h   A *verb* is a word that expresses action or a state of being.

(1) An *action verb* expresses physical or mental activity.

EXAMPLES   shriek, think, hope, break, growl, forget, jog, try, laugh, buy

(2) A *transitive verb* is an action verb that takes an *object*—a noun or pronoun that tells *who* or *what* receives the action of the verb.

EXAMPLES   The cat **emptied** its water bowl. [*Water bowl* receives the action of the verb *emptied*.]
The thunder **rattled** the windows. [*Windows* receive the action of the verb *rattled*.]

(3) An *intransitive verb* is an action verb that does not take an object.

EXAMPLES   Lena's balloon **sailed** away.
An osprey **soared** over the treetops.

A verb can be transitive in one sentence and intransitive in another.

EXAMPLES   You really **burst** my bubble. [transitive]
The dam **burst**. [intransitive]

(4) A *linking verb*, or *state-of-being verb*, connects the subject with a noun, a pronoun, or an adjective that identifies or describes it.

The most commonly used linking verbs are forms of the verb *be*: *am, is, are, was, were, being, been,* and so on. Other common linking verbs include *appear, become, feel, grow, look, remain, seem, smell, sound, stay, taste,* and *turn.*

EXAMPLES   This Mediterranean salad **tastes** delicious.
The night **grew** cold and spooky.

Many linking verbs can be used as action (nonlinking) verbs as well.

EXAMPLES   This milk **has turned** sour. [The verb links the subject, *milk*, to a word that describes it, *sour*.]
A police car **turned** the corner. [The verb describes an action taken by the subject, *police car*.]

(5) A *verb phrase* consists of a *main verb* and at least one *helping*, or *auxiliary*, verb. Common helping verbs are forms of *be*, forms of *have*, forms of *do*, and the auxiliaries *can, could, may, might, must, shall, should, will,* and *would*.

EXAMPLES   **does** know, **must have been** hurrying, **is** now sailing

EXERCISE 6   Identifying Transitive and Intransitive Verbs

In the sentences below, identify each italicized verb as transitive or intransitive.
Write *trans.* for *transitive* or *intr.* for *intransitive* on the line before each sentence.

EX. _____intr._____ 1. The crew *calmed* down after the storm.

_____ 1. The messenger *rode* all night.

_____ 2. We *turned* the dial to the public radio station.

_____ 3. Whom *did* you *elect* treasurer?

_____ 4. Marjorie *flipped* the pancakes as if she were an expert.

_____ 5. Toshiro *wrote* frequently to his uncle.

_____ 6. Please *send* Stamos my best wishes.

_____ 7. The first clouds *looked* fluffy and white.

_____ 8. Yesterday Grace *bowled* a perfect game.

_____ 9. Two coats of paint *work* better than one.

_____ 10. Which hamster *crawled* into your glove?

EXERCISE 7   Identifying Verb Phrases and Helping Verbs

In each of the sentences below, underline the verb phrase once and the helping
verb, or verbs, twice.

EX.   1. Do you play the piano?

1. George will be the first one at the planetarium.

2. That tree was transplanted here from another part of the country.

3. Must everyone shout at once?

4. I can remember it perfectly.

5. The senators are debating the issue right this minute.

6. Sondra had always helped her mother can tomatoes.

7. His package might have been sent to the wrong address.

8. Does Yolanda usually smile so much?

9. Our stuffed animals would definitely win a prize for the best

toy collection.

10. Miguel is thinking about tomorrow's trip.

ADVERBS

10i An *adverb* is a word used to modify a verb, an adjective, or another adverb.

Adverbs modify by telling *how, when, where,* or *to what extent*.

most adverbs end in —ly ending

How?	Todd washed the car **quickly.** Marissa works **fast.**
When?	The patient is resting **now.** Winter came **early** last year.
Where?	May we look **around?** Please come **here.**
To what extent?	We **almost** had an accident. The weather was **extremely** bad.

EXAMPLES   After the operation, Mr. Santos could see **clearly** again. [*Clearly* modifies the verb, telling *how* Mr. Santos *could see.*]
The lions were **quite** hungry. [*Quite* modifies the adjective, telling *to what extent* the lions were *hungry.*]
Chandra dances **more** gracefully than I. [*More* modifies the adverb, telling *to what extent* Chandra dances *gracefully.*]

EXERCISE 8   Identifying Adverbs and the Words They Modify

Underline the adverbs in each of the following sentences. Draw brackets around the word or words that each adverb modifies. On the line before the sentence, identify the word or words that are modified by writing *v.* for *verb,* *adj.* for *adjective,* or *adv.* for *adverb.*

EX.   _____*v.*_____ 1. Giselle [returned] today.

_____ 1. Every morning he quickly turned off the alarm.

_____ 2. Completely happy with the show, the critic wrote a good review.

_____ 3. The building was later finished.

_____ 4. Some sports figures are extremely talented.

_____ 5. Our teacher often likes to tell about her trip to Mexico.

_____ 6. Park the truck closer to the entrance.

_____ 7. Jewel wondered if she would ever get to see Dallas.

133

_____ 8. To open the door, push that lever forward slowly.

_____ 9. Happily, the three of them ran to the park.

_____ 10. Fred claimed he had found a new job almost accidentally.

_____ 11. Hector ran immediately to aid his brother.

_____ 12. The people next door just recently moved in.

_____ 13. Consider yourself quite fortunate to have been chosen.

_____ 14. Several of the most popular games were played at the party.

_____ 15. Rather formally, Melba introduced me to her boyfriend.

EXERCISE 9   Using Adverbs

Complete each sentence below by supplying an appropriate adverb. The word or phrase in parentheses tells you what information the adverb should give. Write the sentences on your own paper.

EX.   1. She worked _(How?)_ at her new job.
    1. She worked hard at her new job.

1. Chad could spell long words _(To what extent?)_ well.

2. The quarterback threw the pass _(How?)_ .

3. Five of our new computers are kept _(Where?)_ in the math room.

4. People who wish to run in marathons should practice _(How?)_ .

5. We'll find out the answer _(When?)_ .

©1993 by Sidney Harris.

"I'VE JUST READ YOUR LATEST BOOK AND FOUND IT FAST MOVING, FULL OF SUSPENSE, AND VERY WELL WRITTEN. YOU'RE PROBABLY JUST THE PERSON WHO COULD CLEAR UP SOMETHING THAT'S BEEN PUZZLING ME FOR YEARS. WHAT'S AN ADVERB?"

REVIEW EXERCISE 1

A. Classifying Nouns

On the line before each sentence below, classify the italicized noun. Write *con.* for *concrete* or *abs.* for *abstract*. Then, if the noun is compound, write *comp.*, and if it is collective, write *coll.* Use a semicolon to separate your answers.

EX. <u>con.; comp.</u> 1. The real *Mother Goose* may have lived in Boston.

_____ 1. There is *evidence* that she was not a kindly bird in a bonnet.

_____ 2. A woman named Elizabeth Foster married *Isaac Goose* in 1682.

_____ 3. Elizabeth took care of her ten *stepchildren*.

_____ 4. She eventually added six of her own children to the *family*.

_____ 5. Elizabeth had a wonderful *memory* for stories, rhymes, and fables.

_____ 6. Thomas Fleet, Mrs. Goose's *son-in-law*, collected and printed some of her tales.

_____ 7. By *tradition*, Mother Goose rhymes have no known author.

_____ 8. Copies of Fleet's *collection* have all disapeared.

_____ 9. Some childhood *favorites*, such as "Old King Cole," are from a French collector.

_____ 10. Elizabeth Goose was buried in a *graveyard* near the Park Street Church.

B. Classifying Verbs

On the line before each sentence below, identify the italicized verb as an action verb or a linking verb. If it is an action verb, tell whether it is transitive or intransitive. Write *a.v.* for *action verb, l.v.* for *linking verb, trans.* for *transitive*, and *intr.* for *intransitive.* Use a semicolon to separate your answers.

EX. <u>a.v.; trans.</u> 1. Eloise *grew* miniature roses in her window box.

_____ 1. Your brother *looks* taller this year.

_____ 2. That airplane can *fly* faster than any other ever built.

_____ 3. Please *stand* those boxes up in the corner.

_____ 4. Hoy *considered* all his options before deciding.

_____ 5. Only ten loyal fans *remained* at the end of the game.

_____ 6. Eat your oatmeal before it *gets* cold.

_____ 7. I have *been* so busy, I haven't had time to call.

_____ 8. *Can* we *see* you tomorrow?

_____   9. The balloon touched the lightbulb and *exploded*.

_____   10. It *might be* better if we left early.

C.   Identifying Adjectives and Adverbs

On the line before each sentence below, identify the italicized word by writing *adj.* for *adjective* or *adv.* for *adverb*. Then underline the word or words that the adjective or adverb modifies.

EX.   __adj.__   1. The prow of the ship cut through the *thick* ice. __

_____   1. Everyone was *formally* dressed for the wedding.

_____   2. I have heard that crocodiles are more *dangerous* than alligators.

_____   3. The *all-American* hamburger most likely originated in Germany.

_____   4. Ricardo explained the topic *clearly*.

_____   5. The settlers stopped to repair the *wagon* wheel.

_____   6. Remind me *later* to fix that window.

_____   7. On the way to Boston, we stopped to see the *most* wonderful museum.

_____   8. The *famous* author spoke at our school.

_____   9. My cousin has always wanted to be an *airline* pilot.

_____   10. Wiggins was six-foot-four, so we had to look *up* when we talked to him.

D.   Using the Parts of Speech to Write a Children's Book

You are writing an alphabet book for small children. Each entry in your book will include a letter of the alphabet, a sentence that includes a word beginning with that letter, and the part of speech of the word.

Write entries for each of the twenty-six letters in the alphabet. Use each of the parts of speech that you have learned at least five times. These parts of speech are *nouns, pronouns, adjectives, verbs,* and *adverbs*.

EX.   A is for **apricot**.
   I ate an apricot.
   Apricot is a **noun**.

PREPOSITIONS

✓ shows relation.

10j   A *preposition* is a word used to show how a noun or a pronoun is related to some other word in the sentence.

A preposition introduces a *prepositional phrase.* The noun or pronoun that ends a prepositional phrase is the *object of the preposition.* In the following examples, the object of the prepositions is *tree.*

Notice how changing the preposition in the following examples changes the relationship between *flew* and *tree.*

EXAMPLES   The bird flew **above** the tree.   The bird flew **beneath** the tree.
The bird flew **into** the tree.   The bird flew **near** the tree.
The bird flew **around** the tree.   The bird flew **toward** the tree.

Commonly Used Prepositions				
aboard	before	by	like	through
about	behind	concerning	near	to
above	below	down	of	toward
across	beneath	during	off	under
after	beside	except	on	until
against	besides	for	onto	up
along	between	from	outside	upon
among	beyond	in	over	with
around	but (meaning	inside	past	within
at	*except*)	into	since	without

Prepositions may also be compound.

Compound Prepositions			
according to	because of	in place of	next to
along with	by means of	in spite of	on account of
as of	in addition to	instead of	out of

NOTE   The same word may be either an adverb or a preposition, depending on its use in a sentence.

EXAMPLES   During the storm, please stay **inside**. [adverb]
The parrot was sleeping **inside** his cage. [preposition]

137

EXERCISE 10   Identifying Prepositions and Their Objects

Underline each preposition in the sentences below. Draw a bracket around its object. Sentences contain more than one answer.

EX.   1. Samuel lives <u>near</u> the[lake] .

1. Mail the peaches to Oregon.

2. Have you ever heard the song "Over the Rainbow"?

3. No one had seen Rip van Winkle for twenty years.

4. During the 1840s, Alexander Cartwright wrote the basic rules of modern baseball.

5. My aunt does not allow elbows on the table.

6. The radio reported that we could expect more sunshine in the afternoon.

7. If the bull charges, don't get in the way.

8. Finding a parking place near that theater can often be difficult.

9. I tried reasoning with him, but he wouldn't listen to me.

10. Her flower arrangement was in a crystal vase.

11. Kent is always racing his bike around the block.

12. If she's not here by noon, give her a call.

13. We were pleased that the team had succeeded against great odds.

14. I wore a jacket instead of a sweater.

15. Do you think life exists outside our solar system?

EXERCISE 11   Writing an Explanation of Services

You and some friends have started a small business entertaining neighborhood children at birthday parties. The Community Service Bureau keeps a register of various businesses in the community. The bureau will list your business if you write a short explanation of your services.

On your own paper, write fifteen sentences explaining what your birthday party service does. You might describe the costumes that you and your friends wear, the kinds of entertainment that you offer, and the games that you have the children play. Use and underline at least ten prepositional phrases in your sentences. Include at least three compound prepositions.

EX.   1. *Our group performs magic tricks, gives puppet shows, and entertains children with <u>many different games.</u>*

CONJUNCTIONS AND INTERJECTIONS

10k A *conjunction* is a word used to join words or groups of words.

(1) A *coordinating conjunction* connects words or groups of words that are used in the same way.

Coordinating Conjunctions
and but for nor or so yet

(handwritten: FANBOY)

EXAMPLES   On the end table were a reading lamp **and** some books.
Have you ever ridden a mule **or** a donkey?
The plane ran out of fuel, **but** the pilot glided it to a safe landing.

(2) *Correlative conjunctions* are pairs of conjunctions that join words or groups of words used in the same way.

(handwritten: word pairs)

Correlative Conjunctions		
both . . . and	neither . . . nor	whether . . . or
either . . . or	not only . . . but also	

EXAMPLES   Do you know **whether** Aunt Camilia **or** Uncle José will be
attending the ceremony?
Neither rain **nor** snow falls in that dry, barren land.
Your boots are **not only** wet **but also** muddy. *(handwritten: ideas that are less important.)*

(3) A *subordinating conjunction* begins a subordinate clause, joining it to
an independent clause. *(handwritten: adds to the main idea.)*

Commonly Used Subordinating Conjunctions			
after	because	since	when
although	before	so that	whenever
as	even though	than	where
as if	how	that	wherever
as much as	if	though	whether
as though	in order that	unless	while
as well as	provided	until	why

EXAMPLES   Sit still **so that** the doctor can examine your bruise.
Because it started raining, we had to rush for shelter.

> **10l**   An *interjection* is a word used to express emotion. It has no
> grammatical relation to other words in the sentence.
>
> EXAMPLES   ah, ouch, hey, oh, well, whew, whoops, wow, yikes

EXERCISE 12   Identifying and Classifying Conjunctions

Underline the conjunctions in the following paragraph. In the space above each
conjunction, write *coor.* for *coordinating conjunction*, *corr.* for *correlative
conjunction*, or *sub.* for *subordinating conjunction*.   *◦ pairs .*

EX.   [1] Snake charmers begin learning their craft at the age of five $\underset{coor.}{\underline{or}}$ six.

[1] Even $\underset{sub.}{\underline{though}}$ Westerners may think it strange, in India and Egypt the

practice of snake charming has been going on for thousands of years. [2] In

India, the snake charmers consider themselves to be a separate group, and

they associate certain beliefs with their practices as well. [3] They see snake

charming not only as an art, but also as a way of life. [4] When they are

successful at it, they become part of a sacred tradition. [5] Since they have no

other source of income, "snakers" stage the most dramatic performances

possible. [6] Because the threat of danger attracts crowds, poisonous cobras are

often used. [7] The snaker seems to be charming the cobra with a flute, but

having no ears, the snake actually can't hear anything. [8] The snake charmer

attracts the snake and uses various techniques to do so. [9] For example, the

snake charmer may splash cold water on it or blow air on it through the flute.

[10] Although any of these methods may be used, the trick is always to keep the

snake harmlessly "entranced" for the length of the show.

EXERCISE 13   Writing Sentences with Interjections

On your own paper, write ten sentences describing a heroic rescue. In your
sentences, use at least four interjections from the list at the top of this page.
Underline the interjections you use.

EX.   1. <u>Wow!</u> That bonfire is getting out of control!

DETERMINING PARTS OF SPEECH

> **10m A word's part of speech is determined by how the word is used in a sentence.**
>
> EXAMPLES   Have a **drink** of this freshly squeezed orange juice. [*Drink* is used as a noun.]
> I **drink** orange juice every morning. [*Drink* is used as a verb.]
> Colandra works **hard.** [*Hard* is used as an adverb to modify *works*.]
> Misha fell onto the **hard** floor of the skating rink. [*Hard* is used as an adjective to modify *floor*.]

EXERCISE 14   Identifying Parts of Speech

On your own paper, write the part of speech of each italicized word in the paragraph below. Write *n.* for *noun*, *pron.* for *pronoun*, *v.* for *verb*, *adj.* for *adjective*, *adv.* for *adverb*, *prep.* for *preposition*, *conj.* for *conjunction*, or *intj.* for *interjection*.

EX.   [1] The case of *Johnny Red had* everyone baffled.

1. n.; v.

[1] It was a crying *shame* that *it* ever came to court. [2] Johnny Red, the *best* horse in the state, had failed to make his last *jump* in the *championship* competition. [3] Many people thought the *horse* trainer *had been* negligent. [4] This *fact* resulted in a *lawsuit* filed *by* Paula, who had been riding Johnny Red. [5] The courtroom was packed, *and* the judge *warned* people not to crowd the aisle. [6] Then the judge advised the seated jurors to listen *carefully to* all the testimony. [7] "Use your *brain* power," he told *them.* [8] "And don't talk to the *press* until the trial is *over.*"

[9] The trainer had done little to win people's *trust* because of *his* strange ways. [10] For example, he was *occasionally* known to shoe his horses in *bright* colors. [11] At last, *his* friend Willimena got up on the *witness stand.*

[12] "*No!*" she exclaimed. "This man is a great trainer and couldn't be *responsible* for this." [13] Then, out of the *blue*, Paula, a witness, remembered seeing Red putting his *head over* the fence to munch on something the day of the competition.

[14] "As a matter of fact," added Paula, "I recall Red faltering *oddly* just before I started *to saddle* him up." [15] Luckily for the trainer, that *very* afternoon *detectives* were able to find out what Red *had eaten.*

REVIEW EXERCISE 2

A. Identifying Parts of Speech

On your own paper, write the part of speech of each italicized word in the following paragraph. Write *n.* for *noun,* *pron.* for *pronoun,* *v.* for *verb,* *adj.* for *adjective,* *adv.* for *adverb,* *prep.* for *preposition,* *conj.* for *conjunction,* or *intj.* for *interjection.* Separate your answers with a semicolon.

EX. [1] Sequoyah will *forever* be remembered as one of the greatest *American Indian* leaders.

    1. adv.; adj.

[1] Born in Tennessee about 1770, Sequoyah *was raised* on a small farm by his *Cherokee* mother. [2] A childhood sickness made him lame *for* life, but it did not destroy *his* brave spirit. [3] *After* his mother died, he married a Cherokee named Sallie and went to Alabama to run a *trading post.* [4] As a result of his own *personal* struggle, he persuaded the *Cherokee Council* to pass prohibition laws. [5] Sequoyah's *family* was interested *in* preserving Cherokee traditions. [6] But Sequoyah wasn't interested *only* in the traditions of the *Cherokee* people. [7] He soon proved *himself* a talented artist, blacksmith, *and* silversmith. [8] *But* his *greatest* accomplishment was still to come. [9] *In* 1791, he saw some letters written by *white* soldiers. [10] He was fascinated *with* the idea *of* communicating by writing. [11] Sequoyah devoted his time to developing a similar form of *communication* for the *Cherokees.* [12] Absorbed in *his* project, he spent *twelve* years inventing a system. [13] *Many* people *tried* to discourage him. [14] *Finally,* though, he created a symbol for each of the *eighty-five* sounds in the Cherokee language. [15] Self-educated, he *had invented* a new alphabet all *by* himself. [16] *Fortunately,* many others found *it* easy to learn. [17] Soon, *some* of the Cherokees used his *system* to write and publish books in their own language. [18] For his achievement, Sequoyah *has earned* a permanent place of *honor* in the legends of his people. [19] Largely thanks to his work, the first issue *of* a *weekly* newspaper, The Cherokee Phoenix, was published in 1828. [20] In *recognition* of his great accomplishment, the giant redwoods of *California* were named for him, "Sequoyah gigantea."

CHAPTER REVIEW

A. Identifying Nouns, Pronouns, and Adjectives

In the sentences below, identify the part of speech of each italicized word or expression. On the line before each sentence, write *n.* for *noun, pron.* for *pronoun,* or *adj.* for *adjective.*

EX. __adj.__ 1. *Bright* sunshine filled the room.

_____ 1. Clarence wore blue jeans and a *cowboy* hat.

_____ 2. We waxed the floor *ourselves.*

_____ 3. The baby in the crib was *cranky* until she got some juice.

_____ 4. *Which* of these tangerines is ripe?

_____ 5. William sent Lulu a *singing* telegram.

_____ 6. *Liberty* and justice for all are fine ideals.

_____ 7. My *cousin* Lyle lives in Massachusetts.

_____ 8. Pick *any* card you like, and I'll tell you what it is.

_____ 9. You take *this* crate, and I'll take that one.

_____ 10. To *whom* was he speaking?

B. Determining the Parts of Speech of Words

In the paragraph below, identify the part of speech of each italicized word or expression. On the line before each sentence, write *n.* for *noun,* adj. for *adjective,* *pron.* for *pronoun, v.* for *verb, adv.* for *adverb, prep.* for *preposition, conj.* for *conjunction,* or *intj.* for *interjection.* Use a semicolon to separate your answers.

EX. __n.; adv.__ 1. Driving on the *right* is a *fairly* new custom.

_____ 1. *Only two* hundred years ago, travelers who met on the road would usually move to the left.

_____ 2. *This* is still the custom *in* England.

_____ 3. Pope Boniface VIII made left-hand travel the *official policy* in Europe in 1300 A.D.

_____ 4. *This* rule applied to all the people coming *to* Rome.

_____ 5. Researchers say the custom makes sense *because* most people *are* right-handed.

_____ 6. Left-handed travel makes it easier for a person to respond *if* trouble occurs.

_____ 7. In countries influenced by Great Britain, *left-handed* travel is still customary.

_____ 8. However, that practice is not carried out in the *United States*.

_____ 9. Believe it *or* not, the reason has to do with wagons.

_____ 10. Most of the North American settlers' wagons *had* no front seats, so the drivers sat instead on the left-rear animal in the team.

_____ 11. Drivers sat to the left so they could *better* control their teams of horses or oxen with their right hands.

_____ 12. In this situation, drivers could also keep an eye *on* each other's wagon wheels passing to their left.

_____ 13. In this way, they more easily *avoided* accidents.

_____ 14. British wagons, meanwhile, had seats, and *their* drivers sat on the right.

_____ 15. Consequently, in modern *British* cars, the steering wheels are also positioned on the right.

C. Writing Sentences with Words Used as Specific Parts of Speech

On your own paper, write fifteen sentences according to the guidelines below.

EX.   1. Use *building* as a verb.
       1. The children are building a sandcastle.

1. Use *both* as an adjective.
2. Use *well* as a noun.
3. Use *whew* as an interjection.
4. Use *turn* as a linking verb.
5. Use *unless* as a subordinating conjunction.
6. Use *next to* as a preposition.
7. Use *outside* as an adverb.
8. Use *climb* as a noun.
9. Use *outside* as a preposition.
10. Use *turn* as an action verb.
11. Use *sign* as a noun.
12. Use *either* as an indefinite pronoun.
13. Use *not only, but also* as a correlative conjunction.
14. Use *sign* as an action verb.
15. Use *that* as a relative pronoun.

SUBJECTS AND PREDICATES

11a **A sentence consists of two parts: the *subject* and the *predicate*. The subject tells *whom* or *what* the sentence is about. The predicate tells something about the subject.**

EXAMPLES

SUBJECT	PREDICATE		PREDICATE	SUBJECT
Water	spilled.		Away on the ship sailed	the boy.

SUBJECT	PREDICATE		PREDICATE	SUBJECT	PREDICATE
Dina	brought the salad.		When will	Sal and you	arrive?

11b **The *simple subject* is the main word or group of words that tells *whom* or *what* the sentence is about.**

EXAMPLES   **Who** was the performer in that concert?
Walking to his car, **Antonio** whistled his favorite song.

11c **The *simple predicate* is a verb or verb phrase that tells something about the subject.**

EXAMPLES   Pauline **was** restless and bored.
Did Omar **memorize** his lines for the show?

NOTE   In this book, the term *subject* refers to the simple subject, and the term *verb* refers to the simple predicate (a one-word verb or a verb phrase) unless otherwise indicated.

EXERCISE 1   Identifying Complete Subjects and Predicates in Sentences

In each of the following sentences, draw a vertical line to separate the complete subject from the predicate.

EX.   1. Waiting for the bus to arrive, Sasha | read two chapters in her mystery book.

1. Who was your favorite actor in that movie?

2. Jorge arranged the grapes, apples, and oranges in a ceramic bowl.

3. George threw back the covers of his bed.

4. Magda noticed the blooming cherry trees in the park.

5. Which herbal tea is the most healthful?

6. Instead of going to the concert, Francesca studied for her Russian exam.

7. The tree boughs drooped under the weight of the wet snow.

8. Into the bushes fled the frightened rabbit.

9. For recreation, I practice yoga every other day.

10. A group of downtown merchants protested the city's street repair plan.

11. Yori recognized the constellation to the south.

12. Meeting at the library, many volunteers prepared for the book sale.

13. The dress rehearsal for *Fiddler on the Roof* will be after school tomorrow.

14. Is the cat sleeping on the windowsill?

15. Lessons in breathing, floating, and kicking were taught to the young swimmers.

16. Feeding on sunflower seeds every day, one gray squirrel grew chubbier than the others.

17. The tired physician leaned back in her chair for a short nap.

18. Blueberry bagels are a popular breakfast item in our household.

19. Having read *The Joy Luck Club*, everyone enjoyed seeing the film adaptation.

20. Did Anton visit his grandparents in St. Petersburg?

EXERCISE 2   Identifying Subjects and Verbs in Sentences

In each sentence below, underline the subject once and the verb twice.

EX.   1. The <u>skier</u> <u>maneuvered</u> expertly through the course.

1. Where did your sister go to college?

2. All of the packages were delivered.

3. Sunning itself on the porch, the dog stretched lazily.

4. Several awards were presented by Congress today.

5. Gregg will play point guard this season.

6. Did Elena ever find her chemistry assignment?

7. Encouraged by her lead, Laura ran swiftly to the finish line.

8. Apples spilled from the basket onto the table.

9. Into the bright sea sailed the tall ship.

10. When will your family return from vacation?

COMPOUND SUBJECTS AND COMPOUND VERBS

> **11d** A *compound subject* consists of two or more subjects that are joined by a conjunction and have the same verb.
>
> Compound subjects are usually joined by *and* or *or*.
>
> ```
>                    COMP S          V
> ```
> EXAMPLES   The cat and her kittens | slept in the hall closet last night.
>
> ```
>                       COMP S           V
> ```
> Sam, Marlon, and Pedro | rode their horses through the woods.
>
> **11e** A *compound verb* consists of two or more verbs that are joined by a conjunction and have the same subject.
>
> Compound verbs are usually joined by *and*, *but*, or *or*.
>
> ```
>               S              COMP V
> ```
> EXAMPLES   Lisette | walks or jogs along that long trail.
>
> ```
>                               S              COMP V
> ```
> For the dinner party, I | prepared pasta and baked bread.

EXERCISE 3   Identifying Compound Subjects and Compound Verbs

In the sentences below, underline the subjects once and the verbs twice.

EX.   1.   Katia and Suzanne write and publish short stories.

1. Water lapped against the sand and tickled our toes.

2. The coach and her team won the game and celebrated their victory.

3. Snow and ice threatened their holiday travel plans.

4. Anticipation and excitement kept Manuel awake most of the night.

5. Each of the children studied and excelled in a different language.

6. Kazuo and Taro flew to Japan and visited their father's family.

7. At home, Tamara and Misha speak in Russian and English.

8. The plane and its passengers had been delayed.

9. Having adapted to arid conditions, many plants and animals live and thrive in the desert.

10. At Sam's party, we ate a lot, played music, and danced.

EXERCISE 4   Using Compound Subjects and Compound Verbs to Combine Sentences

Combine each of the following groups of short sentences into one longer sentence by using compound subjects and compound verbs. Write each new sentence on the lines provided. Underline the subject once and the verb twice.

EX.   1.   The captain alerted his crew to the approaching storm. He ordered everyone to wear life jackets.

<u>The captain</u> <u><u>alerted</u></u> his crew to the approaching storm and <u><u>ordered</u></u>

everyone to wear life jackets.

1.   Before going outside, Rena put on a coat. Rinda put on a coat, too.

2.   The guests arrived on Thursday night. They didn't leave until Monday.

3.   Marta is learning how to play Go. Jamal and Mark are learning, too.

4.   After cleaning the attic, Franklin sorted old photographs. Then he called his sister. Franklin invited his sister to dinner. _____

5.   When steamed and served with fresh lemon, broccoli tastes crisp and zesty. Green beans are crisp and zesty when served this way, too.

6.   Last week, Bruce played in the open jazz competition. He played the saxophone. Roberto played the saxophone, too. _____

7.   After the dress rehearsal, Miriam walked home. Then she ate dinner. Finally, she practiced her lines one more time. _____

8.   The young couple replastered the old ceilings. Then they sanded the plaster. Finally, they painted the ceilings. _____

9.   Amanda took the reins from Kevin. She mounted the horse.

10.   *David Copperfield* is a great novel by Charles Dickens. *Bleak House* and *Great Expectations* are also great novels by Dickens. _____

FINDING THE SUBJECT OF A SENTENCE

11f   To find the subject of a sentence, ask *Who*? or *What*? before the verb.

EXAMPLES   Blocking my view of the harbor was a building. [*What* was blocking my view? A *building* was.]
In her office, Ms. Menino graded papers. [*Who* graded papers? *Ms. Menino* graded.]

(1) The subject of a sentence expressing a command or a request is always understood to be *you*, although *you* may not appear in the sentence.

EXAMPLES   Watch that movie to learn more about oceans. [*Who* is being told to watch? *You* are being told to watch.]
Please listen to my speech, Ann. [*Who* is being asked to listen? *You* listen.]

(2) The subject of a sentence is never in a prepositional phrase.

EXAMPLES   A **group** of students gathered around the bulletin board. [*Who* gathered? A *group* gathered. *Students* is the object of the preposition *of*.]
One of the restaurants on that street has closed down. [*What* has closed down? *One* has closed down. *Restaurants* is the object of the preposition *of*. *Street* is the object of the preposition *on*.]

(3) The subject of a sentence expressing a question usually follows the verb or a part of the verb phrase.

EXAMPLES   Is **Rudy** moving next week? [*Who* is moving next week? *Rudy* is.]
Will the **festival** end on Sunday? [*What* will end on Sunday? *The festival* will end.]

EXERCISE 5   Finding Subjects and Verbs

In each of the following sentences, underline the subject once and the verb twice. Include all parts of a compound subject or a compound verb and all words in a verb phrase. In sentences that give orders or make requests, underline only the verb.

EX.   1.   That night, the radio and the television aired the president's address in its entirety.

1.   Throughout her lifetime, the philanthropist collected and donated works of art.

2.   Swooping over the lake were seagulls and ducks.

3.   A herd of elephants bathed and played in the muddy river.

4. Turn left, and follow the signs at the next intersection.

5. The printmaker and his assistant experimented with different inks.

6. After the exam, Marla, Theresa, and Jamie met in the hallway and walked home together.

7. Lush ferns and May apples carpeted the floor of the pine grove.

8. After her evening jog, Janet steamed clams and made a salad.

9. Gregory and Margaret registered for their first judo class.

10. Sunflower seeds and millet are healthy bread ingredients.

11. After his illness, the musician practiced and started performing again.

12. Each night, the cat paced the hallways and looked for mice.

13. The disc jockey always opened and closed her show with the same song.

14. Mr. Martínez and Ms. Chung have earned good citizenship awards and were honored by the mayor.

15. The diner and the newspaper stand on the corner have closed down.

16. The crumpled paper covered the surface of the drafting table.

17. Whales and icebergs are common sights off the coast of Alaska.

18. Hiding behind the tree were Alice and Anton.

19. City hall has been remodeled and opens tomorrow.

20. In her backyard, Felicia stood and watched the lunar eclipse.

21. The student's excellent academic record and community service earned her a scholarship.

22. Each fall, the northern peninsula of Wisconsin shimmers with changing leaves and hosts thousands of visitors.

23. A group of citizens attended the meeting and voiced their opinions.

24. Peonies in pink, magenta, and crimson grow in that garden.

25. In Mr. Rasko's basement, birdhouses and feeders were being built and painted.

DIRECT OBJECTS AND INDIRECT OBJECTS

11g **A *complement* is a word or a group of words that completes the meaning of a verb.**

Some sentences contain only a subject and a verb.

	S V
EXAMPLES	She ran.

                  V
                Look! [The subject *you* is understood.]

Other sentences require one or more complements to complete their meaning.

INCOMPLETE   Melvin bought
  COMPLETE   Melvin bought a **hamster.**

Generally, a sentence includes at least one complement.

The *direct object* and the *indirect object* are two types of complements.

11h **A *direct object* is a noun or a pronoun that receives the action of a verb or shows the result of the action. A direct object tells *whom* or *what* after an action verb.**

EXAMPLES   Rachel admired **Golda Meir.** [Admired *whom*? *Golda Meir.*]
             That man delivered **flowers** to my house. [Delivered *what*? *Flowers.*]

NOTE   For emphasis, the direct object may come before the subject and the verb.

EXAMPLE   What an exciting **movie** we watched! [Watched *what*? *A movie.*]

11i **An *indirect object* is a noun or a pronoun that comes between an action verb and a direct object. It tells *to whom* or *to what* or *for whom* or *for what* the action of the verb is done.**

EXAMPLES   Diego read **Ms. Hintz** and **Mr. Saenz** his poetry. [Read *to whom*? *Ms. Hintz and Mr. Saenz*]
             I gave the **house** a cleaning. [Gave *to what*? *The house.*]

Don't mistake an object of the preposition *to* or *for* for an indirect object.

INDIRECT OBJECT   The teacher gave **Todd** and **me** a makeup test.
OBJECT OF PREPOSITION   The teacher gave a makeup test to **Todd** and **me.**

EXERCISE 6   Identifying Direct and Indirect Objects

Underline the direct and indirect objects in each of the following sentences. In the space above the underlined words, write *d.o.* for *direct object* and *i.o.* for *indirect object*. Some sentences have more than one answer, and not all sentences contain an indirect object.

EX.   1. Derek showed the <u>volunteer</u> his voter registration <u>card</u>.
i.o. *d.o.*

1. Nana gave her granddaughter the ruby ring.

2. The journalist interviewed the scientists before they entered the laboratory.

3. After the snowfall, Uncle Vanya sculpted my cousins and me a statue out of ice and snow.

4. Mrs. Mantuano feeds the cardinals small, black sunflower seeds.

5. Sylvana's strong language skills have earned her a scholarship.

6. For dinner my father made us barley soup, salad, and braided egg bread.

7. We rode the elevator to the top floor of the John Hancock building.

8. After much persuasion, Mother finally showed us photos of her as a child.

9. Franz Schubert composed sonatas, quartets, and symphonies.

10. Erica donates her time and skills to the area literacy center.

11. What a stunning exhibit about Egypt we saw!

12. Before leaving, Helen gave Frank instructions about collecting the mail.

13. Tomas covers sporting events for the West High *Herald*.

14. Jasper gave Bill the term paper and asked for his opinion.

15. Stanley offered us excellent seats in the theater.

16. Jacob declined the apples and took the pitcher of cider.

17. Flooding destroyed many houses and farms.

18. Cam handed his father a birthday card.

19. Ice covered the roads and kept us from traveling.

20. We welcomed the Chan's invitation to the party.

21. Kendra showed me photographs from her trip to Poland.

22. The clerk sold the customer two pairs of pants and a sweater.

23. Warm weather brightened our spirits.

24. What a marvelous performance the madrigal singers gave us!

25. Sheila practiced the long list of vocabulary words for her French exam.

OBJECTIVE COMPLEMENTS

11j An *objective complement* is a word or group of words that helps complete the meaning of an action verb by identifying or modifying the direct object.

EXAMPLES   Kyle called Rita a brilliant **mathematician.**
                     Jerome painted the model airplane **gray.**

Only a few verbs take an objective complement: *consider, make,* and verbs that can be replaced by *consider* or *make,* such as *appoint, call, choose, elect, name, cut, paint,* and *sweep.*

EXERCISE 7   Identifying Objective Complements

Underline each objective complement in the sentences below.

EX.   1. Computer experts considered the new software program <u>brilliant</u>.

1. Stefan painted the front porch steps green.

2. Many found the Supreme Court's decision amazing.

3. Advertisements called the new automobile sleek and sophisticated.

4. Always forgetful, John considered his brother a fountain of knowledge.

5. The sleet and snow made the rural routes treacherous.

6. Taylor called Jiro a true and trusted friend.

7. The school board appointed Ms. Guerra interim president.

8. Elena and Bob named their daughter Lara.

9. An art expert called the painting a fake, but others disagreed.

10. Friends nominated Jerry co-chair of the food collection drive.

11. Frank named his two gerbils Romeo and Juliet.

12. Every Saturday morning, the shop owner wipes the windows clean.

13. Deeply concerned, the physician thought the patient's condition serious.

14. Officials found the heavy voter turnout a surprise.

15. Even my friend Marsha called the story sad.

REVIEW EXERCISE

A. Finding Subjects and Verbs

For each sentence below, underline the subject once and the verb twice. Include all parts of a compound subject or a compound verb.

EX. 1. On Saturday mornings, Sharon and Ivan walk to the community center.

1. At the center, they meet their reading partners, Joel and Yolanda.

2. Joel and Sharon are reading short stories and poems by Raymond Carver.

3. Stories and plays by Anton Chekhov are familiar to Ivan, but not to Yolanda.

4. Yolanda has read some of Chekhov's descriptions and does like them.

5. Ivan agrees, but he does not enjoy some of the sadder stories.

B. Identifying Direct Objects, Indirect Objects, and Objective Complements

On the line before each sentence below, identify each italicized complement by writing *d.o.* for *direct object*, *i.o.* for *indirect object*, or *obj. cmpt.* for *objective complement*.

EX. _obj. cmpt._ 1. We considered the tomato a *fruit*.

_____ 1. Between the pages, the old dictionary contained numerous pressed *flowers*.

_____ 2. Lettuce picked from the garden makes a salad *fresh* and tasty.

_____ 3. Dogs have tremendous *abilities* as thoughtful, inquisitive, and loyal companions.

_____ 4. The environmentalists gave our *company* advice on irrigation.

_____ 5. Carla thought the mountain path treacherous and *beautiful*.

_____ 6. Some of the ancient Egyptian jars contained *honey*.

_____ 7. Shannon's portrait of her grandfather won the grand *prize* at the Missouri State Fair.

_____ 8. The hostess gave the *chef* several compliments on the fine meal.

_____ 9. We painted the old car *green*.

_____ 10. After much debate, the panel finally called the matter *closed*.

SUBJECT COMPLEMENTS

11k A *predicate nominative* is a word or group of words that follows a linking verb and refers to the same person or thing as the subject of the verb.

EXAMPLES   Dr. Chan is a **pediatrician**. [The noun *pediatrician* refers to the subject, *Dr. Chan*.]
The three contestants are **Juliana, Lucian,** and **Marco**. [The compound *Juliana, Lucian, and Marco* refers to the subject, *contestants*.]

11l A *predicate adjective* is an adjective that follows a linking verb and modifies the subject of the verb.

EXAMPLES   Iona looks **relaxed**. [The adjective *relaxed* modifies the subject, *Iona*.]
My new puppy is **active**. [The adjective *active* modifies the subject, *puppy*.]

EXERCISE 8   Identifying Linking Verbs and Subject Complements

In each of the following sentences, underline the subject complement once and the linking verb twice. On the line before the sentence, identify the complement by writing *p.n.* for *predicate nominative* or *p.a.* for *predicate adjective*.

EX.   _p.a._   1. Does that apple taste tart?

_____   1. Of these three fabrics, the velvet is the one I'll buy.

_____   2. Our state's chief industries are agriculture and tourism.

_____   3. After the storm subsided, the lake became calm.

_____   4. Grapefruit can taste bitter or sour.

_____   5. The tall stalk with broad green leaves is a Brussels sprouts plant.

_____   6. All of the contestants looked nervous.

_____   7. Ava's drawings are sensitive and powerful.

_____   8. After her walk, Mrs. Petrakis felt energetic and refreshed.

_____   9. Peanut butter is a good energy source for birds.

_____   10. Before the announcement, the mood in the room was electric.

_____   11. The two candidates for class president are Julia and Eli.

_____   12. Wearing a cape and dark glasses, the man looked mysterious.

_____ 13. The pine cones and evergreen boughs felt sticky from the sap.

_____ 14. Of the two fragrances, this one smells sweeter.

_____ 15. The tree with the crimson leaves is a red maple.

_____ 16. After the reading, the young author looked relieved.

_____ 17. During the flood, the citizens remained hopeful of saving their homes.

_____ 18. Many species of eucalyptus trees are aromatic.

_____ 19. We learned that our neighbor is an accomplished pianist.

_____ 20. Toward the end of the long lecture, the professor's voice sounded raspy and dry.

Writing Complements

Complete each of the sentences below with the type of subject complement named in parentheses. Write your answers on the lines provided.

EX.   1. The tall pines in the forest are _____. (*predicate adjective*)

1. During a summer storm, the sound of rain on the roof is _____.
    (*predicate adjective*)

2. Our great-aunt Isabel was _____. (*predicate nominative*)

3. Waiting in the lobby, the applicants for the position looked_____
    and_____ . (*compound predicate adjective*)

4. The owner of the small bungalow on our block is _____.
    (*predicate nominative*)

5. My two favorite performers are_____ and _____.
    (*compound predicate nominative*)

6. Especially without their leaves, the trees look _____
    and_____. (*compound predicate adjective*)

7. Why does the vegetable soup taste_____? (*predicate adjective*)

8. Two popular apples are_____ and _____. (*compound
    predicate nominative*)

9. The chorus sounded_____. (*predicate adjective*)

10. After the announcement, the winner looked _____ and
    _____. (*compound predicate adjective*)

CHAPTER REVIEW

A. Identifying Subjects and Verbs in a Paragraph

For each sentence in the paragraph below, underline the subject once and the verb twice.

EX. [1] Surprisingly, bagpipes originated in Asia.

[1] Some people find bagpipes a shrill instrument, but others fall in love with them. [2] Actually, bagpipes are two instruments in one. [3] Blowing into the instrument, the player fills the bag with air. [4] Then the player squeezes the bag with her or his arm and forces air through two kinds of pipes. [5] Three drones and a chanter are the pipes for a modern bagpipe. [6] Air goes into the drones to create predetermined notes. [7] After starting a song the player cannot tune the drones. [8] The rest of the air goes to the chanter. [9] The chanter has seven finger stops and a thumb stop. [10] To produce different notes, the musician places fingers on the stops in the chanter.

B. Identifying Complements in Sentences

Underline the complement or complements in each of the following sentences. On the line before the sentence, classify each complement by writing *d.o.* for *direct object*, *i.o.* for *indirect object, obj cmpt.* for *objective complement*, *p.n.* for *predicate nominative*, or *p.a.* for *predicate adjective.*

EX. __p.n.__ 1. As a young woman, our grandmother was a seamstress.

_____ 1. Famous for his sophistication and wry humor, Cary Grant made many films.

_____ 2. After kneading the dough, Dad formed two round loaves.

_____ 3. The guitarist was a master of Spanish flamenco music.

_____ 4. Even the most experienced art critics considered her photographs wonderful.

_____ 5. Before putting out the campfire, Ben poured Sam a mug of hot cider.

_____ 6. After calling, please confirm your order by letter.

_____ 7. The blue satin evening gown looked elegant and refined.

_____ 8. The seemingly quiet, well-mannered cat was an accomplished hunter.

_____ 9. In a strong, clear voice, she read her poems to the hushed audience.

_____ 10. Some analysts predict high inflation before an economic recession.

_____ 11. The new play at the Center for Performing Arts is a guaranteed success.

_____ 12. After a vigorous swim, Alisha usually feels refreshed.

_____ 13. To avoid fines, please return your library books on time.

_____ 14. What an outstanding athlete she is!

_____ 15. Halim missed the concert by hours.

C   Writing a News Article

You are a rewrite specialist for the *Boston World Newspaper*. Your job is to take notes over the telephone from a reporter and write a first draft of a news article. Use the notes below to write an article of at least fifteen sentences. You will need to create other details to finish the article. Underline and label at least one compound verb, one compound subject, one direct object, and one indirect object in your article. Write the article on your own paper. Don't forget to give your article a headline.

Who?   Roberto and Sarah Serran
What?   an alligator crashing through a screen door to get into the house
When?   August 3, 2008; 3:45 P.M.
Why?   seemed to be after the people's pet poodle
Where?   Neiberville, Florida
How?   used its strength to ram the screen, tearing a hole in it

EX.

A Strange Guest

comps   *comps*
Yesterday afternoon a Florida couple and their pet poodle were relaxing in their living room.

PREPOSITIONAL PHRASES

12a   A *phrase* is a group of words that is used as a single part of speech and does not contain a verb and its subject.

12b   A *prepositional phrase* is a group of words consisting of a preposition, a noun or pronoun that serves as the object of the preposition, and any modifiers of that object.

EXAMPLES   The tiny room **off the kitchen** is Maria's study. [The noun *kitchen* is the object of the preposition *off*.]
The lawsuit finally went **to the grand jury.** [The compound noun *grand jury* is the object of the preposition *to*.]
According to her, a larger room would never feel cozy. [The pronoun *her* is the object of the preposition *According to*.]

The object of a preposition may be compound.

EXAMPLE   She has covered the walls **with posters and photographs.**

   REFERENCE NOTE: For lists of prepositions, see page 137.

EXERCISE 1   Identifying Prepositional Phrases and Their Objects

Find the prepositional phrases in the following sentences. Underline each preposition once and the object of the preposition twice.

EX.   1.   My baseball cards are <u>in</u> the <u><u>closet</u></u>.

1.   They made dinner reservations for the prom.

2.   The woman in the blue coat is a store detective.

3.   Have you ever seen a scarf on a collie?

4.   Please take the package to the post office.

5.   There's not enough room on my desk for this project.

6.   Could we go to the football game, Mom?

7.   I lost my pen through a hole in my backpack.

8.   These boots are quite warm because they are lined with wool felt.

9.   Lee slung his jacket over his shoulder and suavely departed.

10.   Does hanging a horseshoe above a door bring good luck?

11. I haven't a superstitious bone in my body.

12. Tala scrubbed the whitewalls on the car with steel wool.

13. If a tree falls in the forest, only the birds will hear it.

14. Put it there, near the Dutch oven.

15. They heard a disturbing, grating noise after each shifting of the gears.

16. I walked around the block first.

17. If you moved from here, where would you go?

18. No, don't go that way; go over the bridge and turn right.

19. Shelly lined the first pitch into short right field.

20. Guess how many pinto beans are in the barrel and win a pumpkin pie.

EXERCISE 2   Revising Sentences Using Prepositional Phrases

For each of the sentences below, add at least one prepositional phrase as a modifier. Write your sentences on your own paper.

EX.   1. Botan forgot his jacket.
       1. Botan forgot his jacket at school.

1. Don't be alarmed.
2. We are invited.
3. Have you ever gone swimming?
4. My brother has a blister.
5. I took this picture.
6. Have you any money?
7. We brought our own shovels.
8. If Jody doesn't take the tapes, who will?
9. That bobsled run looks awfully dangerous.
10. Lon bought a great used bicycle.
11. I like to wear a sweater.
12. We went and nearly got lost.
13. The Drapers had a great time.
14. Did you see U2 when they came?
15. Floyd sat.
16. I packed a cheese sandwich.
17. The dog took a long nap.
18. My friends arrived.
19. A vegetable pizza is baking.
20. That wool sweater is something I could make.

ADJECTIVE PHRASES AND ADVERB PHRASES

12c An *adjective phrase* is a prepositional phrase that modifies a noun or a pronoun.

An adjective phrase tells *what kind, how many,* or *which one.*

EXAMPLES   Two cups **of peppermint tea** is my limit. [*Of peppermint tea* modifies the noun *cups.*]
Everyone **in the classroom** was absolutely silent. [*I   the classroom* modifies the pronoun *Everyone.*]

12d An *adverb phrase* is a prepositional phrase that modifies a verb, an adjective, or an adverb.

An adverb phrase tells *how, when, where, why,* or *to what extent* (*how long* or *how far*).

EXAMPLES   New Zealand was first inhabited **by the Maori.** [*By the Maori* modifies the verb *was inhabited.*]
The Maori canoes were full **of people, animals, plants, and tools.** [*Of people, animals, plants, and tools* modifies the adjective *full.*]
Why did the Maori travel so far **from their home?** [*From their home* modifies the adverb *far.*]

EXERCISE 3   Identifying Adjective Phrases and Adverb Phrases and the Words They Modify

In the following sentences, underline each adjective phrase once and each adverb phrase twice. Draw an arrow from the phrase to the word or words it modifies.

EX.   1.   Dad and I went to the grocery store on the corner.

1. We bought food for our two-night backpacking trip.

2. Dad took a day's vacation from work.

3. He told his boss about our plans.

4. We had been planning the trip since last month.

5. At home we prepared the food.

6. Everything except the water went into little plastic bags.

7. Instead of throwing them away, we bring the bags home and reuse them.

8. Sitting in front of all that food made me feel hungry.

9. We loaded our backpacks with socks, sweaters, and the food.

10. Dad had saved some cooking gear from his time in the service.

11. Unlike him, all I had was a shiny new knife.

12. Finally, we tied our sleeping bags to the bottoms of our backpacks.

13. After a long hike, we reached our campsite.

14. I slept soundly until morning.

15. The next morning, we awoke before sunrise.

16. We loaded the sleeping bags and backpacks into the car again.

17. It was still dark as we drove along the empty freeway.

18. Not a single car was in front of us or behind us.

19. At last we arrived at the trailhead parking lot.

20. This time Dad didn't lock the keys in the car.

21. We put our boots on and walked beside each other for a while.

22. As the trail grew steeper, I led the way across the first ridge.

23. We rested once or twice along the way.

24. Dad sat down next to me, and we looked at the morning sky together.

25. Sometimes I think the nicest thing about a hiking trip is the start.

EXERCISE 4   Writing Directions

You are writing to your friend who lives in another city. Your friend is coming to visit you. On your own paper, write a letter and give directions to your house. Include at least five adjective phrases and five adverb phrases. Underline each adjective phrase once and each adverb phrase twice. You may include a map if you wish.

EX.   November 14, 2008

    Dear Mason,

        I can't wait until I next month when you come to my house. We live in a
    house at the top of a steep hill.

PARTICIPLES AND PARTICIPIAL PHRASES

12e   A *participle* is a verb form that can be used as an adjective.

Two kinds of participles are the *present participle* and the *past participle*. The perfect tense of a participle is formed with a past participle and the helping verb *having*.

PRESENT   **Waving,** the boy dwindled to a speck as the boat went west. [*Waving*, a form of the verb *wave*, modifies the noun *boy*.]
Did you see anyone **walking** through the back yard? [*Walking*, a form of the verb *walk*, modifies the pronoun *anyone*.]

PAST   Di and Wendy tossed the **baked** potato back and forth to cool it. [*Baked*, a form of the verb *bake*, modifies the noun *potato*.]
Battered and **soaked,** we held on to the overturned skiff. [*Battered*, a form of the verb *batter*, and *soaked*, a form of the verb *soak*, modify the pronoun *we*.]

PERFECT   The Tewa performer, **having dressed** like an Apache, took part in the Deer Dance. [*Having dressed*, a form of the verb *dress*, modifies the noun *performer*.]
Having napped, the four-year-old was ready to play. [*Having napped*, a form of the verb *nap*, modifies the compound noun *four-year-old*.]

12f   A *participial phrase* consists of a participle and all of the words related to the participle.

EXAMPLES   **Talking to her dog,** Mildred repotted the four azaleas. [The phrase modifies the noun *Mildred*.]
The outfielder, **having scooped up the grounder,** threw the ball to first base. [The phrase modifies the noun *outfielder*.]
Paco, **having already learned the secret,** laughed at our impatient curiosity. [The phrase modifies the noun *Paco*.]

EXERCISE 5   Identifying Participles

Underline the participles used as adjectives in each of the following sentences.

EX.   1.   Are those antique <u>cooking</u> utensils?

1.   The shingled house on the point barely survived the storm.

2.   My grandpa likes stewed tomatoes.

3.   In the fading light, Bly liked to sit at the edge of the water and watch the shorebirds gather.

163

4. Having showered, Dan was dismayed to find there were no clean towels.

5. I understand the northern spotted owl is an endangered species.

6. Lucy wanted a new fishing pole to replace the broken one.

7. All main dishes come with salad and a baked potato.

8. How much spending money do you have each week?

9. Do you suppose Al Unser's family buys him driving gloves for his birthday?

10. He carefully placed the polished guitar in its case.

11. Arnie ran away from the honking geese.

12. A draft blew the wrinkled curtains away from the sill.

13. Toshi, having walked to school, had snow on her hair and shoulders.

14. Bagged newspapers are easy for the recycling crew to handle.

15. Running children and crying babies seemed to fill the tiny room.

EXERCISE 6   Identifying Participial Phrases and the Words They Modify

In each of the sentences below, underline the participial phrase once. Then underline twice the word or words each participial phrase modifies.

EX.   1. Having grown up in a poor family, Pancho Gonzales certainly was not a member of a tennis club.

1. The name given to him at birth was Richard Alonzo Gonzales.

2. Born in Los Angeles in 1928, Pancho became the best U.S. tennis player of his day.

3. Living in Southern California, he could play tennis year-round.

4. It was difficult competing at a high level without a coach.

5. His playing, known for its speed and fierce attack, was always exciting.

6. Having turned professional in 1949, Pancho held several amateur titles.

7. Completing his final year as an amateur, he won six major tournaments.

8. As a professional, he dominated the U.S. men's singles circuit, winning the championship seven years in a row.

9. Whether playing on clay or on grass courts, he would win.

10. Admired for his powerful serves, Pancho always had a great number of enthusiastic fans.

GERUNDS AND GERUND PHRASES

12g A *gerund* is a verb form ending in *–ing* that is used as a noun.

SUBJECT	**Skipping** rope is good exercise.
PREDICATE NOMINATIVE	A popular activity at Leo's house is **singing.**
DIRECT OBJECT	For two hours the forwards practiced **dribbling.**
INDIRECT OBJECT	Why not give **bricklaying** a try?
OBJECT OF A PREPOSITION	I talked to Amanda about **bowling.**

Don't confuse a gerund with a present participle used as an adjective or as part of a verb phrase.

GERUND	My favorite hobby is **working** on my car. [*Working* is the predicate nominative referring to the noun *hobby.*]
PRESENT PARTICIPLES	The crew was no longer **working.** [*Working* is the main verb in the verb phrase *was working.*]
	Working for this company, you will get excellent benefits. [*Working* is the adjective modifying the pronoun *you.*]

 NOTE   When you use a noun or a pronoun just before a gerund, use the possessive form.

EXAMPLES	**Bertha's** reading was getting better.
	Ms. Uno was impressed by **her** reading.

12h A *gerund phrase* consists of a gerund and all of the words related to the gerund.

Like participles, gerunds may have modifiers and complements.

EXAMPLES	**Having two national languages** can be an asset. [The phrase is the subject of the verb *can be.*]
	My immediate goal is **running in the marathon.** [The phrase is the predicate nominative explaining the noun *goal.*]
	My brother tried **singing the blues.** [The phrase is the direct object of the verb *tried.*]
	Everyone applauded Harry and Bill for **boxing fairly.** [The phrase is the object of the preposition *for.*]

EXERCISE 7   Identifying Gerunds and Their Uses

Underline the gerunds in the sentences below. On the line before each sentence, identify how each gerund is used. Write s. for *subject*, p.n. for *predicate nominative*, d.o. for *direct object*, or o.p. for *object of a preposition*.

EX. ___s.___ 1. Travis's singing is terrific.

_____ 1. Jogging is great, but you shouldn't overdo it.

_____ 2. I took the train home in December because I don't enjoy flying.

_____ 3. My cousin Alma gave a speech about marketing last Tuesday afternoon.

_____ 4. I know that studying for this class is important.

_____ 5. On the baseball field, we practiced sliding.

_____ 6. Abner's favorite art form is sculpting.

_____ 7. Tracing is a good way to create a design.

_____ 8. My kitten's purring can be heard across the room.

_____ 9. Ralph knows a lot about cooking.

_____ 10. One helpful and important skill is reading.

EXERCISE 8   Identifying Gerund Phrases and Their Uses

Underline the gerund phrases in the paragraph below. Above each gerund phrase, identify its use by writing s. for *subject*, p.n. for *predicate nominative*, d.o. for *direct object*, or o.p. for *object of a preposition*.

EX.   [1] <u>Writing a résumé</u> requires some research the first time.
           s.

[1] I started my research by going to the town library. [2] My favorite pastime there is browsing in the stacks of books. [3] Going to the reference room took me by the science fiction shelves, where a book caught my eye. [4] I suppose whoever arranged the library enjoys trapping unwary researchers that way. [5] The next thing I knew, the librarian was talking about closing the library.

INFINITIVES AND INFINITIVE PHRASES

12i   An *infinitive* is a verb form that can be used as a noun, an adjective, or an adverb. An infinitive usually begins with *to*.

NOUN   Parents are excited once their baby learns **to smile.**
ADJECTIVE The loan officer is the one **to ask.**
ADVERB   Molly came **to help.**

The word *to*, the sign of the infinitive, is sometimes omitted.

EXAMPLES   Let's **[to] visit** the Neimans.
           Would you help Nalani **[to] stand** on her head?
           The paint fumes made me **[to] faint.**

12j   An *infinitive phrase* consists of an infinitive and all of the words related to the infinitive.

EXAMPLES   Do you try **to eat a balanced diet?** [The phrase is the direct object of the verb *Do try*.]
           To read the morning paper in her robe and slippers seems indulgent to Rosa. [The phrase is the subject of the verb *seems*.]
           Richard made a promise **to go to Tula Springs.** [The phrase modifies the noun *promise*.]
           With a high-pressure hose, Joann was able **to scrape the paint in one day.** [The phrase modifies the predicate adjective *able*.]

NOTE   Unlike other verbals, an infinitive may have a subject. Such a construction is called an *infinitive clause*. The subject of an infinitive is in the objective case.

       EXAMPLES   We thought **Paola to be the best choice.** [*Paola* is the subject of the infinitive *to be*. The entire clause is the direct object of the verb *thought*.]
                  Mr. Suro expected **him to come back for his change.** [*Him* is the subject of the infinitive *to come*. The entire clause is the direct object of the verb *expected*.]

EXERCISE 9   Identifying Infinitives

Underline the infinitives in the following paragraph.

   EX.   [1] Lani wanted <u>to run</u> for the student senate.

       [1] While running, she began to learn more about democracy. [2] She

decided to read a book about different governments. [3] In some ways the students were able to govern themselves democratically. [4] The students voted to choose the best candidate for the senate. [5] Like the U.S. Congress, the elected students met to talk about issues and to vote on rule changes. [6] If people want to dismiss their representative, a democracy allows impeachment. [7] However, the students in Lani's class had never tried to dismiss their senator. [8] To impeach a student senator had not been necessary in the school. [9] Lani and her supporters wanted to add this ability to the school rules. [10] After Lani was elected, she was able to propose this rule change to the senate.

EXERCISE 10   Identifying Infinitive Phrases and Their Functions

Underline the infinitive phrases in each of the sentences below. On the line before the sentence, identify the way the phrase is used by writing *n.* for *noun, adj.* for *adjective,* or *adv.* for *adverb.* If the infinitive phrase is used as a noun, identify its function by writing *s.* for *subject, d.o.* for *direct object,* or *p.n.* for *predicate nominative.* If the infinitive phrase is used as a modifier, circle the word it modifies.

EX. _n.; d.o._   1. Everyone wanted <u>to taste the punch</u>.

_____ 1. Darla wants to visit the Grand Ole Opry in Nashville.

_____ 2. Rutger is the person to give your receipts to.

_____ 3. We went to the church bazaar to buy some of Lottie Walker's famous baked goods.

_____ 4. Those people over there tried to talk to us about the movie.

_____ 5. To drive in the Indy 500 is Sallie's latest dream.

_____ 6. My great-grandfather once walked forty miles to listen to Duke Ellington play.

_____ 7. Matthew thought it would be fun to get a crew cut.

_____ 8. Are you happy to be leaving tomorrow?

_____ 9. Cornelius designed the chair to fit at his new desk.

_____ 10. Aunt Jess gave us some money to buy a poster for our bedroom.

APPOSITIVES AND APPOSITIVE PHRASES

12k An *appositive* is a noun or pronoun placed beside another noun or pronoun to identify or explain it.

EXAMPLES   Dad's brother **Orville** was named for one of the Wright brothers.
Ma Chan protested that she, a true **pacifist,** could never support a war.

12l An *appositive phrase* consists of an appositive and its modifiers.

EXAMPLES   The pigs, **three animals whose story is well known,** built three types of houses.
An intermingling of Europeans and American Indians, the Métis developed a unique culture.

EXERCISE 11   Identifying Appositives

Underline the appositive in each sentence below. Then circle the word or words the appositive identifies or explains.

EX.   1. (Katya), my friend, is learning to speak Russian.

1. Those envelopes on the desk, the white ones, belong to Rafael.

2. Ms. Lin and Mr. Rinaldo, my favorite teachers, are planning a school musical for the spring.

3. Shanna will use pine, her favorite wood, to make that large picture frame.

4. Percy's solar energy science project, the first-place winner, will be on display in the school library today.

5. I am interested in learning more about Jesse Owens, the runner.

6. The new community center location, 6 Carlos Street, is near my grandmother's apartment.

7. My raincoat, the gray one in the closet, is new.

8. Our house guest, an expert on antique furniture, will give a lecture today.

9. Have you ever tried tortellini soup, my specialty?

10. She bought a red carnation, her favorite flower.

EXERCISE 12   Identifying Appositive Phrases

Underline the appositive phrase in each sentence below. Then circle the word or words the appositive phrase identifies or explains.

EX. 1. (Akeem) , a novice on the ice, tried to stand up on his skates.

1. After the party, we proved to Dad that Shep, our new dog, can fetch a tennis ball from the creek.

2. Everyone at the show, over two hundred people, loved Masie's new band.

3. Steven's stepfather, a former fighter pilot, now flies passenger planes for one of the major airlines.

4. Buford's sister, his company's cashier, moved to Maine, where she has a highly successful business.

5. Betty actually has an appointment with a publisher to discuss her book, a novel called *The Life of a Sixteen-Year-Old.*

6. I can never get enough fresh corn on the cob, my favorite vegetable.

7. In the 1860s, some of my ancestors came to this country from Ireland, the "Emerald Isle."

8. My brother, the "planner," asked Ines to go with him to the dance.

9. If I could raise enough cash, I would like to own stock in that company, a lawn-furniture manufacturer.

10. The owners of the new theater, a posh tenplex, promise to sweep and wash the aisles after each screening.

11. Can you believe that my uncle, a professor at Tufts University, has published more than two hundred articles?

12. The newspaper said that that auto dealer, the one with the crazy TV commercials, is running for mayor.

13. Ms. Lawson said she would have a party at the end of the year for our class, third period English.

14. After I did my homework, fifty geometry problems, I helped my little brother build a balsa wood model boat.

15. Sara, Sue's cousin, and I found that we got along really well.

CHAPTER REVIEW

A. Identifying Adjective and Adverb Phrases

In the sentences below, classify each italicized phrase. On the line before the sentence, write *adj. phr.* for *adjective phrase* or *adv. phr.* for *adverb phrase*. Then circle the word that the phrase modifies.

EX. <u>adv. phr.</u>   1. The car (swerved) away *from the tree.*

_____ 1. A cup *of fish chowder* would make a nice lunch.

_____ 2. My friend Frieda walked carefully *around the stage.*

_____ 3. My arms were covered *with poison ivy.*

_____ 4. *During the blizzard,* we kept candles nearby.

_____ 5. Rena likes the view *from the fourth floor.*

_____ 6. The island *near the shore* attracts many tourists.

_____ 7. Luigi cleaned his room completely *except for his closet.*

_____ 8. My stamps are those *on the counter.*

_____ 9. The baby's forehead was warm *with a fever.*

_____ 10. Keith opened a can *of chick peas.*

B. Classifying Verbal Phrases and Identifying Their Function

On the line before each sentence, classify each italicized phrase by writing *part. phr.* for *participial phrase, ger. phr.* for *gerund phrase,* or *inf. phr.* for *infinitive phrase.* Then identify the phrase's function by writing *adj.* for *adjective, adv.* for *adverb, d.o.* for *direct object, o.p.* for *object of a preposition, p.n.* for *predicate nominative,* or *s.* for *subject.*

EX. <u>inf. phr.; adj.</u>   1. It is time *to go to school.*

_____ 1. I expect his mother would be worried about the boy *swinging from that branch.*

_____ 2. But I don't like *cleaning my room.*

_____ 3. Perhaps you don't understand the difficulties of *running a business.*

_____ 4. *Peeking under the table,* Isaiah smiled at Rover.

_____ 5. After what Esperanza said, we tried *to accompany her.*

_____ 6. Because of the summer humidity, the clothes *stored in the garage* had mildewed.

_____ 7. Our goal is to *sell ten billion almonds*, and we know it can be done if everyone contributes.

_____ 8. *Tanning too much* is now generally agreed to be unhealthful, especially for people with a history of skin problems.

_____ 9. The rules committee asked me to *remove some posters that my friends and I had put up*.

_____ 10. *To bid on a print* is why I went to the auction.

_____ 11. Besides *driving at night in a storm*, I also hate driving in heavy mist and fog.

_____ 12. Because we had a sunny day, the clothes *hung on the line* were now dry and ready to be folded.

_____ 13. Do you think that I like *waiting for the train* any more than you do?

_____ 14. We received tremendous praise for *standing our ground against so many hostile people*.

_____ 15. Is anyone here ready *to present his or her oral report today*?

C. Writing Sentences with Phrases

On your own paper, write ten sentences according to the following guidelines. In each of your sentences, underline the italicized phrase given.

EX. 1. Use *after the show* as an adverb phrase.
    1. The director asked us to meet with her after the show.

1. Use *because of the festival* as an adverb phrase.
2. Use *from Belgium* as an adjective phrase.
3. Use *leaping over us* as a participial phrase.
4. Use *moved from its usual spot* as a participial phrase.
5. Use *replacing a flat tire* as a gerund phrase that is the object of a preposition.
6. Use *applying for a job* as a gerund phrase that is the subject.
7. Use *to taste* as an infinitive phrase that is a direct object.
8. Use *to wear* as an infinitive phrase that is an adjective or an adverb.
9. Use *to see the local rock band* as an infinitive phrase that is a predicate nominative.
10. Use *one of my teammates* as an appositive phrase.

KINDS OF CLAUSES

13a An *independent* (or *main*) *clause* expresses a complete thought and can stand by itself as a sentence.

EXAMPLES **Mr. Yellowhair drove to Yuma.** [one independent clause]
Memdi turned the corner, but **Nara ran in the opposite direction.** [two independent clauses joined by a comma and a conjunction]
We picked up empty cans on our walk; we filled two thirty-gallon trash bags. [two independent clauses joined by a semicolon]
Although the ground was bare, **we had a great time on our ski trip.** [one independent clause combined with a subordinate clause]

Usually, an independent clause by itself is called a sentence. It is called an independent clause when it is combined with at least one other clause (independent or subordinate) to form a sentence.

13b A *subordinate* (or *dependent*) *clause* does not express a complete thought and cannot stand alone as a sentence.

Subordinate means "less important." The meaning of a subordinate clause is complete only when the clause is attached to an independent clause. Words such as *whom*, *because*, or *that* usually signal the beginning of a subordinate clause.

EXAMPLES **whom** I introduced to Ms. Miltos
We had a visitor from Chicago **whom I introduced to Ms. Miltos.**

because Mom needed more space
Because Mom needed more space, we finally cleaned out the storage bin.

that she liked
Cam caught sight of a quilted jacket **that she liked** and pointed it out to Tran.

As the examples show, subordinate clauses can be located at the beginning, in the middle, or at the end of a sentence.

EXERCISE 1   Identifying Independent and
              Subordinate Clauses in Paragraphs

In the paragraphs below, classify each italicized clause as independent or subordinate. On your own paper, write *indep.* for *independent* or *sub.* for *subordinate*.

EX.   [1] The Hmong (pronounced "mung") are an Asian people *who have recently entered the United States.*

1. sub.

[1] Before 1960, *few Westerners had heard of the Hmong.* [2] This group had moved into the mountains of Southeast Asia *when they left China about 150 years ago.* [3] In China, *where they had lived for thousands of years,* they had been an unwanted minority. [4] In their own language, <u>Hmong</u> means "free people," but *to the Chinese they were merely peasants.*

[5] *After the Hmong moved southwest of China,* the men farmed and hunted, and some made beautiful necklaces from silver. [6] Among the women, *fine sewing was the most valued skill.* [7] The cloths *that the women decorated with intricate designs of embroidery and appliqué* were called <u>pa ndau</u>, meaning "cloth beautiful as a flower."

[8] *Then the Vietnam War began,* and the United States became involved in Southeast Asia. [9] *Because Hmong men had earned a reputation as courageous fighters against the Japanese during World War II,* U.S. forces asked them for help against the communists of North Vietnam. [10] Hmong men and boys as young as twelve years old served as guides, interpreters, and fighters; *entire villages aided U.S. fliers who were shot down over the mountains.*

[11] *When the United States pulled its forces out of Vietnam in 1973,* the Hmong were left surrounded by enemies. [12] Taking only *what they could carry,* families made their way down mountains and across rivers, often under enemy fire. [13] *It has been estimated* that half of all Hmong died during the war and in the flight after it.

[14] Most of the Hmong *who reached Thailand* were sent into refugee camps. [15] Many families emigrated to the West, hoping *that someday they could return to their mountain homes.* [16] For those admitted to the United States, *life has not been easy.* [17] But these people have learned *what they need to do* to survive. [18] Women *who are skilled at <u>pa ndau</u>* have discovered that Americans appreciate the beauty of their sewing. [19] *The next generation is attending school and learning to read and write English.* [20] *As their children grow up in America,* many Hmong families struggle to keep their traditions alive.

13c An *adjective clause* is a subordinate clause that modifies a noun or a pronoun.

An adjective clause always follows the word or words it modifies and tells *which one* or *what kind*. An adjective clause is usually introduced by a *relative pronoun*—a word that relates the clause to the word or words the clause modifies.

Relative Pronouns
that   which   who   whom   whose

EXAMPLES   Primo chose the pumpkin **that was shaped like an egg.** [The adjective clause modifies the noun *pumpkin*, telling *which one*.]
The Pineyard Inn, **which has a small dining room,** served excellent Chinese food. [The adjective clause modifies the noun *Pineyard Inn*, telling *what kind* of restaurant.]
The man **who was president of the United States from 1977 to 1981** was born in Georgia. [The adjective clause modifies the noun *man*, telling *which one*.]
Sonia enjoyed the speech by Ms. Graham, **whom people called an expert in real estate.** [The adjective clause modifies the noun *Mrs. Graham*, telling *which* person.]
Ms. Barkin, **whose dog frequently barks all night,** does not live far enough away. [The adjective clause modifies the noun *Ms. Barkin*, telling *which* person.]

An adjective clause may also begin with a relative adverb, such as *when* or *where*.

EXAMPLES   I began to wish for the day **when class would be over.**
Is the shop **where Kameko bought the wooden combs** in Kyoto?

The relative pronoun or relative adverb is sometimes not expressed, but its meaning is understood.

EXAMPLES   Can you look for the catalog **[that] you received last week?**
I can't recall the time **[when] we are supposed to meet the train.**

EXERCISE 2   Identifying Adjective Clauses and the Words They Modify

In each sentence below, underline each adjective clause once and each relative pronoun or relative adverb twice. Then circle the noun or pronoun that the clause modifies.

EX.   1. The jack-o'-lantern that Von carved is getting moldy.

1. Molly, who enjoys swimming, is going to Edgewater Beach.

2. Lincoln delivered his "Gettysburg Address" near a battlefield where thousands had died.

3. The eruption of Mount Vesuvius, which occurred in A.D. 79, buried the city of Pompeii in lava.

4. This mahogany desk, which my stepfather built, has six drawers.

5. In November 1922, Howard Carter, who had been exploring for twenty-five years, discovered the tomb of King Tutankhamen.

6. Mr. Weiman will play the tape that he had made of the band's concert.

7. Mr. Cata is going to the kiva where the kachina ceremony will be held.

8. Ms. Carlin spoke excitedly of the evening when she watched the eclipse.

9. Wilson enjoyed the film he saw last night.

10. Jody had laryngitis during the time the choir rehearsed the Slovenian song.

EXERCISE 3   Revising Sentences by Using Adjective Clauses

Revise each of the sentences below by adding an adjective clause. Write the revised sentences on your own paper.

EX.   1. The bicycle had lost a pedal.
       1. The bicycle that the boys were trying to sell had lost a pedal.

1. The bus departed from the station at noon.

2. Jacy used the red toothbrush.

3. The door led to the basement.

4. The baseball pitcher was elated.

5. Does the battery still have a charge?

6. Hira may sleep on the futon.

7. A large crowd gathered in the park.

8. Fran must fix a flat tire on the bicycle.

9. Enrique walked quickly to the store.

10. Joan enjoyed the stew.

THE ADVERB CLAUSE

13d **An *adverb clause* is a subordinate clause that modifies a verb, an adjective, or an adverb.**

An adverb clause tells *how, when, where, why, to what extent,* or *under what condition.*

EXAMPLES **If you need a subject for your essay,** start by reading a weekly newsmagazine. [The clause modifies the verb *start,* telling *under what condition.*]
That hamster seems happier **because we gave it a new wheel.** [The clause modifies the·adjective *happier,* telling *why.*]
Sonia enjoys ice skating more **than her sister does.** [The clause modifies the adverb *more,* telling *to what extent.*]

An adverb clause that introduces a sentence is set off by a comma.

EXAMPLE **As soon as the sun shines,** the ice on the sidewalk will melt.

An adverb clause is introduced by a ***subordinating conjunction***—a word that shows the relationship between the adverb clause and the word or words the clause modifies. Some subordinating conjunctions can also be used as prepositions.

Common Subordinating Conjunctions			
after	as though	since	when
although	because	so that	whenever
as	before	than	where
as if	how	though	wherever
as long as	if	unless	whether
as soon as	in order that	until	while

13e **Part of a clause may be left out when the meaning can be understood from the context of the sentence. Such a clause is called an *elliptical clause.***

EXAMPLES Trish likes Eric Clapton better **than [she likes] any other musician.**
When [you are] driving, you should be able to hear the traffic sounds and not just the radio.

EXERCISE 4   Identifying Adverb Clauses and the Words They Modify

In the following sentences, underline each adverb clause once and underline twice the verb, adjective, or adverb that the clause modifies.

EX.   1. Dena arrived at school a half hour <u>sooner</u> <u>than her brother did</u>.

1. Although the work was not difficult, it took a long time.

2. The engine on your car should run smoothly unless there is below-zero weather.

3. Harry ate his salad more slowly than anyone else at the table.

4. As Akoni's catamaran sped across the lake, the clouds darkened rapidly.

5. You may use my bicycle as long as you take proper care of it.

6. The snow was deeper than anyone had ever seen it before.

7. We go to the movies whenever we hear about a worthwhile film.

8. If we mail our orders in November, we should receive our calendars before the start of the new year.

9. While he was waiting for the bus, Turner practiced the song he was to perform later in the day.

10. For Kari, the exercises in yoga class were difficult because she had not tried them before.

11. The potato soup will be ready as soon as you add the spices.

12. Whenever her baby sister is asleep, Kim works on her tapestry.

13. Sometimes Chen speaks so quickly that I can't understand him.

14. Davis is better at mowing and edging than I am.

15. The rain fell steadily until our street became one enormous puddle.

EXERCISE 5   Writing Sentences with Adverb Clauses

On your own paper, write five sentences by joining clauses from the list below. Use five different subordinating conjunctions from the chart on the previous page. Underline the adverb clauses once and the subordinating conjunctions twice.

a cold rain fell	Young Bear wanted to make the team
the thread was worn	the sun went down
the jacket was not warm enough	it was not a bitterly cold day
Nancy arrived at school early	the most difficult test was over
she felt relieved	the button fell off
One Feather was in the first rank	

EX.   1. <u>When a cold rain fell</u>, the jacket was not warm enough.

THE NOUN CLAUSE

13f A *noun clause* is a subordinate clause used as a noun.

A noun clause may be used as a subject, a predicate nominative, a direct object, an indirect object, or an object of a preposition.

SUBJECT	**Whatever you want to do** is all right with me.
PREDICATE NOMINATIVE	Home is **wherever I can cook a meal.**
DIRECT OBJECT	Kung doesn't know **whether he can join the team.**
INDIRECT OBJECT	The children handed **whoever walked by** a pamphlet protesting a longer school year.
OBJECT OF A PREPOSITION	No one could agree about **how the baby bird should be fed.**

COMMON INTRODUCTORY WORDS FOR NOUN CLAUSES				
Relative Pronouns				
that	whatever	whichever	whoever	whomever
what	which	who	whom	
Relative Adverbs				
how	when		where	whether
if	whenever		wherever	why

Sometimes the word that introduces a noun clause is not expressed.

EXAMPLE   I heard **[that] the class might travel to Baltimore in April.**

EXERCISE 6   Identifying and Classifying Noun Clauses

Underline the noun clause in each of the following sentences. On the line before the sentence, identify the part of speech of the clause. Write *s.* for *subject*, *p.n.* for *predicate nominative*, *d.o.* for *direct object*, *i.o.* for *indirect object*, or *o.p.* for *object of a preposition*.

EX. ⎯ *d.o.* ⎯ 1. Sabrina wondered which of the neighborhood dogs was barking.

⎯⎯⎯⎯ 1. The mechanic described how an engine works.

⎯⎯⎯⎯ 2. Whichever piece Lawanda plays will be the highlight of the concert.

⎯⎯⎯⎯ 3. The question is whether we should buy or rent snorkeling equipment.

_____   4. Pilar provided a copy of her diploma to whomever she asked for a job.

_____   5. The wallpaper choice was whatever my mother selected.

_____   6. The apprentice does well what is assigned to her.

_____   7. Whoever was awarded the prize must have been pleased.

_____   8. On Saturday Joe will give whoever is interested a ride on his snowmobile.

_____   9. Only the bus driver paid attention to where construction blocked traffic.

_____ 10. The speaker gave whoever heckled him a fast and funny answer.

_____ 11. How much students practice affects their playing ability.

_____ 12. You can order whatever is on the menu.

_____ 13. The banyan tree provides shade to whoever sits underneath it.

_____ 14. The mystery was which of the keys had been stolen and replaced.

_____ 15. Tanya brought whoever seemed interested a copy of her poem.

EXERCISE 7   Writing Sentences with Noun Clauses

Finish each sentence below by replacing each blank with a noun clause. Use the word in parentheses to introduce the noun clause. Write your completed sentences on your own paper.

EX.   1. The rain washed away _____ . (Use *whatever*.)
         1. The rain washed away whatever tracks the bear had left.

1. Put _____ at the front of the stage. (Use *whichever*.)

2. Mr. Ramírez agreed to sell _____ . (Use *whatever*.)

3. _____ should switch off the lights. (Use *Whoever*.)

4. _____ pleases Ms. O'Toole greatly. (Use *That*.)

5. Mei Hua didn't know _____ . (Use *whether*.)

6. I sent _____ a map and directions. (Use *whoever*.)

7. _____ need water only twice a month. (Use *Whichever*.)

8. Nobody knows _____ . (Use *when*.)

9. Mr. Hirata explained _____ . (Use *why*.)

10. The letter carrier will deliver _____ . (Use *whatever*.)

SENTENCE STRUCTURE

13g According to their structure, sentences are classified as *simple, compound, complex,* or *compound-complex.*

(1) A *simple sentence* **has one independent clause and no subordinate clauses.**

EXAMPLES   Please turn down the volume for a moment.
Do you know another way out of town?
I could have walked even farther in these new shoes.

(2) A *compound sentence* **has two or more independent clauses but no subordinate clauses.**

Independent clauses may be joined by (1) a comma and a coordinating conjunction (*and, but for, nor, or, so,* or *yet*); (2) by a semicolon; or (3) by a semicolon and a conjunctive adverb or transitional expression followed by a comma.

EXAMPLES   The Sherpas of Nepal are known as good mountaineers**, and** they often guide people in the Himalayas.
The park has occupied that corner since 1891**;** it was a gathering place for hippies in the sixties**;** now people seldom use it.
Tranh agreed to take the hen**; however,** he felt unhappy about the trade.

(3) A *complex sentence* **has one independent clause and at least one subordinate clause.**

EXAMPLES   The Japanese thought **that dolls could draw disease out of a sick person.**
Although the Parks took us sightseeing, we stayed with the Kims because they have an extra room.

(4) A *compound-complex sentence* **has two or more independent clauses and at least one subordinate clause.**

EXAMPLES   Sequoyah created an alphabet **that has eighty-six symbols;** the Cherokee people still use it today.
After the bread rose, Meg punched it down**, and** Lily formed the dough into loaves.

EXERCISE 8   Classifying Sentences According to Structure

Identify the structure of each of the sentences below. On the line before each sentence, write *simp.* for *simple, comp.* for *compound, cx.* for *complex,* and *cd.-cx.* for *compound-complex.*

EX. ___cx.___ 1. One of the most remarkable examples of multifamily housing that you can see on this continent is the cliff dwelling at Mesa Verde in southwestern Colorado.

_____ 1. The ancient structures of Mesa Verde give historians and tourists a glimpse into a fascinating culture.

_____ 2. Between A.D. 550 and the late 1300s, this area of southwestern Colorado was busy, but now the ancient buildings contain only memories.

_____ 3. Though the Anasazi were well known by other peoples in their own time, today relatively little is known about their way of life.

_____ 4. For about 750 years, the Anasazi lived and farmed on top of Mesa Verde.

_____ 5. The ancestors of the Anasazi were called Basket Makers; they perfected the art of making baskets that were both beautiful and useful.

_____ 6. Around A.D. 550, some Basket Makers moved to Mesa Verde, where they developed a method of building dwellings called pithouses.

_____ 7. Soon the Anasazi learned to build square rooms with vertical walls, and their round pithouses were used only as ceremonial rooms.

_____ 8. Anasazi pottery has been found all over Mesa Verde; it is easily recognized by designs that were painted with black paint in intricate lines, squares, and other geometric shapes.

_____ 9. Because the plateaus usually received enough rain, the Anasazi managed to grow corn, beans, and squash.

_____ 10. Thousands of Anasazi lived in cliff dwellings of Mesa Verde until the late 1300s, when they mysteriously abandoned their homes.

Peanuts reprinted by permission of UFS, Inc.

SENTENCE PURPOSE

13h Sentences are classified according to purpose as *declarative, imperative, interrogative,* or *exclamatory.*

(1) A *declarative sentence* **makes a statement. All declarative sentences end with periods.**

EXAMPLE   Children in Great Britain celebrate Guy Fawkes Day with bonfires and fireworks**.**

(2) An *imperative sentence* **gives a command or makes a request. Imperative sentences usually end with periods, but a very strong command may end with an exclamation point.**

EXAMPLES   First, take the pine needles out of your basket**.**
Run for the hills**!**

(3) An *interrogative sentence* **asks a question. Interrogative sentences end with question marks.**

EXAMPLES   Do you keep spoke wrenches in stock**?**
Where are those T-shirts with the school's name on them**?**

 Any sentence may be spoken in such a way that it is interrogative. If so, the sentence should end with a question mark.

EXAMPLE   You called me**?**

(4) An *exclamatory sentence* **expresses strong feeling. Exclamatory sentences end with exclamation points.**

EXAMPLES   What a singer Faye is**!**
How glamorous you look**!**

 Any sentence may be spoken in such a way that it is exclamatory. If so, the sentence should end with an exclamation point.

EXAMPLE   What happened to all of the apples**!**

EXERCISE 9   Classifying Sentences According to Purpose

Identify the purpose of each of the following sentences. On the line before each sentence, write *dec.* for *declarative, imp.* for *imperative, inter.* for *interrogative,* or *excl.* for *exclamatory.* Also add the correct end marks.

EX.   __*dec.*__ 1. I read this book of fairy tales when I was very young

_____ 1. At 10:00 P.M., the last train will leave the station

_____ 2. How many hours will Agoyo need to bake enough bread for everyone

183

_____ 3. In certain parts of the tropics, it usually rains every day, but only for a short period of time

_____ 4. Those two cats curl up together when they're cold

_____ 5. Get this lawn mowed today

_____ 6. How quickly can you do your homework and still answer all the problems correctly

_____ 7. Alas, I will not be able to see my friends again for six full weeks

_____ 8. The program for tonight's concert has been changed

_____ 9. Chung Sook enjoys the institute so much that he plans to take additional courses

_____ 10. Is it necessary to soak the beans overnight before we cook them

_____ 11. Oh, what an annoying sound that machine makes

_____ 12. Are all of the children who are going on the field trip here yet

_____ 13. Write to your U.S. senator about your views on the recycling issue

_____ 14. Watch out for the icy steps

_____ 15. When was the last time you practiced your typing

_____ 16. After the festival, Benally and Wauneka walked home together

_____ 17. How is it that you have never met him before

_____ 18. Do the dishes as soon as you finish eating

_____ 19. Tell me how long it takes you to peel a potato

_____ 20. Yuck, what an ugly mess that muddy shirt is

_____ 21. Stop what you're doing, and come here immediately

_____ 22. Walter caught a golden trout and then cooked it over the campfire

_____ 23. This year the last snowfall before the solstice was on December 19

_____ 24. Do you expect that Abeyto will return from the mountain before sunset

_____ 25. Go to the convenience store at the minimall and get a box of cereal

CHAPTER REVIEW

A. Identifying Independent and Subordinate Clauses

Classify the italicized clauses in each of the sentences below. On the line before each sentence, write *indep. cl.* for *independent clause*, *adj. cl.* for *adjective clause*, *adv. cl.* for *adverb clause*, or *n. cl.* for *noun clause*.

EX. <u>adj. cl.</u> 1. Nels paused and stared at the sky, *which had suddenly darkened*.

_____ 1. Kenya, a country on the east coast of Africa, *became independent in 1963*.

_____ 2. Vo, *whose hair was still uncombed*, went out to collect the newspaper from the lawn.

_____ 3. *What I learned in school today* will be of use when I go to take my driver's license exam.

_____ 4. Sarah left for school *after Molly came home from her morning run*.

_____ 5. *Although nothing could have warned him of the danger*, Angelo suddenly moved off in another direction.

_____ 6. A short but fascinating story is *how Franklin won the election*.

_____ 7. Len emerged briefly from the shadows *in which he had been running* into bright sunlight.

_____ 8. *The kiwi bird lives in New Zealand, has wings, but cannot fly*.

_____ 9. *Whoever moves fastest* will become our starting forward.

_____ 10. Mrs. Fung is reading her daughter's favorite book, the one about mothers *who were brought up in traditional ways* and their very modern daughters.

B. Identifying Sentences by Structure and Purpose

Identify the structure of each of the following sentences. On the line before each sentence, write *simp.* for *simple*, *comp.* for *compound*, *cx.* for *complex*, and *cd.-cx.* for *compound-complex*. Then identify the purpose of each sentence. On the line before each sentence, write *dec.* for *declarative*, *imp.* for *imperative*, *inter.* for *interrogative*, or *excl.* for *exclamatory*.

EX. <u>cx.; imp.</u> 1. While exiting a building during a fire drill, do not talk with other students.

_____ 1. The 2006 Winter Olympic games were held in Turin, Italy.

_____ 2. Once they had their grandmother's approval, Elena stripped the old paint from the chair, and Diane sanded the surface.

_____ 3. Does a kitten, unless it is taught, know how to hunt?

_____ 4. Read the chapter; then respond to questions 1 through 15.

_____ 5. Some of the planets have moons, and one of the planets has rings; can you identify all of these planets?

_____ 6. If Tisa does one hundred pushups, I'll be amazed!

_____ 7. Roald Amundsen was a courageous explorer and became the first man to reach the South Pole.

_____ 8. Even if we're losing by sixty points, don't even think of quitting the game!

_____ 9. If the plumber cleaned out the drain, why can't we use the sink?

_____ 10. Mindy wants to shop for sweaters, and Cao must buy a new jacket before the weather turns cold.

C. Using Clauses to Write a Poem

Create a poem by filling in each line below. Use and label at least one adverb clause, one adjective clause, and one noun clause.

EX.   1. I believe _that I have a purpose_ . (noun cl.)

Today

I believe _____ .

I dream _____ .

I want _____ .

I fear _____ .

Yesterday

I learned much_____ .

When _____ , I stayed silent.

The people _____ didn't hear me.

But _____ .

Tomorrow

If _____ , I will succeed with my plans.

I will _____ because _____ .

Listen to _____ .

You _____ .

SUBJECT-VERB AGREEMENT

Number is the form of a word that indicates whether the word is singular or plural.

14a A word that refers to one person or thing is *singular* in number. A word that refers to more than one is *plural* in number.

SINGULAR employer   theory   woman   that   either   it
PLURAL   employers   theories women   those   both   they

Most nouns that end in *s* are plural; most present-tense verbs that end in *s* are singular. Past-tense verbs (except *be*) have the same form in both the singular and the plural.

NOTE The singular pronouns *I* and *you* almost always take plural verbs. The only exceptions are the forms *I am* and *I was*.

14b A verb should agree with its subject in number.

(1) Singular subjects take singular verbs.

EXAMPLE   The falcon **flies** above the rabbit warren.[The singular verb *flies* agrees with the singular subject *falcon*.]

(2) Plural subjects take plural verbs.

EXAMPLE   The falcons **fly** above the rabbit warren.[The plural verb *fly* agrees with the plural subject *falcons*.]

Like the one-word verb in each of the preceding examples, a verb phrase must also agree in number with its subject. The number of a verb phrase is indicated by the form of its first auxiliary (helping) verb.

EXAMPLES   My aunt **is rebuilding** a classic Thunderbird.[singular subject and verb phrase]
My aunts **are rebuilding** a classic Thunderbird.[plural subject and verb phrase]

EXERCISE 1   Selecting Verbs That Agree in Number with Their Subjects

For each of the following phrases, underline the verb or verb phrase in parentheses that agrees in number with its subject.

EX.   1. she (*run, runs*)

1. thoroughbred (*gallops, gallop*)
2. roses (*blooms, bloom*)
3. fans (*is shouting, are shouting*)
4. candidate (*announces, announce*)
5. Rachel (*is practicing, are practicing*)
6. chefs (*slices, slice*)

7. we (*decides, decide*)

8. judge (*hears, hear*)

9. fingers (*flexes, flex*)

10. elephant (*is charging, are charging*)

11. skyscrapers (*towers, tower*)

12. gazelles (*leaps, leap*)

13. scrolls (*is crumbling, are crumbling*)

14. helicopter (*hovers, hover*)

15. reporter (*is waiting, are waiting*)

16. radio signals (*carries, carry*)

17. spaghetti (*boils, boil*)

18. students (*is uniting, are uniting*)

19. performer (*dazzles, dazzle*)

20. Carlos (*forgets, forget*)

EXERCISE 2   Identifying Subjects and Verbs That Agree in Number

For each sentence below, underline the verb or verb phrase in parentheses that agrees in number with its subject.

EX. 1. Athletes (*trains, train*) rigorously for the demanding triathlon.

1. The oceanographers (*is collecting, are collecting*) samples of algae.

2. Every year, several million tourists (*visits, visit*) Europe.

3. Alaska (*covers, cover*) the most area of any state in the United States.

4. Alma (*maneuvers, maneuver*) the bike down the path expertly.

5. The interpreter (*translates, translate*) the ambassador's speech.

6. Julia (*is refinishing, are refinishing*) the woodwork on the antique dresser.

7. The computer program (*alphabetizes, alphabetize*) automatically.

8. In our school, many students (*speaks, speak*) more than one language.

9. The cultural festival (*has, have*) crafts from over ten countries.

10. Storm clouds (*is gathering, are gathering*) above the plain.

11. The acrobats (*is performing, are performing*) on Saturday.

12. The accountant (*is totaling, are totaling*) the figures.

13. Bees (*plays, play*) a vital role in the pollination of flowers.

14. We (*collects, collect*) newspapers for recycling.

15. The librarians (*is shelving, are shelving*) the new books.

16. The Rio Grande (*marks, mark*) the border between Texas and Mexico.

17. Keiko (*is throwing, are throwing*) a surprise party for her sister.

18. The museum (*is holding, are holding*) a special exhibit on Chinese textiles.

19. The orioles (*is nesting, are nesting*) outside the kitchen window.

20. Our teachers (*urges, urge*) us to read the material twice.

INTERVENING PHRASES AND CLAUSES

14c **The number of the subject is not changed by a phrase or a clause following the subject.**

EXAMPLES The **boxes are** filled with videotapes.
The **boxes** under the bed **are** filled with videotapes. [The prepositional phrase *under the bed* does not affect the number of the subject *boxes*.]

Leonard Bernstein earned fame as a composer.
Leonard Bernstein, one of this country's most noted conductors, **earned** fame as a composer. [The appositive phrase *one of this country's most noted conductors* does not affect the number of the subject *Leonard Bernstein*.]

The **jerseys are** purple, yellow, and black.
The **jerseys** that we ordered **are** purple, yellow, and black. [The adjective clause *that we ordered* does not affect the number of the subject *jerseys*.]

A prepositional phrase may begin with a ***compound preposition*** such as *together with, in addition to, as well as,* or *along with*. These phrases do not affect the number of the verb.

EXAMPLES **Lanny,** as well as his brother, **is planning** a trip. [singular subject and verb]
Your **socks,** along with your hat, **are** in the closet. [plural subject and verb]

 REFERENCE NOTE: For lists of prepositions, see page 137.

EXERCISE 3   Identifying Subjects and Verbs That Agree in Number

For each of the following sentences, underline the verb or verb phrase in parentheses that agrees in number with its subject.

EX. 1. The package that I sent (*contains, contain*) the information.

1. Mr. Delgado, one of my co-workers, (*bakes, bake*) his own bread.

2. The bins for the clothing drive (*is filling, are filling*) quickly.

3. Rice, as well as pasta, (*is, are*) a good source of complex carbohydrates.

4. The books on the bottom shelf (*is, are*) oversized.

5. Many houses along the river (*was, were*) damaged by the flood.

6. Our next-door neighbors (*plants, plant*) bulbs in their garden.

7. George Washington, the first president of the United States, (*is, are*) known as the father of his country.

8. The jets that just landed (*needs, need*) refueling.

9. Raisins, together with granola, (*makes, make*) trail mix.

10. The students who attended the meeting (*supports, support*) the school board's new policies.

EXERCISE 4   Proofreading a Paragraph for Subject-Verb Agreement

In the paragraph below, draw a line through each verb or verb phrase that does not agree with its subject. Write the correct form of the verb or verb phrase in the space above the error. Some sentences may contain no errors.

EX.   [1] The floor ~~are~~ a central part of Japanese houses. *is*

. [1] For thousands of years, the floor have been the center of activity in Japanese houses. [2] Sitting, as well as sleeping, are done on the floor. [3] A *tatami* are the floor covering used in Japanese housing. [4] These rectangular mats is made from rice straw. [5] A typical *tatami* measure about six feet by three feet and is two inches thick. [6] In some houses space are left between the mats. [7] In others, the mats completely covers the floor. [8] People take off their shoes at the door to protect the floor and the mats. [9] The foot covering that they put on are called a *tabi*, which is like a slipper. [10] The regular size of the *tatami* have greatly influenced Japanese architecture. [11] The height of *shoji*, which are sliding doors, match the length of the tatami. [12] A *toko-no-ma*, an area for displaying art, are also influenced by the *tatami*. [13] The *toko-no-ma* is positioned at eye-level of a person sitting on a *tatami*. [14] A person often describe a room by the number of mats that cover the floor. [15] For example, a six-mat room is a room whose floor is covered by six *tatami*.

AGREEMENT WITH INDEFINITE PRONOUNS

14d **The following indefinite pronouns are singular:** *anybody, anyone, anything, each, either, everybody, everyone, everything, neither, nobody, no one, nothing, one, somebody, someone,* **and** *something.* **A singular indefinite pronoun takes a singular verb.**

EXAMPLES **Each** of you **is** my friend.[singular subject, singular verb]
Everything he does **is** a success.[singular subject, singular verb]
No one who has seen the show **says** it is worth fifty dollars. [singular subject, singular verb]

14e **The following indefinite pronouns are plural:** *both, few, many,* **and** *several.* **A plural indefinite pronoun takes a plural verb.**

EXAMPLES **Both** of my aunts **say** they will vote.[plural subject, plural verb]
Many in my neighborhood **are** complaining about the graffiti. [plural subject, plural verb]

14f **The following indefinite pronouns may be either singular or plural:** *all, any, most, none,* **and** *some.*

These pronouns are singular when they refer to a singular word and are plural when they refer to plural words.

EXAMPLES **Most** of the river **runs** through the Great Plains.[*Most* refers to the singular noun *river.*]
Most of the windows **are** open.[*Most* refers to the plural noun *windows.*]

Some of the wharf **was** rebuilt after the hurricane.[*Some* refers to the singular noun *wharf.*]
Some of the stores **offer** computer services.[*Some* refers to the plural noun *stores.*]

NOTE The word *none* is singular when it means "not one" and plural when it means "not any."

EXAMPLES **None** of the spots **shows.**[*Not one* shows.]
None of the spots **show.**[*Not any* show.]

EXERCISE 5   Identifying Subjects and Verbs That Agree in Number

For each of the following sentences, underline the verb or verb phrase in parentheses that agrees in number with its subject.

EX.   1. Everyone who waited in line (*was*, *were*) able to buy tickets.

1. Both of the songs (*sounds, sound*) familiar.

2. Some of the meat (*needs, need*) to be defrosted.

3. For the tryouts, each of the actors (*prepares, prepare*) an audition piece.

4. Most of the classes (*has, have*) small enrollments.

5. Neither of the restaurants (*accepts, accept*) reservations.

6. Each thread in the tapestry (*is, are*) made of handspun silk.

7. Someone in the bleachers (*is waving, are waving*) to you.

8. Some of the runners (*looks, look*) tired.

9. Any of the dresses (*is, are*) appropriate for the occasion.

10. Some of the trains (*runs, run*) on weekends.

11. Both of the newspapers (*offers, offer*) excellent local news coverage.

12. Some of my sources (*is, are*) firsthand.

13. All of the meteorologists (*is predicting, are predicting*) a severe thunderstorm.

14. Most of my colleagues (*attends, attend*) the conference.

15. None of the defendant's alibis (*holds, hold*) up in court.

16. Everyone who reads the book (*has, have*) a different interpretation.

17. Most of Siri's arguments (*makes, make*) sense.

18. Many of the diners (*orders, order*) the vegetarian chili.

19. One of the artists (*incorporates, incorporate*) recycled materials into her paintings.

20. Most of the council members (*votes, vote*) on the proposal.

21. Many at the airport (*is experiencing, are experiencing*) travel delays.

22. Everyone (*understands, understand*) the director's instructions.

23. Either of your plans (*is, are*) acceptable.

24. Anyone who wants to attend (*is, are*) welcome.

25. No one (*wants, want*) the festival to end.

THE COMPOUND SUBJECT

A *compound subject* consists of two or more nouns or pronouns that are joined by a conjunction and have the same verb.

14g Subjects joined by *and* usually take a plural verb.

(1) Compound subjects joined by *and* that name more than one person or thing always take plural verbs.

EXAMPLES   **Doug** and **Mika met** at Bruno's party.
                Corn, wheat, and **soybeans are** that country's main crops.

(2) Compound subjects joined by *and* that name only one person or one thing take a singular verb.

EXAMPLES   My best **friend** and **tutor is** Devon. [one person]
                Red beans and **rice is** a staple at our house. [one thing]

14h Singular subjects joined by *or* or *nor* take a singular verb.

EXAMPLES   Either **he** or **Kathie needs** to stay here.
                Neither **Spike** nor **Brandy** ever **wears** a sweater.

14i When a singular subject and a plural subject are joined by *or* or *nor*, the verb agrees with the subject nearer the verb.

EXAMPLES   Either my **sister** or my **cousins are going** to pick you up.
                [The plural subject *cousins* is nearer the verb.]
                Either my **cousins** or my **sister is going** to pick you up.
                [The singular subject *sister* is nearer the verb.]

EXERCISE 6   Correcting Errors in Subject-Verb Agreement

In the following sentences, draw a line through each verb that does not agree in number with its subject. Write the correct form of the verb in the space above the error. Some sentences may not contain any agreement errors.

EX.   1.   Both Damon and Krista ~~enjoys~~ *enjoy* jazz music.

1. Law and order were the main theme of the mayoral campaign.

2. Bicycling and in-line skating is enjoyable and healthful forms of exercise.

3. Sandra and her cousins sees each other every year at their family reunion.

4. The project head and computer analyst are my aunt.

5. Neither Nicole nor Tracy takes credit for the rally's success.

6. Your sister and your mother looks alike.

7. Mushrooms and zucchini is my favorite vegetables.

8. Either my father or I usually makes dinner.

9. Neither my swimming coach nor my history teacher know Ms. Kim.

10. The ode and the sonnet is forms of poetry.

11. Firsthand accounts and historical evidence supports the archeologist's claim.

12. Either the director or the committee members schedules the meeting.

13. Margo and Brian is learning Japanese.

14. Dogs and wolves belongs to the canine family.

15. Nuts and milk are my favorite snack.

16. Neither palm trees nor cactuses grows in northern climates.

17. James Baldwin and Ralph Ellison were two of the writers Tom wrote about in his English paper.

18. Hot peppers and curry powder makes the dish very hot.

19. Either Josh or Anthony bat after the shortstop.

20. Plants, plush carpeting, and subdued lighting softens the lobby's severe appearance.

21. Roses, azaleas, and tulips grows well in our climate.

22. Neither the Senate nor the House of Representatives is in session.

23. Either the cat or the dogs sleeps on the hallway rug.

24. The authors and the illustrator of the new children's book is coming to the bookstore.

25. Cindy and Tanya works as cashiers every Saturday.

EXERCISE 7   Using Verbs That Agree in Number with Compound Subjects

Write five sentences on your own paper about your cultural heritage. In each sentence, use a compound subject joined by *and, or,* or *nor.* Include one example of two singular subjects joined by *either/or* or *neither/nor* and one singular and one plural subject joined by *either/or* or *neither/nor.* Pay special attention to subject-verb agreement.

EX.   1. My Shawnee heritage and my Irish heritage are very special to me.

14j Collective nouns may be either singular or plural.

A *collective noun* is singular in form, but it names a group of persons or things.

Common Collective Nouns			
alliance	class	flood	public
army	club	group	series
assembly	committee	herd	squad
audience	crowd	jury	staff
band	faculty	majority	swarm
choir	family	number	team
clan	flock	panel	troop

Use a plural verb when the noun refers to the members of the group as individuals. Use a singular verb with a collective noun when the noun refers to the group as a unit.

EXAMPLES   The audience **is** getting louder.
The audience **are** screaming the names of their favorite songs.

The band **is** unwilling to play an encore.
The band **disagree** about what song to play next.

EXERCISE 8   Writing Sentences with Collective Nouns

From the chart above, select ten collective nouns. On your own paper, write a pair of sentences using each noun. Each pair of sentences should show how the collective noun may be either singular or plural.

EX. 1. a. The jury finds the defendant not guilty.
b. The jury disagree on how the defendant should be compensated.

REVIEW EXERCISE 1

A. Identifying Correct Verbs in Sentences

In each of the sentences below, underline the verb or verb phrase in parentheses that agrees in number with its subject.

· EX.   1. Those olives (*is*, *are*) extremely salty.

1. Many of my friends (*studies*, *study*) together before exams.

2. The flamenco dancers (*is wearing*, *are wearing*) authentic costumes.

3. Nuna, one of the researchers, (*dedicates*, *dedicate*) herself to her job.

4. Centimeters and decimeters (*is*, *are*) metric units of measurement.

5. My sister, as well as my parents, (*shares*, *share*) my enthusiasm.

6. Some of the buildings (*is*, *are*) visible through the fog.

7. The class (*assigns*, *assign*) responsibilities to different groups of students.

8. Neither Rhonda nor Emilio (*wants*, *want*) to leave.

9. Rhythm and blues (*is*, *are*) Carla's favorite type of music.

10. The doctor (*is expecting*, *are expecting*) your visit.

B. Making Verbs Agree with Their Subjects

In each sentence below, draw a line through any verb that does not agree in number with its subject. Then, on the line before the sentence, write the correct form of the verb. If a sentence contains no errors, write C.

EX. _____needs_____   1. Each of the potatoes need to be peeled.

_____   1. A swarm of bees are heading toward the hive.

_____   2. Many of the younger campers miss their parents.

_____   3. Wax from the candles are dripping on the table.

_____   4. Either the magician or the band provide the entertainment.

_____   5. "The song that we heard remind me of summer," said Jill.

_____   6. Both of those articles reports on recent military events.

_____   7. Confidence and determination is important qualities.

_____   8. Some species of bamboo grows nearly three feet a day.

_____   9. The magazine, along with the journals, have arrived.

_____   10. Most of the shops in this mall offer discounts on seasonal items.

OTHER PROBLEMS IN AGREEMENT

14k   A verb agrees with its subject, not with its predicate nominative.

EXAMPLES   **Science labs are** my favorite school activity. [plural subject, plural verb]

My favorite school activity is science labs. [singular subject, singular verb]

14l   A subject preceded by *every* or *many a/an* takes a singular verb.

EXAMPLES   **Every** new day **promises** something new.
Many a day **has** passed since I sent her that letter.

14m   An expression stating an amount may be singular or plural.

(1) An expression stating an amount is singular when the amount is thought of as a unit and is plural when the amount is thought of as many parts.

EXAMPLES   If you ask me, **six cars is** a caravan. [The *cars* are thought of as a unit.]

Six cars are leaving from school for Memphis later this afternoon. [The *cars* are thought of separately.]

(2) A fraction or a percentage is singular when it refers to a singular word and plural when it refers to a plural word.

EXAMPLES   **Three fourths** of the committee **is** a quorum. [The percentage refers to the singular noun *committee*.]

Three fourths of the committee members **are** present. [The percentage refers to the plural noun *members*.]

Seventy percent of the student body **agrees** with the decision. [The percentage refers to the singular noun *body*.]

Seventy percent of the students **agree** with the decision. [The percentage refers to the plural noun *students*.]

(3) Expressions of measurement (length, weight, capacity, area) are usually singular.

EXAMPLE   **Eight hundred meters is** a long way to run.

14n   The title of a creative work (such as a book, song, film, or painting) or the name of a country (even if it is plural in form) takes a singular verb.

EXAMPLES   Louisa May Alcott's ***Little Women* was** largely autobiographical.
The United States elects its president every leap year.

14o   Many nouns that are plural in form are singular in meaning.

(1) The following nouns always take singular verbs.

civics	genetics	news
economics	mathematics	physics
electronics	linguistics	

EXAMPLE   **Civics is** more than just the study of the law.

(2) The following nouns always take plural verbs.

binoculars   pliers   shears   trousers   eyeglasses   scissors

EXAMPLE   My **eyeglasses are** no longer strong enough.

(3) The name of an organization (even if it is plural in form) usually takes a singular verb.

EXAMPLES   **General Motors is** a large company.
The United Nations is composed primarily of the General Assembly and the Security Council.

(4) Many nouns ending in -ics, such as *acoustics, athletics, ethics, politics, statistics,* and *tactics,* may be singular or plural.

EXAMPLES   **Politics is** what I plan to study in college.
My **politics are** similar to my parents'.

14p   In the expression *number of*, the word *number* is singular when preceded by *the* and is plural when preceded by *a*.

EXAMPLES   **The number of** dogs in our building **has skyrocketed**.
A number of people **have** acquired them recently.

14q   When the subject follows the verb, as in questions and in sentences beginning with *here* and *there*, identify the subject and make sure that the verb agrees with it.

The verb usually comes before the subject in sentences beginning with *Here* or *There* and in questions.

EXAMPLES   Here **is** the **flower** you brought.
Here **are** the **flowers** you brought.

There **was** a **horse** in the field.
There **were** no **horses** in the field.

When **is your brother** coming to visit?
When **are your brothers** coming to visit?

NOTE   Contractions such as *Here's, There's, When's,* and *Where's* incorporate the verb *is.* Use such contractions only with subjects that are singular in meaning.

NONSTANDARD   When's your classes?
STANDARD   When **are** your **classes**?

NONSTANDARD   Here's my new shoes.
STANDARD   Here **are** my new **shoes**.
STANDARD   Here's my new **pair** of shoes.

14q   When a relative pronoun (*that, which,* or *who*) is the subject of an adjective clause, the verb in the clause agrees with the word to which the relative pronoun refers.

EXAMPLES   My yoga class, **which meets** on Monday, is scheduling an extra session. [*Which* refers to the singular noun *class.*]
I know people **who design** clothes. [*Who* refers to the plural noun *people.*]

NOTE   A relative pronoun takes a plural verb when its antecedent is preceded by *one of those* or *one of these.* When its antecedent is preceded by *the only one of those* (or *these*), the relative pronoun takes a singular verb.

EXAMPLES   Ursula is **one of those runners who are** on both the cross-country and the track teams.
The portrait over the fireplace is **the only one of those paintings that is** not by my father.

EXERCISE 9   Selecting Verbs That Agree in Number with Their Subjects

In each of the following sentences, underline the verb or contraction in parentheses that agrees in number with its subject.

EX.   1.   Where (*is, are*) the pliers?

1.   Sore muscles (*is, are*) the first sign that I have exercised too hard.

2.   Many a president (*has, have*) sat in this room.

3.   There (*is, are*) nine players on a baseball team.

4.   The Peace Corps (*is, are*) headquartered in Washington, D.C.

5.   The city hall is the only one of those buildings that (*is, are*) scheduled for demolition.

6.   The number of mosquitoes (*has, have*) decreased this month.

7.   *One Writer's Beginnings* (*is, are*) Eudora Welty's account of growing up in Jackson, Mississippi.

8.   Twenty percent of the orange crop (*was, were*) affected by the frost.

9. "My goal (*is, are*) increased sales and salary increases," the manager announced.

10. Mathematics (*has, have*) always been Charlotte's best subject.

11. Every hesitation in Branford's speech (*reveals, reveal*) his discomfort.

12. The drivers of the snowplows in my town, which (*is, are*) in the Adirondacks, work very hard.

13. Your binoculars (*is, are*) in the case.

14. My debating tactics (*isn't, aren't*) the same as yours.

15. Two weeks (*has, have*) passed since we last spoke.

EXERCISE 10   Proofreading a Paragraph for Subject-Verb Agreement

In the paragraph below, underline any verb or verb phrase that does not agree in number with its subject. Write the correct form of the verb on your own paper. Some sentences may not contain any agreement errors.

EX.   [1] Jacqueline Cochran's career and achievements <u>is</u> outstanding.

    1. *are*

[1] By age 22, Cochran's successful business tactics was making her well-known in the cosmetics industry. [2] After she learned to fly to promote her business in 1932, every speed, distance, and altitude record were hers to break. [3] It was her record-breaking abilities and her gender that brought her fame. [4] Two air-speed records was set in 1938, one of them by Cochran. [5] Military service and working as a pilot instructor was another part of Cochran's success. [6] During World War II, the United States were finally allowing women to work at jobs traditionally held by men. [7] A number of female pilots was trained by Cochran during the war. [8] The Women's Air Force Service Pilots were the organization that Cochran headed in 1943. [9] Many a flying record were broken by the skilled pilot in the years that followed. [10] Flying faster than the speed of sound and flying twice the speed of sound was among Cochran's many firsts. [11] Another first for a woman, 1,429 miles per hour were the speed record Cochran set in 1964. [12] The titles Air Force Reserve colonel and NASA consultant was added to Cochran's list of achievements before her death in 1980. [13] Cochran's book *Stars at Noon* tell the story of her life. [14] The number of records set by Cochran show her talent and skill. [15] Aeronautics owe a great deal to Jacqueline Cochran.

REVIEW EXERCISE 2

A. Identifying Verbs That Agree in Number with Their Subjects

In each sentence below, underline the verb or contraction that agrees in number with its subject.

EX. 1. (*Where's*, *Where are*) the reference materials?

1. Phonetics (*is*, *are*) the subject of today's discussion.

2. Nearly three fourths of the earth's surface (*is*, *are*) covered by water.

3. This is one of those companies that (*leads*, *lead*) tours of the Grand Canyon.

4. Ravi's trousers (*needs*, *need*) to be hemmed.

5. The United Auto Workers (*is*, *are*) a powerful union.

6. The law firm's ethics (*is*, *are*) always honorable.

7. Those two singers (*is*, *are*) performing a duet.

8. The new shears (*makes*, *make*) trimming the bushes much easier.

9. Ten miles (*is*, *are*) not a long distance to travel by car.

10. Jogging and reading (*is*, *are*) what I do to relax.

11. The Netherlands (*observes*, *observe*) a national holiday on April 30.

12. Thirty percent of the renovation (*remains*, *remain*) to be finished.

13. Those sea lions, which live off the California coast, (*has*, *have*) been thriving.

14. (*What's*, *What are*) the organization's politics?

15. The United States (*ranks*, *rank*) fourth in population among countries.

16. News from the battlefield (*was*, *were*) encouraging.

17. A number of the applications that (*was*, *were*) made for the job opening interested the director.

18. Vivaldi's *Four Seasons* (*is*, *are*) being performed by the Boston Symphony Orchestra.

19. What the documentary reveals (*is*, *are*) corruption and criminal activity.

20. Four boxes (*is*, *are*) inside the crate.

B.   Proofreading a Paragraph for Errors in Subject–Verb Agreement

In the paragraphs below, draw a line through any verb or verb phrase that does not agree in number with its subject. Write the correct form of the verb in the space above the incorrect word. Some sentences may contain no agreement errors.

EX.   [1]   American architect I. M. Pei's sense of beauty ~~please~~ *pleases* museum-goers around the world.

[1] A number of public buildings in the United States, France, and China has been designed by Pei. [2] Although Pei was born in China in 1917, the United States have been home to the architect since 1935. [3] His bold designs for museums in Washington, D.C. and Paris has made Pei famous. [4] In 1978, Pei designed the East Building of Washington's National Gallery of Art. [5] When visitors enter the gallery, they sees a large triangular space and a small number of paintings. [6] Pei's use of open space and light leave a lasting impression.

[7] Paris's Louvre Museum celebrated its bicentennial in 1993 with the opening of a newly renovated wing. [8] One billion dollars were the price tag for the renovation, headed by Pei. [9] Two thirds of the renovation were completed in time for the bicentennial celebration. [10] Three courtyards was renovated in the Richelieu Wing. [11] Enormous skylights is Pei's trademark, and Pei installed them over each courtyard. [12] The ninety feet of space between the floors and paned ceilings bring light to the once dim halls. [13] The twenty-two thousand square meters gained by the renovation are twice the old exhibition space. [14] These statistics suggest that the renovation was both practical and pleasing. [15] Since the renovation, many a visitor have passed through Pei's glass pyramid, which serves as the museum's entrance.

PRONOUN AGREEMENT

A pronoun usually refers to a noun or another pronoun. The word to which a pronoun refers is called its *antecedent*. The *number* of a noun or pronoun is either *singular* or *plural*.

14s   A pronoun should agree with its antecedent in number and in gender.

(1) Use a singular pronoun to refer to a singular antecedent; use a plural pronoun to refer to a plural antecedent.

EXAMPLES   **Esperanza** sold **her** bicycle to buy in-line skates. [The singular pronoun *her* refers to the singular antecedent *Esperanza*.]
Before I was born, **the Dodgers and the Giants** moved **their** teams to California. [The plural pronoun *their* refers to the plural antecedent *the Dodgers and the Giants*.]

The *gender* of a singular noun or pronoun is either *masculine, feminine*, or *neuter* (neither masculine nor feminine).

(2) The singular pronouns *he, him, his,* and *himself* refer to masculine antecedents. The singular pronouns *she, her, hers,* and *herself* refer to feminine antecedents. The singular pronouns *it, its,* and *itself* refer to antecedents that are neuter.

EXAMPLES   **Watson** built this model of the Golden Gate bridge **himself**. [The masculine pronoun *himself* refers to the masculine antecedent *Watson*.]
Ruby knew the blue ribbon would be **hers**. [The feminine pronoun *hers* refers to the feminine antecedent *Ruby*.]
After years of use, the **table** had lost **its** shine. [The neuter pronoun *its* refers to the neuter antecedent *table*.]

If a singular antecedent may be either masculine or feminine, use both the masculine and feminine pronouns to refer to it.

EXAMPLES   **Anyone** who is going on the trip should bring **his or her** sketchbook.
Everybody who saw the trick tried to do it **himself or herself**.

Often, you can avoid the "his or her" construction by revising the sentence, using the plural forms of both the pronoun and its antecedent.

EXAMPLES   **All** of the persons going on the trip should bring **their** sketchbooks.
All of those who saw the trick tried to do it **themselves.**

14t   Use a singular pronoun to refer to the following antecedents: *anybody, anyone, each, either, everybody, everyone, neither, nobody, no one, one, somebody,* **and** *someone.*

These words do not indicate gender. To determine their gender, look at the phrases following them.

EXAMPLES   **Each** of the **girls** has worn **her** cap.
One of the **men** forgot **his** wallet.

14u   Use a singular pronoun to refer to two or more singular antecedents joined by *or* or *nor.*

EXAMPLES   **Either Mitchell or Marcel** promised to bring **his** amplifier.
Neither Grace nor Ludmilla said **she** knew how far it was to Sacramento.

14v   Use a plural pronoun to refer to two or more singular antecedents joined by *and.*

EXAMPLES   If you see **Luca and Troy**, tell **them** Ms. Yamamoto wants **them** to come to her office.
Carl, Antonia, and Feng have finished editing **their** film.

NOTE   Revise awkward constructions caused by antecedents that are different genders.

AWKWARD   Either Ernest or Alice will play his guitar.
REVISED   Either Alice will play her guitar, or Ernest will play his.

14w   When a singular and a plural antecedent are joined by *or* or *nor*, the pronoun usually agrees with the nearer antecedent.

EXAMPLES   Neither the **puppies nor** our full-grown **dog** likes **its** new dishes.
Neither our full-grown **dog nor** the **puppies** like **their** new dishes.

Whenever possible, revise the sentence to avoid such an awkward construction.

EXAMPLE   The **puppies** don't like **their** new dishes, and our full-grown **dog** doesn't like **its** new dishes either.

EXERCISE 11   Using Pronouns That Agree with Their Antecedents

In the following sentences, fill in each blank with a pronoun that agrees with its antecedent.

EX.   1.   All of the women completed _____*their*_____ work.

1.   Before the debate, Miguel reviewed _____ note cards.

2.   The stock doubled _____ value within a year.

3.   How does the snake shed _____ skin?

4.   Carl, Sara, and Reggie had _____ essays published in a literary journal.

5.   Does the film live up to _____ reputation?

6.   The fruit stand _____ is stocked with organic produce.

7.   Wendy identified the unclaimed gloves as _____ .

8.   Will either Mom or Emily volunteer _____ time?

9.   Robert practiced _____ German with the exchange student.

10.   My friend Zoe has been performing Indian classical dance since _____ was six years old.

11.   The photo essay speaks for _____ .

12.   When I see Gerald and Patti, I'll tell _____ about the party.

13.   Everyone who is going on the class trip needs to bring _____ deposit on Monday.

14.   All who have a suggestion should put _____ comments in writing.

15.   Neither John nor Adam is ready to give _____ report.

16.   Contestants must submit _____ artwork before next Friday.

17.   Dawn developed the advertising campaign _____ .

18.   Neither Pedro nor Walter took _____ case to court.

19.   Will scientists from several countries share _____ findings at the conference?

20.   The cabinet's shelves are made from the same wood as _____ doors.

21.   All of the spectators showed _____ appreciation by applauding and cheering.

22. Lana's blouse, _____ birthday gift, has a colorful design.

23. Each of the Girl Scouts wore _____ uniform.

24. Is Ms. Gutiérrez visiting _____ niece in Arizona?

25. The geese are returning from _____ winter homes.

EXERCISE 12   Proofreading a Paragraph for Pronoun-Antecedent Agreement

In the paragraphs below, draw a line through the errors in pronoun–antecedent agreement. Write your corrections above the error. Some sentences may be correct.

EX. [1] In the world of Impressionist painting, Mary Cassatt made their *(her)* work known.

[1] Like many other female painters, Mary Cassatt found himself surrounded by the works and ideas of men. [2] Neither the painters she studied nor the instructors who taught her were female. [3] However, what Cassatt learned on his own she applied to her paintings. [4] The pastel colors that Cassatt used characterize their best work. [5] After some Impressionist artists saw some of Cassatt's paintings at an 1874 exhibit, nearly everyone agreed that her work was among the best of any artists that they had ever seen. [6] Certainly no one could truthfully claim that their work was better than hers was.

[7] Edgar Degas suggested that Cassatt create a series of paintings, and she accepted her suggestion. [8] All of the paintings in the series had mothers and children as its subject. [9] Many critics think the series themselves is Cassatt's most important work. [10] Cassatt painted women and children in her everyday domestic lives with few traces of sentimentality. [11] Each of the women seemed to have their own identity. [12] *The Bath* shows a mother washing their daughter's feet and is typical of Cassatt's affection for her subjects.

[13] The men and women Impressionist painters allowed Cassatt to act as a sort of art dealer for his and her paintings. [14] Cassatt had wealthy friends and relatives in the United States who bought their paintings and those of other Impressionist artists. [15] Some American painters today are aware of Cassatt's influence on his work.

CHAPTER REVIEW

A. Proofreading Sentences for Subject-Verb and Pronoun-Antecedent Agreement

In each of the sentences below, draw a line though any errors in subject-verb agreement or pronoun-antecedent agreement. Then, on the line before the sentence, write your correction. If a sentence contains no errors, write C.

EX. _____is_____ 1. The jewelry that Inez makes are based on Navajo designs.

_____ 1. Ten feet are the average height for a sunflower.

_____ 2. Computer programmer and analyst is one of the jobs in which I am interested.

_____ 3. All of the teachers have her master's degrees.

_____ 4. A number of squirrels has made their home in that tree.

_____ 5. The dancers from the ballet company is rehearsing their parts.

_____ 6. Either David or Kyle will read their poem next.

_____ 7. Marta, as well as her parents, are joining us for dinner.

_____ 8. Some of the exhibit showcases Japanese textile arts.

_____ 9. The scissors is kept in a locked drawer.

_____ 10. The orchestra is disagreeing about the concert schedule.

_____ 11. Both New York and New Jersey held its elections this year.

_____ 12. Neither Jupiter nor its moons is visible under these conditions.

_____ 13. The quartet are performing several Mozart compositions.

_____ 14. Designing computers requires specialized training.

_____ 15. Many in the community participates in a neighborhood watch program.

_____ 16. What Jen is doing to earn extra money are shoveling snow and chopping firewood.

_____ 17. The mare tended its foal.

_____ 18. Two thirds of the vote assures a victory.

_____ 19. Neither of the undefeated teams expect to lose the game.

_____ 20. All of the reporters showed his or her credentials.

B.   Proofreading a Paragraph for Errors in Subject-Verb and Pronoun-Antecedent Agreement

In the paragraph below, draw a line through any errors in subject-verb agreement or pronoun-antecedent agreement. Write your correction in the space above the incorrect word. Some sentences may contain no agreement errors.

EX.   [1] Many cultures ~~has~~ *have* unique methods of decorating cloth.

[1] Batik is one of those methods that has existed for many years.

[2] People in Southeast Asia has used the batik method for thousands of years. [3] In batik dyeing, wax is placed on cotton cloth to form a pattern. [4] The cloth under the wax receive no dye. [5] When the cloth is dyed and the wax is removed, the pattern appear on the cloth. [6] Brown, blue, and red is the traditional colors for batik. [7] Either multicolored designs or a blended pattern are a variation of basic batik. [8] Wax from the first design is boiled off. [9] Each new application of wax create a new pattern. [10] In Java, many advancements was made in the art of batik. [11] The Javanese artists' innovations allowed her to create highly detailed patterns. [12] In the 1700s, they was applying the wax with a specialized copper instrument. [13] One hundred years later the Javanese were using a wood-block process to apply the wax. [14] Today, modern machines duplicates the batik process. [15] However, authentic batik cloth are still made by this centuries-old process.

C.   Writing a Journal Entry

You are the first reporter from Earth sent to examine the first space colony on Venus. On your own paper, write an entry in your journal that records what you see and do there. Use at least five of the words below in your log entry. Be sure your verbs agree with their subjects.

inhabitants	people	we	many	all	troop
everybody	some	most	any	none	flock

Day 142, A.D. 2217

EX.   We reached the hot and rocky surface early this morning. The people who have greeted us seem as excited about us as we are about them.

CASE OF PERSONAL PRONOUNS

Case is the form that a noun or a pronoun takes to indicate its use in a sentence. In English, there are three cases: *nominative*, *objective*, and *possessive*.

The form of the noun is the same for both the nominative case and the objective case. For example, a noun used as a subject (nominative case) will have the same form when used as an object (objective case).

NOMINATIVE CASE   The **cashier** returned the change. [subject]
OBJECTIVE CASE   Give the **cashier** your money. [indirect object]

A noun changes its form for the possessive case, usually by adding an apostrophe and an *s* to most singular nouns and only the apostrophe to most plural nouns.

POSSESSIVE CASE   I appreciated the **cashier's** courtesy. [singular]
                  I admired the **cashiers'** uniforms. [plural]

☞   **REFERENCE NOTE:** For more information on forming possessive nouns, see pages 317–318.

Many pronouns have special forms for the nominative, objective, and possessive cases. Notice in the chart that *you* and *it* have the same form in the nominative and the objective case. All other personal pronouns have different forms for each case. Notice also that only third person singular pronouns indicate gender.

PERSONAL PRONOUNS		
Singular		
Nominative Case	**Objective Case**	**Possessive Case**
I	me	my, mine
you	you	your, yours
he, she, it	him, her, it	his, her, hers, its
Plural		
Nominative Case	**Objective Case**	**Possessive Case**
we	us	our, ours
you	you	your, yours
they	them	their, theirs

NOTE   Some teachers prefer to use the term *adjective* to describe a possessive pronoun, such as *my* or *their*, that precedes a noun. Follow your teacher's directions in labeling possessive forms.

Within each case, the forms of personal pronouns indicate *number, person,* and *gender*. **Number** is the form a word takes to indicate whether it is *singular* or *plural*. **Person** is the form a word takes to indicate the one(s) speaking (*first person*), the one(s) spoken to (*second person*), or the one(s) spoken of or about (*third person*). **Gender** is the form a word takes to indicate whether it is *masculine, feminine,* or *neuter* (neither masculine nor feminine).

EXERCISE 1   Identifying Personal Pronouns and Their Cases

On the line before each sentence below, identify the case of the italicized pronoun by writing *nom.* for *nominative, obj.* for *objective,* or *poss.* for *possessive.*

EX. _poss._ 1. *Our* class studied the Athabaskan people of the Yukon.

_____ 1. Ms. Schultz, the social studies teacher, told *us* that many American Indians live in Alaska.

_____ 2. *I* was fascinated by the Athabaskans, many of whom live along the Yukon River.

_____ 3. They have lived along *its* banks for at least 2,500 years.

_____ 4. *Their* language is related to both Navajo and Apache.

_____ 5. *My* friend Kele is Navajo.

_____ 6. He also became interested in the Athabaskans when I told *him* about the similarity of the languages.

_____ 7. To refer to the Athabaskans in their native language, you would call *them* Dene, which means "the people."

_____ 8. Dene make their livings in traditional ways, by hunting and fishing, but *they* also work in nontraditional jobs, such as oil drilling.

_____ 9. Dene try to live *their* lives in harmony with nature.

_____ 10. That sounds like a reasonable philosophy to *me*.

_____ 11. Never in *my* life have I grown food or fished for my dinner.

_____ 12. Like many people in the United States, *I* am out of touch with the natural world that supports me.

_____ 13. *They* may be like me in this regard.

_____ 14. *We* could learn much from the Athabaskans, or Dene.

_____ 15. *Theirs* is a way of life worth preserving.

THE NOMINATIVE CASE

15a   The subject of a verb is in the nominative case.

EXAMPLES   **She** feeds the fish. [*She* is the subject of *feeds*.]
Della and **I** wired the lights. [*Della and I* is the compound subject of *wired*.]
Ted told the manager that **we** had been working all day. [*Ted* is the subject of *told*, and *we* is the subject of *had been working*.]

A subject may be a compound with a pronoun appearing in combination with a noun or another pronoun. To help you choose the correct pronoun form in a compound subject, try each form as the subject of the verb.

EXAMPLE   (*She, Her*) and (*I, me*) took karate lessons.
Her and *me* took karate lessons. [incorrect use of objective case]
She and *I* took karate lessons. [correct use of nominative case]

ANSWER   **She** and **I** took karate lessons.

15b   A predicate nominative is in the nominative case.

A *predicate nominative* is a noun or pronoun that follows a linking verb and explains or identifies the subject of the sentence. A pronoun used as a predicate nominative always follows a form of the verb *be* or a verb phrase ending in *be* or *been*.

EXAMPLES   The goalie of the team is **she**. [*She* follows the linking verb *is* and identifies the subject *goalie*.]
The best speaker has been **he**. [*He* follows the linking verb *has speaker*.]
The last people in the theater were **he** and **I**. [*He* and *I* follow the linking verb *were* and identify the subject *people*.]

NOTE   In informal usage, expressions such as *It's me* and *That's her* are acceptable. Avoid them in more formal speaking situations, such as job interviews. In your written work, do not use them unless you are creating casual conversation in dialog.

Like a subject, a predicate nominative may be compound.

EXAMPLES   The only students who participated were **Laura** and **Minnie**. [*Laura* and *Minnie* follow *were* and identify the subject *students*.]
The co-captains of the team are **he** and **I**. [*He* and *I* follow *are* and identify the subject *co-captains*.]

EXERCISE 2   Proofreading for the Correct Use of Pronouns in the Nominative Case

In the paragraph below, draw a line through each incorrect pronoun form. Write the correct pronoun in the space above the word. A sentence may be correct.

EX.   [1] If you and ~~me~~ want to become auto mechanics, we should study

electronics and computers.

[1] Jake and me visited the science museum last Saturday. [2] Him and I

wanted to see the exhibit on cars of the future. [3] It was he who suggested

that we go because he knows of my interest in becoming a mechanic. [4] Jake

introduced me to the exhibit's organizer, Ms. Cochran, and then Jake and her

showed me some amazing things. [5] Them and I peeked under the hoods of

electric cars and examined some computers that control engine functions and

air conditioning and heating systems.

EXERCISE 3   Using Personal Pronouns as Subjects and as Predicate Nominatives

On the line before each sentence below, write a personal pronoun that can be substituted for the word or words in italics.

EX.   _he_   1. Rafe and *Aaron* took a snorkeling class at the YMCA.

_____ 1. The instructors of the class were John Powers and *Emily Pratt*, two dive masters with lots of experience.

_____ 2. The best swimmers in the class were *Paulo and I*.

_____ 3. The most skilled divers in that YMCA class were Marsha and *Tyrone*.

_____ 4. We paired up into two-person teams, and Ms. Pratt said that one team would be *Mark* and I.

_____ 5. *Mark and I* practiced putting on our fins, clearing our snorkels, replacing our masks under water, and lifesaving techniques.

THE OBJECTIVE CASE

15c   A direct object and an indirect object are in the objective case.

A *direct object* is a noun or pronoun that receives the action of the verb or shows the result of the action.

EXAMPLES   The phone call made **her** happy. [*Her* tells whom the phone call made happy.]
Someone asked **them** for free tickets. [*Them* tells whom someone asked.]

An *indirect object* is a noun or pronoun that tells *to whom* or *for whom* or *to what* or *for what* the action of the verb is done.

EXAMPLES   Christos told **us** an incredible story. [*Us* tells *to whom* Christos told an incredible story.]
Gerd sent **him** an invitation to the party. [*Him* tells *to whom* Gerd sent an invitation.]

15d   An object of a preposition is in the objective case.

A noun or pronoun used as an *object of a preposition* comes at the end of a phrase that begins with a preposition.

EXAMPLES   for **her**   under **them**   next to **you** and **us**

    REFERENCE NOTE: For a list of commonly used prepositions, see page 137.

To choose the correct pronoun in a compound direct object, compound indirect object, or compound object of a preposition, try each form of the pronoun separately in a sentence.

EXAMPLE   Desi informed him and I.
Desi informed him is correct.
Desi informed I is incorrect.
ANSWER   Desi informed **him** and **me.**

EXAMPLE   We served him and they lunch.
We served him is correct.
We served they is incorrect.
ANSWER   We served **him** and **them** lunch.

EXAMPLE   The teachers gave apples to them and we.
The teachers gave apples to them is correct.
The teachers gave apples to we is incorrect.
ANSWER   The teachers gave apples to **them** and **us.**

EXERCISE 4   Using Correct Forms of Objective Case Pronouns

For each sentence below, underline the correct pronoun in parentheses.

EX.   1. Wanda told (*he, him*) about that exhibit.

1. The strong wind pushed Dwayne and (*I, me*) as we walked down the sidewalk.

2. In fifteen minutes, Paco will join (*they, them*) on the stage for the musical's grand finale.

3. "Would you deliver these carnations and roses to (*he, him*) on your way home?" Kasia asked.

4. For three hours on Wednesday, I walked beside (*she, her*) in the neighborhood park.

5. Because Aaron is such a good friend, I wrote (*he, him*) a song about some of our experiences.

6. Parker told (*we, us*) all about his plans to go to junior college next September.

7. Rosa roasted the chilies and then served (*they, them*) to her guests.

8. I would like for my cousin Rashid and (*I, me*) to play a game of chess this afternoon.

9. I went with (*he, him*) to buy candles for our menorah.

10. Please tell (*we, us*) when the eclipse will begin.

11. I would like to invite (*he, him*) as well.

12. Give (*they, them*) information for the report.

13. You may borrow the books next to Dad and (*me, I*).

14. Ted reminded (*she, her*) that vacation would begin in two weeks.

15. I asked Tanya to help (*I, me*) pick out a bonsai tree.

16. Help Sam and (*she, her*) paint the fence.

17. My mother tutored Pedro and (*he, him*) in algebra.

18. Give (*we, us*) good directions to the African American Meeting House.

19. Mr. Weitz showed (*they, them*) his handmade porcelain dolls.

20. "She crossed the finish line ahead of (*I, me*)," Brent said to the coach.

THE POSSESSIVE CASE

15e **The possessive pronouns *mine, yours, his, hers, its, ours,* and *theirs* are used in the same ways that the pronouns in the nominative and the objective cases are used.**

SUBJECT	Your shoes and **mine** are getting muddy.
PREDICATE NOMINATIVE	That bracelet is **his.**
DIRECT OBJECT	Patty, fill **theirs** first.
INDIRECT OBJECT	Can't you give **ours** a try?
OBJECT OF PREPOSITION	Compare these sample answers to **yours.**

15f **The possessive pronouns *my, your, his, her, its, our,* and *their* are used as adjectives before nouns.**

EXAMPLES   **My** dog has no fleas.
              His pants need mending.
              Have I told you **our** group is going to Toronto?

15g **A noun or a pronoun preceding a gerund is in the possessive case.**

A *gerund* is a verb form that ends in *–ing* and functions as a noun. Since a gerund acts as a noun, the noun or pronoun that comes before it must be in the possessive case in order to modify the gerund.

EXAMPLES   **His** swimming was incredibly smooth. [*His* modifies the gerund *swimming*. Whose swimming? His swimming.]
              Their jogging was a regular lunchtime activity. [*Their* modifies the gerund *jogging*. Whose jogging? Their jogging.]

Do not confuse a gerund with a present participle, which is also a verb form that ends in *–ing.* A gerund acts as a noun; a present participle serves as an adjective. A noun or pronoun that is modified by a present participle should not be in the possessive case.

EXAMPLE   We watched **people** riding in horse-drawn carriages. [*People* is modified by the participial phrase *riding in horse-drawn carriages*.]

The form of a noun or pronoun before an *-ing* word often depends on the meaning you want to express. If you want to emphasize the *–ing* word, use the possessive form. If you want to emphasize the noun or pronoun preceding the *–ing* word, avoid the possessive form.

EXAMPLES   The **Russian Club's** planning an international theme party drew much attention. [The emphasis is on the gerund *planning. Russian Club's* modifies *planning*.]
              The **Russian Club** planning an international theme party received praise. [The emphasis is on *Russian Club*. The participle *planning* modifies *Russian Club*.]

EXERCISE 5   Using Possessive Pronouns

Complete each of the sentences below with an appropriate possessive pronoun. Do not use the same pronoun twice.

EX.   1.   After we won _____our_____ game, we shook hands.

1.   It's _____ necklace. I bought it at the fair last year.

2.   I gave the diary to Lisa because I thought it was _____ .

3.   Is that _____ mother I saw you with?

4.   If it's _____ toy, then give it back to him.

5.   My mother made borscht using _____ great-great-grandmother's recipe.

6.   Since the limousine was parked in your driveway, I thought it was

_____ .

7.   _____ cousins are coming to visit us from Karachi.

8.   Jon noticed the bee because of _____ buzzing.

9.   _____ writing an original play was Maria's idea.

10. No, it's not _____ . I've never seen it before.

EXERCISE 6   Proofreading Sentences for Correct Use of Possessive Pronouns

In each of the sentences below, draw a line through each incorrect pronoun and write the correct pronoun in the space above the correct word.

EX.   1.   Tina tugged at ~~hers~~ *her* boots.

1.   We saw their walking together to the corner.

2.   Phil writing always deserves praise.

3.   "Her salad and your are ready," the server said.

4.   Them playing a duet was my favorite part of the show.

5.   Our searching turned up some terrific props for the show.

SPECIAL PRONOUN PROBLEMS

15h Pronouns used as appositives should be in the same case as the word they refer to.

An *appositive* is a noun or pronoun used with another noun or pronoun to identify or explain it.

EXAMPLES　The two best spellers, **he** and **she,** will compete in the finals. [The pronouns are in the nominative case because they are in apposition with the subject *spellers.*]
The trophy was given to the entire team, **him, her,** and **me.** [The pronouns are in the objective case because they are in apposition with the object of the preposition *team.*]

15i A pronoun following *than* or *as* in an elliptical construction is in the same case as it would be if the construction were completed.

An *elliptical construction* is a clause from which words have been omitted.

ELLIPTICAL　Ella was much more effective under the basket **than she.**
COMPLETED　Ella was much more effective under the basket **than she was.**

ELLIPTICAL　The dripping faucet bothered her brother as much **as her.**
COMPLETED　The dripping faucet bothered her brother as much **as it bothered her.**

The pronoun form in an elliptical construction determines the meaning of the elliptical phrase or clause. Be sure to use the pronoun form that expresses the meaning you intend. Notice how the meaning of each of the following sentences depends on the pronoun form in the elliptical construction.

EXAMPLES　I have been Luanne's friend longer **than she.** [I have been Luanne's friend longer *than she has been Luanne's friend.*]
I have been Luanne's friend longer **than hers.** [I have been Luanne's friend longer *than I have been her friend.*]

15j A pronoun ending in *–self* or *–selves* should not be used in place of a simple personal pronoun.

NONSTANDARD　Jerome and myself rode to the gym.
STANDARD　Jerome and **I** rode to the gym.

NONSTANDARD　Eva and Nolan brought gifts for ourselves.
STANDARD　Eva and Nolan brought gifts for **us.**

EXERCISE 7   Selecting the Correct Pronouns

For each of the sentences below, underline the correct pronoun in parentheses.

EX.   1. He gave the extra tickets to Warren and (*me*, *myself*).

1. Rhonda has been a gymnast longer than (*he*, *him*).

2. Ray, please give a set of chopsticks to each of the dinner guests, Geraldo and (*she*, *her*).

3. Because we had lived in town the longest, Mia and (*I*, *me*) gave the tour to the visitors.

4. The coach gave the captains, (*she*, *her*) and me, certificates of appreciation for our hard work.

5. I don't know the Bova family as well as I know (*they*, *them*).

6. "Are you unhappy with (*myself*, *me*)?" the puppy seemed to ask, as it sat by the broken vase.

7. The scientists, both (*she*, *her*) and he, discovered the vaccine.

8. Avery and (*I*, *myself*) are trying to make a latchhook rug.

9. Two employees, Jose and (*she*, *her*), will bring their children to the company picnic.

10. The best drummers in the band, you and (*she*, *her*), should enter the competition.

11. Zora gave Roberto and (*me*, *myself*) some fresh oranges she had received from her grandmother in Miami.

12. My sister is more outgoing than (*he*, *him*) most of the time.

13. Reggie wants to invite his best friends, (*they*, *them*) and you, to the outdoor concert this weekend.

14. My brother Sheldon told us how they, (*he*, *him*) and his friends, used to put on plays.

15. Do you like the Indian dish *saag panner* as much as (*I*, *me*)?

16. "I am as dedicated as (*they*, *them*) when it comes to raising money for our library," the mayor said.

17. Those two people, he and (*she*, *her*), are the photographers who created that brochure.

18. That ladder is as tall as (*he*, *him*).

19. Will you give Charlotte and (*me*, *myself*) a ride home from basketball practice?

20. We helped the children, him and (*she*, *her*), mold clay into animals.

WHO *AND* WHOM

Nominative	Objective	Possessive
who whoever	whom whomever	whose whosoever

15k The pronoun *who* is called an *interrogative pronoun* when it is used to form a question. When *who* is used to introduce a subordinate clause, it is called a *relative pronoun*.

(1) The form an interrogative pronoun takes depends on its use in a question.

Who is used as a subject or as a predicate nominative. *Whom* is used as an object of a verb or as an object of a preposition.

NOMINATIVE   **Who** wants to make popcorn? [*Who* is the subject of the verb *wants.*]

OBJECTIVE   With **whom** did you go to the movies? [*Whom* is the object of the preposition *with.*]

NOTE   In spoken English, the use of *whom* is gradually disappearing. Today it is acceptable to begin a spoken question with *who* regardless of whether the nominative or the objective form is grammatically correct. In writing, though, it is still important to distinguish between *who* and *whom.*

(2) The form a relative pronoun takes depends on its use in a subordinate clause.

To choose between *who* or *whom* in a subordinate clause, follow these steps.

Step 1:   Find the subordinate clause.
Step 2:   Decide how the relative pronoun is used in the clause—*subject, predicate nominative, direct object, indirect object,* or *object of a preposition.*
Step 3:   Determine the case for this use of the relative pronoun.
Step 4:   Select the correct case form of the relative pronoun.

EXAMPLE   She is the person (*who, whom*) I told you about.
Step 1:   The subordinate clause is (*who, whom*) *I told you about.*
Step 2:   In this clause, the pronoun is the object of the preposition *about.*
Step 3:   As an object of a preposition, the pronoun should be in the objective case.
Step 4:   The objective form is *whom.*
ANSWER   She is the person **whom** I told you about.

EXAMPLE	Do you know (*who, whom*) he meant?
Step 1:	The subordinate clause is (*who, whom*) *he meant.*
Step 2:	In this clause, the pronoun is the direct object of the verb *meant.*
Step 3:	As a direct object, the pronoun should be in the objective case.
Step 4:	The objective form is *whom.*
ANSWER	Do you know **whom** he meant?

EXERCISE 8   Using *Who* and *Whom* Correctly

In the sentences below, underline the correct form of the pronoun in parentheses.

EX.   1.   (*Who, Whom*) were you calling?

1. Nolan Ryan was a ballplayer (*who, whom*) I admired.
2. Dad will give an extra helping to (*whoever, whomever*) asks for one.
3. (*Who, Whom*) is responsible for this confusion?
4. Do you know (*who, whom*) the president of Mexico is?
5. To (*who, whom*) shall we write this thank-you note?
6. Ms. Groat, (*who, whom*) is a chemist, will talk about her recent discoveries.
7. After I visited Austria, I began to read avidly about Mozart, (*who, whom*) was born there.
8. The class elected me to write to Steven Spielberg, (*who, whom*) may visit our town soon.
9. Can you predict (*who, whom*) will win the speech tournament?
10. Was it Lionel (*who, whom*) the band director asked to perform?
11. The Spanish Club served flan to everyone (*who, whom*) had a ticket.
12. I'd really like to know (*who, whom*) the judges selected.
13. Wilson is the only student in the class (*who, whom*) completed both an essay and an art project.
14. The senator (*who, whom*) I sent a complaint to wrote back to explain her vote.
15. Ophelia will gladly be partners with (*whoever, whomever*) is left.
16. The principal said, "We need someone on (*who, whom*) we can depend to keep this project going strong."
17. When jogging, I smile at (*whoever, whomever*) I pass.
18. All the jugglers asked, "(*Who, Whom*) dropped the torch?"
19. Hal can't decide (*who, whom*) to ask to the prom.
20. Did you tell anyone (*who, whom*) did it?

CHAPTER REVIEW

A. Proofreading Sentences for Correct Pronoun Forms

In each of the sentences below, draw a line through any incorrect pronoun forms. On the line before the sentence, write the correct form of the pronoun. If the sentence contains no errors, write C.

EX.   _him_   1. Did you send a postcard to ~~he~~ and Emilio?

_____ 1. For who are you ringing that bell, Kesi?

_____ 2. Clem and myself wrote a program to compute batting averages.

_____ 3. At the audition, Andrea was called back more often than me.

_____ 4. The winners, Latoya and me, received free concert tickets.

_____ 5. The most popular actor in Hollywood is probably him.

_____ 6. Jeb told Libby and we some tall tales from Arkansas.

_____ 7. Him and Bert are making a movie about vampire bats.

_____ 8. We ran into Cara and them at the shoe store in the mall.

_____ 9. The man whom you saw on stage is the mayor's son.

_____ 10. I could never be as good a quarterback as him.

_____ 11. Lori and myself bought new snowshoes at the trading post.

_____ 12. The next performers, Mario and me, will do some magic tricks.

_____ 13. Marco and them will be on a float in the parade.

_____ 14. It could have been us who got caught in that avalanche!

_____ 15. The stock market crash bankrupted her and him.

B. Proofreading for Correct Pronoun Forms

Draw a line through the incorrect pronoun in each of the following sentences. Write the correct form above it. Some sentences may have more than one error.

EX.   1. Aldo and ~~myself~~ wrote a play about talking housepets, a dog, two cats, and a parrot.

[1] Him acting isn't very good, but Aldo's writing is excellent. [2] He writes more quickly than me. [3] However, I am the one whom does all

221

the editing. [4] Ms. Carson asked Aldo and I to show the finished script
to the drama director and she. [5] We four, Ms. Carson, the director,
Aldo, and me, met to discuss the script. [6] "Ms. Carson and myself love
the idea," said the drama director. [7] "For who did you write the play?"

[8] "I have a little brother in preschool," I answered, "and as we
wrote, I kept the preschoolers in mind and thought that there would be
no better audience than them."

[9] "Well, Ms. Carson liked the play as much as me," said the director,
"and we think that we'll produce it in the spring."

[10] "But first," said Ms. Carson, "our playwrights, Aldo and yourself,
need to make a few revisions."

C.   Writing Notes for a Report

You are the U.S. ambassador to a foreign country. You have just returned to
Washington, D.C., to give a report to the president. Select a country, and, on
your own paper, write fifteen sentences to use as notes for your report. You
might include details about natural resources, industry, recreation, foods, and
customs. Use an encyclopedia, an atlas, and other reference books to research
your country. In your sentences, use, underline, and label pronouns in all three
cases. Also be sure to use forms of *who* and *whom*, and appositives.

EX.   Many people in China sew their own clothes. (poss.)

They seem to prefer comfort rather than style. (nom.)

AMBIGUOUS REFERENCE

16a   A pronoun should always refer clearly to its antecedent.

In the following examples, arrows point from the pronouns to their antecedents.

EXAMPLES   **Phoebe** closed **her** math **book** and put **it** away.

When the **bells** rang, we could hear **them** for miles.

If **Sonny** arrives, tell **him** the news.

(1) Avoid an *ambiguous reference*, which occurs when a pronoun can refer to either of two antecedents.

A simple way to correct some ambiguous references is to replace the pronoun with an appropriate noun.

AMBIGUOUS   Kurt sent Henry a copy of the picture he had drawn. [The antecedent of *he* is unclear.]

CLEAR   Kurt sent **Henry** a copy of the picture **Henry** had drawn.

AMBIGUOUS   After the server brought my sister dessert, she asked her for her check. [The antecedents of *she* and *her* are not clear.]

CLEAR   After the server brought dessert, my **sister** asked for **her** check.

CLEAR   My **sister** asked for **her** check after the server had brought dessert.

(2) Avoid a *general reference*, which occurs when a pronoun refers to a general idea rather than to a specific word or group of words.

The pronouns commonly used in making general references are *it*, *this*, *that*, *which*, and *such*. To correct a general pronoun reference, either replace the pronoun with an appropriate noun or rephrase the sentence.

GENERAL   Luis made it home with the papers, which made us happy! [*Which* has no clear antecedent.]

CLEAR   We were happy Luis made it home with the papers.

GENERAL   A siren rang out and the smell of smoke was in the air. This made the pedestrians leave the street. [*This* has no clear antecedent.]

CLEAR   When they heard the siren ring out and noticed the smell of smoke, the pedestrians left the street.

EXERCISE 1   Revising Sentences to Correct
Ambiguous and General Pronoun References

On your own paper, rewrite each of the sentences below, correcting the ambiguous or general pronoun references. If a sentence is correct, write C.

EX.   1. Pedro was arguing with Bill about a letter he had written.

    1. *Pedro and Bill were arguing about the letter Bill had written.*
            or
       Pedro and Bill were arguing about the letter Pedro had written.

1. My cousin Freda writes poems and stories, which I think is quite admirable.
2. The mayoral candidate spoke clearly and to the point. That should show up his opponents.
3. Nika was surprised to find a parking ticket on her windshield.
4. There was a concert at the beach on the same night as the bowling tournament, and it caused some confusion.
5. The corporal reported to the lieutenant that his patrol was missing.
6. While I had the flu, I received a card from my brother and a book from my aunt, which made me happy.
7. Until they were out of film, the divers photographed the fish.
8. After Lauren's pony bumped into the fence, it kept right on going.
9. More than two hundred people came to see the play on opening night, which pleased the cast.
10. Helen called Marie while she was out.
11. Digging a deep hole and hiding the chest in it, the pirates thought that would protect their treasure.
12. The sky grew dark and lightning flashed, which meant a storm was on the way.
13. Julio noticed that Ken was wearing his Western boots.
14. Our English teacher chose Lenore to represent the class because she spoke so well in public.
15. Wapi rode the roller coaster on an empty stomach, which he later regretted.
16. The birds flew right into the trees, but they weren't hurt.
17. Our college has an excellent science department and a beautiful campus, which makes us proud.
18. Before leaving for Brazil, Cesar told Juan his cousin was going with him.
19. Kai observed the moon through the telescope until it was covered with clouds.
20. The fire chief asked Stan to bring his hat.

WEAK AND INDEFINITE REFERENCE

16b Avoid a *weak reference*, which occurs when a pronoun refers to an antecedent that has not been expressed.

To correct a weak pronoun reference, either replace the pronoun with an appropriate noun or give the pronoun a clear antecedent.

WEAK   I attended the tennis tournament yesterday and saw Stefi win every one.[The antecedent of *one* is not expressed.]

CLEAR   I attended the tennis tournament yesterday and saw Stefi win every match she played.

WEAK   Every school likes enthusiastic students, so let's see some of it at the next student council meeting.[The antecedent of *it* is not expressed.]

CLEAR   Every school likes enthusiastic students, so let's see some enthusiasm at the next student council meeting.

16c In formal writing, avoid the indefinite use of the pronouns *it, they,* and *you.*

An *indefinite reference* occurs when *you, it,* or *they* has no specific person or thing as its antecedent. To correct an indefinite reference, rephrase the sentence, eliminating the personal pronoun.

INDEFINITE   In dance class they teach us how to move our feet to the music. [*They* does not refer to any specific group of people.]

CLEAR   In dance class we learn how to move our feet to the music.

INDEFINITE   In the advertisement it read, "Don't miss New England in the fall!"[*It* does not refer to any specific thing.]

CLEAR   The advertisement read, "Don't miss New England in the fall!"

INDEFINITE   You don't want to get caught napping in Ms. Finch's chemistry class.[*You* does not refer to any specific person.]

CLEAR   None of us wants to get caught napping in Ms. Finch's chemistry class.

NOTE   The indefinite use of *it* in familiar expressions such as *it is early, it is raining,* and *it seems* is acceptable.

EXERCISE 2   Revising Sentences to Correct Weak and Indefinite References

Most of the following sentences contain weak and indefinite references. Revise each faulty sentence on your own paper. [Note: There may be more than one way to revise a sentence.] If a sentence is correct, write C.

EX.   1.   You know scientists have discovered over thirty thousand distinct species of fish?

      1. Scientists have discovered over thirty thousand distinct species of fish.

    1. Katie enjoys using her new in-line skates and says it is her favorite sport.

2. Duc is an excellent pianist, but he has never owned one.

3. Some fish are saltwater fish. They require this to live.

4. In politics, they don't always know all the answers.

5. In the index, it does not list a page reference for information about the Canadian flag.

6. On television, they will present a documentary on the wolf.

7. In the editorial section of the newspaper, it discusses the forthcoming presidential election.

8. In the ocean it is sometimes the survival of the cleverest that prevails.

9. We stopped at the record store at the mall, but we didn't buy any.

10. Ms. Wilson said that the museum was worth visiting, but it would take more than two hours.

11. We missed the bus this morning. That is why we were late for school.

12. Most people prefer truthful leaders, but some people think it is not important.

13. Each December, our village strings colored lights on a twelve-foot fir tree.

14. You need a sharp eye to find a well-camouflaged female bird.

15. In many Japanese restaurants, they serve tea with each meal.

16. The almanac lists outstanding world events of the most recent year.

17. Kari is very shy, but she doesn't show it when she's with our family.

18. Each time Marvin hears country music, he wants to become one of them.

19. The aerobics class worked so hard that it made them breathless.

20. In early motion pictures, they show the actors moving and walking very fast.

21. My father is an art teacher at the high school, but I know nothing about it.

22. On Thursday, Sara spent an hour at the library, but she didn't find any.

23. Al is interested in stamp collecting, so he wants to learn all he can about them.

24. Derek enjoys his career in architecture, and it explains why he measures carefully before he draws.

25. Clay and Jody entered the chess tournament, but Clay didn't win one.

CHAPTER REVIEW

A. Revising Sentences to Correct Faulty Pronoun Reference

The sentences below contain ambiguous, general, weak, or indefinite references of pronouns. Revise the sentences on your own paper to correct each faulty pronoun reference.

EX. 1. On many of the radio stations in Nashville they play country music.
   1. *Many of the Nashville radio stations play country music.*

1. Ben wondered if Sam knew what he looked like up on stage.
2. Write me a letter, and send it overnight, which will make me happy.
3. Blanche ran to the water's edge, dived in, and had a terrific one.
4. Have Sergio climb those three trees, using the correct ropes and handholds. This will be good practice for him.
5. Dad congratulated me, and gave me a slap on the back, which made me feel good.
6. In the polls it showed the challenger cutting into the incumbent's popularity.
7. From the riverbank, we could see the canoes coming our way and our friends waving. That caused us to wave back.
8. The dish crashed to the floor, and it broke.
9. My brother likes my cousin, even though he's always borrowing his jacket.
10. She paid ten dollars for the two packages and four dollars for lunch, which made her grumpy.

B. Revising Sentences by Correcting Faulty Pronoun Reference

Revise the following sentences to correct each ambiguous, general, weak, or indefinite reference. If a sentence is correct, write C.

EX. 1. Mattie took a deep breath and blew out all the birthday candles, which made her guests cheer.
   1. *When Mattie took a deep breath and blew out all her birthday candles, her guests cheered.*

1. In these statistics it indicates that inflation was lower last year.
2. My brothers traveled to see the famous band in concert during their final appearance in this country.
3. Try not to mix the molasses with the honey because it might make the recipe too sweet.
4. Pietro caught the pass, took three fast steps toward the basket, and, at the last minute, made it one-handed.

227

5. Hetty kept singing that song over and over, which brought sentimental tears to her mother's eyes.

6. That clock, which is on the mantle, has needed fixing for the past three months.

7. The team put on their uniforms and then went out to play it.

8. In Pop's old store you knew there would always be bargains.

9. Serena noticed Lorenzo was applauding more than anyone else, and that pleased her very much.

10. When the egg landed on the sidewalk, it exploded.

C. Writing a Story Line

You are a writer for a television network. You are creating a story line for one segment of a new show that will air next season. The new show will be titled *Time Travels*. The basic story involves three friends who travel to different time periods and countries because their time machine doesn't work correctly and won't take them home. In a memo to your boss, explain the story line you propose for your segment. Include time, place, characters, and plot for one episode. Use travel books, history books, and reference books to get ideas. Be sure you use correct pronoun-antecedent agreement.

EX.   To: J.D.

From: Bill Blaze, Head Writer

Dear J.D.,

   I think that of all the shows the network's done so far, this is going to be the best. You asked for a great first segment, and this is it! When the time machine malfunctions, brilliant and studious Raphael Robbins, who is interested in exploring the future, gets his wish and is sent to the year 3201 A.D., a time in which the whole world has gone high-tech. Jenny Frost, the environmentalist who joined the team to find out what life was like before cities were built and everything got polluted, is thrown back into the very primitive, prehistoric past. Meanwhile, Mason McBean, the brave leader, winds up being captured by Confederate soldiers at Richmond. Unfortunately for Raphael and Jenny, Mason is the one who knows how to fix the machine, so he must escape before the machine can be used again.

   Each of the three characters has an exciting adventure in his or her own time and place. In the last scene, the audience gets just a glimpse of Mason, Jenny, and Raphael being sent to new times and places.

REGULAR VERBS

17a **Every verb has four basic parts called its** *principal parts:* **the** *base form,* **the** *present participle,* **the** *past,* **and the** *past participle.* **All other verb forms are derived from these principal parts.**

When the present participle and the past participle forms are used as main verbs (simple predicates) in sentences, they always require helping verbs

EXAMPLES   I **park** the car. [base form of *park*]
I **am parking** the car. [present participle of *park*]
I **parked** the car. [past of *park*]
I **have parked** the car. [past participle of *park*]

17b **A** *regular verb* **forms the past and past participle by adding** *–d* **or** *–ed* **to the base form.**

Base Form	Present Participle	Past	Past Participle
drip	(is) dripping	dripped	(have) dripped
patch	(is) patching	patched	(have) patched
propose	(is) proposing	proposed	(have) proposed
report	(is) reporting	reported	(have) reported

 REFERENCE NOTE: For more information about spelling words with suffixes, see pages 329–331.

When forming the past and past participle of regular verbs, don't make the common mistake of leaving off the *–d* or *–ed* ending. Pay particular attention to the forms of the verbs *ask, attack, drown, prejudice, risk, suppose,* and *use.*

NONSTANDARD   We use to have several huskies.
STANDARD   We **used** to have several huskies.

 A few regular verbs have an alternate past and past participle forms ending in *–t.* For example, the past form of *burn* is *burned* or *burnt.*

EXERCISE 1 Writing the Correct Forms of Regular Verbs

For each of the following sentences, decide what the correct form of the italicized verb should be. Write the correct verb form on the line before each sentence.

EX.   _repeated_   1. Frank *repeat* the definition to himself twice so that he would remember it.

_____ 1. The whole room was silent as Mary *play* her flute solo.

_____ 2. Manuel *burn* dinner because he was watching a television program about night life in the United States.

_____ 3. For exercise, Claire *walk* to school every day, except when the weather was bad.

_____ 4. I am *watch* that bird carefully because it may be a rare species for this area.

_____ 5. The package I am *expect* contains travel information for my trip to Oaxaca, Mexico, including some useful information on Oaxaca's customs and culture.

_____ 6. The remarks by the witness have *prejudice* the jury against the defendant.

_____ 7. Since we moved to San Francisco, I have *celebrate* the Chinese New Year each year with Won and his family.

_____ 8. Carlotta's mother has *list* on this recipe card the ingredients for her famous salsa.

_____ 9. I am reading right now, but when I have *finish*, I will help you with your math.

_____ 10. The painting was of Wolf Chief, a leader of the Mandan Indians who *use* to occupy much of the northern Great Plains.

_____ 11. We *phone* every member to tell them the meeting was canceled.

_____ 12. While Ben is *pay* for his lunch, let's find a table and save him a seat.

_____ 13. Many firefighters have *risk* their lives to save people from burning homes.

_____ 14. Jack is *paint* a portrait of his mother for her birthday.

_____ 15. After thirty years of teaching social studies, Mrs. Polanski is *retire* next spring.

_____ 16. Did you know that the first toothbrush was *develop* in China hundreds of years ago?

_____ 17. I got nervous giving my speech, so I *imagine* the audience was not there.

_____ 18. Mr. Klein is *staple* an answer key to each test so we can correct our mistakes.

_____ 19. Not knowing what his shadow was, my cat has *attack* it several times.

_____ 20. Jane *ask* the usher which line to stand in to buy tickets for the movie.

IRREGULAR VERBS

17c An *irregular verb* forms the past and past participle in some other way than by adding *–d* or *–ed* to the base form.

Base Form	Present Participle	Past	Past Participle
hit	(is) hitting	hit	(have) hit
leave	(is) leaving	left	(have) left
ride	(is) riding	rode	(have) ridden
sing	(is) singing	sang	(have) sung

When forming the past and past participle of irregular verbs, avoid these common errors.

(1) Do not use the past form with a helping verb.

NONSTANDARD	Has Velma rode that hobbyhorse before?
STANDARD	**Has** Velma **ridden** that hobbyhorse before?

(2) Do not use the past participle form without a helping verb.

NONSTANDARD	I sung the national anthem at the game.
STANDARD	I **sang** the national anthem at the game.

(3) Do not add *–d*, *–ed*, or *–t* to the base form.

NONSTANDARD	The batter hitted the ball with a satisfying crack.
STANDARD	The batter **hit** the ball with a satisfying crack.

 NOTE If you are not sure about the principal parts of a verb, look in a dictionary. Entries for irregular verbs give the principal parts.

COMMON IRREGULAR VERBS			
Base Form	**Present Participle**	**Past**	**Past Participle**
be	(is) being	was, were	(have) been
become	(is) becoming	became	(have) become
begin	(is) beginning	began	(have) begun
bite	(is) biting	bit	(have) bitten *or* bit
blow	(is) blowing	blew	(have) blown
break	(is) breaking	broke	(have) broken
bring	(is) bringing	brought	(have) brought

COMMON IRREGULAR VERBS

Base Form	Present Participle	Past	Past Participle
build	(is) building	built	(have) built
burst	(is) bursting	burst	(have) burst
buy	(is) buying	bought	(have) bought
catch	(is) catching	caught	(have) caught
choose	(is) choosing	chose	(have) chosen
come	(is) coming	came	(have) come
cost	(is) costing	cost	(have) cost
do	(is) doing	did	(have) done
draw	(is) drawing	drew	(have) drawn
drink	(is) drinking	drank	(have) drunk
drive	(is) driving	drove	(have) driven
eat	(is) eating	ate	(have) eaten
fall	(is) falling	fell	(have) fallen
feel	(is) feeling	felt	(have) felt
find	(is) finding	found	(have) found
forget	(is) forgetting	forgot	(have) forgotten
freeze	(is) freezing	froze	(have) frozen
get	(is) getting	got	(have) gotten *or* got
give	(is) giving	gave	(have) given
go	(is) going	went	(have) gone
grow	(is) growing	grew	(have) grown
hold	(is) holding	held	(have) held
hurt	(is) hurting	hurt	(have) hurt
keep	(is) keeping	kept	(have) kept
know	(is) knowing	knew	(have) known
lead	(is) leading	led	(have) led
lend	(is) lending	lent	(have) lent
lose	(is) losing	lost	(have) lost
make	(is) making	made	(have) made
meet	(is) meeting	met	(have) met
put	(is) putting	put	(have) put
ride	(is) riding	rode	(have) ridden
ring	(is) ringing	rang	(have) rung
run	(is) running	ran	(have) run
say	(is) saying	said	(have) said

COMMON IRREGULAR VERBS			
Base Form	**Present Participle**	**Past**	**Past Participle**
see	(is) seeing	saw	(have) seen
sell	(is) selling	sold	(have) sold
send	(is) sending	sent	(have) sent
show	(is) showing	showed	(have) shown
shrink	(is) shrinking	shrank *or* shrunk	(have) shrunk *or* (have) shrunken
sing	(is) singing	sang	(have) sung
sink	(is) sinking	sank *or* sunk	(have) sunk
speak	(is) speaking	spoke	(have) spoken
stand	(is) standing	stood	(have) stood
steal	(is) stealing	stole	(have) stolen
swim	(is) swimming	swam	(have) swum
swing	(is) swinging	swung	(have) swung
take	(is) taking	took	(have) taken
tell	(is) telling	told	(have) told
throw	(is) throwing	threw	(have) thrown
wear	(is) wearing	wore	(have) worn
win	(is) winning	won	(have) won
write	(is) writing	wrote	(have) written

EXERCISE 2   Writing Past and Past Participle Forms of Irregular Verbs

Complete the following sentences by writing the correct past or past participle form of the verb in italics on the line in each sentence.

EX.   1.   Kim (*lend*) _____lent_____ me her art supplies for the weekend so that I could finish my project.

1.   Ian has (*sing*) _____ a solo in the spring concert for the last four years.

2.   My uncle Nikimo will take us ice fishing when the lake has

(*freeze*) _____ .

3.   I have (*make*) _____ many new friends since I became a member of the hospital volunteers group.

4.   We have (*buy*) _____ our fruits and vegetables at Mr. Coviello's farm stand for years.

5. The bags were so full of apples that they (*burst*) _____ at the seams.

6. I have (*forget*) _____ how to program the VCR, so I'll have to read the directions.

7. For the science fair, we decided on an idea, (*draw*) _____ sketches, then built our inventions.

8. Joe (*run*) _____ ten miles every other day for a month to prepare for today's race.

9. We (*go*) _____ to the youth center on Saturdays until we moved.

10. The Berlin Wall was constructed in 1961 and (*stand*) _____ until 1989.

11. My great-great-grandfather (*build*) _____ our house in 1896.

12. Lynette (*come*) _____ with us to see the virtual reality exhibit.

13. She (*ring*) _____ the doorbell three times, but no one answered.

14. Mr. Bell has (*send*) _____ me a copy of a book by the poet Julia Alvarez to read during spring break.

15. I (*eat*) _____ so much at breakfast yesterday that I was still full at lunchtime.

EXERCISE 3   Proofreading a Paragraph for Past or Past Participle Forms of Verbs

In the paragraph below, draw a line through the incorrect past or past participle verbs. Write the correct form in the space above the error. Some sentences may contain no errors.

EX.   [1] The Hmong women ~~begun~~ *began* a new way to keep their culture alive through the textile art of *pa ndhau*, or story cloths.

[1] Traditionally, the Hmong have gave hand-stitched squares as wedding or birth gifts. [2] The purpose of these squares was to honor the spiritual beliefs of the people and to bring luck and prosperity. [3] The Hmong women who were confined to refugee camps taked a look at what was happening to them; they realized that in moving from one place to another their culture could easily disappear. [4] They also knowed that they had no cameras or writing skills to preserve their culture, so they decided to use a skill they did have—sewing. [5] Hmong story cloths vividly tell the story of the Hmong people; the beautifully stitched cloths have became graphic accounts of the Hmong history and culture.

LIE *AND* LAY

17d The verb *lie* means "to rest," or "to stay, to recline," or "to remain in a certain state or position." *Lie* never takes an object. The verb *lay* means "to put (something) in a place." *Lay* usually takes an object.

PRINCIPAL PARTS OF *LIE* AND *LAY*			
Base Form	**Present Participle**	**Past**	**Past Participle**
lie (to rest)	(is) lying	lay	(have) lain
lay (to put)	(is) laying	laid	(have) laid

When deciding whether to use *lie* or *lay*, ask yourself two questions.

Question 1:   What do I want to say? Is the meaning "to be in a lying position," or is it "to put something down"?

Question 2:   What time does the verb express, and which principal part is used to show this time?

EXAMPLE   The baby (*lay, laid*) among the pillows on the sofa.

Question 1:   Meaning? The meaning is "to be in a lying position." Therefore, the verb should be *lie*.

Question 2:   Principal part? The verb expresses the past, and the sentence requires the past form. The past form of *lie* is *lay*.

ANSWER   The baby **lay** among the pillows on the sofa.

EXERCISE 4   Choosing the Correct Forms of *Lie* and *Lay*

Underline the correct form of *lie* or *lay* in parentheses in each of the following sentences.

EX.   1.   Pam (*lay, laid*) her books down next to mine on the kitchen table.

1.   Lusita is (*lying, laying*) on the sand, watching the waves and listening to the gulls.

2.   They have (*lain, laid*) down their brushes and are taking a break from painting the house.

3.   Libya (*lies, lays*) north of Niger and Chad in Africa.

4.   Earline has (*lain, laid*) on the couch for three days, recuperating from the flu.

5.   While Kwam is (*lying, laying*) out the bases, the players are warming up.

6.   Before she began her workout, she (*lay, laid*) down on the mat and stretched.

7. The children are (*lying, laying*) in the grass to count the leaves on that tree.

8. A commemorative stone honoring the German and Italian immigrant families who settled the town was (*lain, laid*) in front of the town hall.

9. I (*lay, laid*) my books on the counter and handed the librarian my card.

10. I was so exhausted last night that I fell asleep as soon as I (*laid, lay*) on the bed.

11. My dog (*lies, lays*) next to the dinner table even after we've finished eating.

12. The problem (*lay, laid*) in his negative attitude.

13. Mr. Nakai was shocked when we (*lay, laid*) our finished reports about the end of the Soviet Union on his desk two days early.

14. After my uncle (*lay, laid*) on a waterbed, he wanted one for himself.

15. The bizcochitos Mrs. Lopez made are (*lying, laying*) on the table.

EXERCISE 5   Proofreading Sentences for the Correct Use of *Lie* and *Lay*

In the sentences below, draw a line through each incorrect form of *lie* and *lay*, and write the correct verb form on the line before each sentence. If a sentence is correct, write *C*.

EX. _____lain_____ 1. The book had laid on the shelf for so long that it was covered with dust.

_____ 1. He will dive to get the coins that are laying at the bottom of the pool.

_____ 2. If you see Lin, tell her I am lying down to take a nap.

_____ 3. Joe lay the last brick and stood back to admire his new chimney.

_____ 4. Your skates are probably still laying on the bench at the rink where you left them.

_____ 5. For the last three nights, I have laid in bed, unable to fall asleep.

_____ 6. Benjamin Banneker was appointed by President Washington to help lie a plan for the city of Washington, D.C.

_____ 7. The Bohemian Forest lays to the west of the Elbe River and the Baltic Sea.

_____ 8. In terrible pain, Bill has laid flat on his back for a week.

_____ 9. Rosita lay her quilt on the table and nervously waited for the judges' decision.

_____ 10. They had not seen the "Wet Paint" sign before they laid their bags on that bench.

SIT *AND* SET *AND* RISE *AND* RAISE

17e The verb *sit* means "to rest in an upright, seated position." *Sit* almost never takes an object. The verb *set* means "to put (something) in a place." *Set* usually takes an object.

PRINCIPAL PARTS OF *SIT* AND *SET*			
Base Form	**Present Participle**	**Past**	**Past Participle**
sit (to rest)	(is) sitting	sat	(have) sat
set (to put)	(is) setting	set	(have) set

EXAMPLES **Sit** on the bench.   **Set** your umbrella in the corner.
Who **sat** here last?   Jo **set** the tiny chair on the shelf.

17f The verb *rise* means "to go up" or "to get up." *Rise* never takes an object. The verb *raise* means "to cause (something) to rise" or "to lift up." *Raise* usually takes an object.

PRINCIPAL PARTS OF *RISE* AND *RAISE*			
Base Form	**Present Participle**	**Past**	**Past Participle**
rise (to get up)	(is) rising	rose	(have) risen
raise (to lift up)	(is) raising	raised	(have) raised

EXAMPLES In a pink haze, the sun **rose** over Los Angeles.
Ticket prices **rise** every summer.
Raise the signal flag of a disabled vessel.
Has the electric company **raised** its rates again?

EXERCISE 6 Proofreading Sentences for Correct Use of *Sit* and *Set* and *Rise* and *Raise*

In the following sentences, draw a line through each incorrect form of *sit*, *set*, *rise*, and *raise*, and write the correct verb form on the line before each sentence. If a sentence is correct, write C.

EX. _____raised_____ 1. Bill rose the flag while the band played the national anthem.

_____ 1. Thurgood Marshall set on the Supreme Court for twenty-four years.

237

_____ 2. The lawn hasn't been mowed in five weeks, and the grass has rose above my knees.

_____ 3. When the sun is shining and the temperature is raising, I like to jump in the car and head for the shore.

_____ 4. Vanna is sitting out corn and squash as part of her display on American Indian farming techniques.

_____ 5. You should wait to begin eating until the waiter has sat down each person's meal.

_____ 6. The morning sun is raising above the horizon.

_____ 7. Our town has risen a monument to commemorate the Civil War battle fought here.

_____ 8. Sometimes, I have set in the waiting room for an hour before I could see my dentist.

_____ 9. Rob rises early every July Fourth so that he can find a good spot for our family picnic and for watching the fireworks.

_____ 10. Sit that package on the table, and I'll open it when I get back from lunch.

_____ 11. We set in our seats and waited for Dr. Spitz to begin his lecture on the renowned anthropologist Margaret Mead.

_____ 12. The choir rose money to supplement their annual food-and-clothing drive.

_____ 13. If I rise the height of my chair, I can work more comfortably at my desk.

_____ 14. The book Mrs. Stern has sat on my desk is by sculptor Isamu Noguchi, who carved a sculpture garden from a mountain at the Jerusalem Museum.

_____ 15. The fans raised to their feet as the home team scored its first touchdown of the year.

_____ 16. Please sit your knife and fork down when you are speaking.

_____ 17. The price of movie tickets has raised again.

_____ 18. For three years, I have set behind Antonio in math class.

_____ 19. Don raised his hand to ask a question about Luis W. Alvarez, who won the Nobel Prize for physics in 1968.

_____ 20. Every afternoon, I walk through the door, and my dog is setting there, waiting for me.

VERB TENSE

17g The *tense* of a verb indicates the time of the action or the state of being expressed by the verb.

(1) The *present tense* is used mainly to express an action or a state of being that is occurring now. The present tense is also used to show a customary or habitual action or state of being; to convey a general truth— something that is always true; and to summarize the plot or subject matter of a literary work (such use is called the *literary present*).

EXAMPLES   On Mondays, Marcelo **attends** a yoga class. [customary action]
            The Red Sea **gets** larger every year. [general truth]
            Goldilocks **eats** the bears' porridge. [literary present]

(2) The *past tense* is used to express an action or state of being that occurred in the past but did not continue into the present.

EXAMPLE   Last Monday, Marcelo **attended** a yoga class.

(3) The *future tense* is used to express an action or a state of being that will occur. The future tense is formed with *will* or *shall* and the verb's base form.

EXAMPLE   Next Monday, Marcelo **will attend** his next yoga class.

The future tense may also be expressed by using the present tense of *be* followed by either *going to* or *about to* and the infinitive form of a verb or by using a word or phrase that expresses future time.

EXAMPLES   Soon, we **are going to plan** the clean-up weekend.
            Mr. Davidson **is about to begin** his opening remarks.
            Our canned food collection **begins tomorrow**.

(4) The *present perfect tense* is used mainly to express an action or a state of being that occurred at some indefinite time in the past or that began in the past and continues into the present. The present perfect tense always includes the helping verb *have* or *has*.

EXAMPLE   **Has** Marcelo ever **attended** an advanced yoga class?

(5) The *past perfect tense* is used mainly to express an action or a state of being that was completed in the past before some other past occurrence. The past perfect tense always includes the helping verb *had*.

EXAMPLE   Marcelo attended the class because we **had talked** to him about its health benefits.

(6) The *future perfect tense* is used to express an action or a state of being that will be completed in the future before some other future occurrence. The future perfect tense always includes *will have* or *shall have*.

EXAMPLE   When his yoga classes are over, Marcelo **will have become** much more flexible.

Each tense has an additional form called the *progressive form*, which expresses continuing action or state of being. In each tense, the progressive form of a verb consists of the appropriate tense of *be* plus the verb's present participle. Some tenses also include one or more helping verbs.

Form	Examples
Present Progressive	am, are, is attending
Past Progressive	was, were attending
Future Progressive	will (shall) be attending
Present Perfect Progressive	has been, have been attending
Past Perfect Progressive	had been attending
Future Perfect Progressive	will (shall) have been attending

EXERCISE 7   Identifying Verb Tense

For each of the following sentences, identify the tense of the italicized verb. On the line before each sentence, write *pres.* for *present, past* for *past, fut.* for *future, pres. perf.* for *present perfect, past perf.* for *past perfect,* or *fut. perf.* for *future perfect.*

EX. _____pres._____ 1. The Erie Canal *connects* the Hudson River to Lake Erie.

_____ 1. The governor of New York State *had decided* in 1800 to link the West to the Northeast.

_____ 2. In 1817, the New York legislature *voted* in support of the governor's idea.

_____ 3. Many Irish immigrants *worked* to dig the Erie Canal, which was originally four feet deep and forty feet wide.

_____ 4. The State of New York *spent* many millions of dollars to construct the canal.

_____ 5. The canal has a system of locks, which *fill* or empty to raise or lower a boat to its next level.

_____ 6. Boats *had traveled* part of the Erie Canal in 1820, but it wasn't completed until 1825.

_____ 7. In the beginning, travel along the canal was not fast; mules *pulled* the boats along slowly.

_____ 8. Merchants and sightseers *have made* the long, slow journey.

_____ 9. During the first years of the canal's use, a ride *cost* only pennies a mile.

_____ 10. In the mid-1800s, the ease and speed of the railroad *replaced* difficult canal travel.

_____ 11. It is difficult to use the canal all year because it *will have frozen* by the end of winter.

_____ 12. Since it was first constructed, workers *have increased* the size of the Erie Canal to seven feet deep and seventy feet wide.

_____ 13. Over three thousand miles of canals *connect* various bodies of water in North America.

_____ 14. Today, most travelers *rely* on airplanes for long distances and cars for shorter ones.

_____ 15. Some day we *will have* a new method of transportation, and we may consider cars and planes slow and difficult.

_____ 16. Of course, the Erie Canal *was used* primarily for moving goods on barges.

_____ 17. Railroads and the interstate highway system *have caused* a great decrease in canal use.

_____ 18. Trucks *have* also largely *replaced* the railroads.

_____ 19. *Will* a more efficient means for hauling large loads *have made* trucks obsolete in our lifetimes?

_____ 20. Devising truck fuels that *cause* less pollution may preserve the trucking industry.

EXERCISE 8   Using Different Tenses and Forms of Verbs in Sentences

In each of the following sentences, change the tense of the verb or the form of the verb according to the directions given after the sentence. Write your revised sentence on the line provided.

EX.   1. She played basketball in college. (Change to present progressive.)
       She is playing basketball in college.
       _____

1. Pamela has completed a five-hundred piece jigsaw puzzle. (Change to present perfect progressive.)

_____

2. Jason is building a wooden bird feeder as a present for Mr. Petner. (Change to future.)

_____

3. The rings-and-jewelry set includes seed beads, wire, and directions. (Change to past.)

_____

4. After a long bus ride from Phoenix, the reggae band arrived in town. (Change to future progressive.)

_____

5. Peter Jacobson has been playing music on the harpsichord for five years. (Change to present perfect.)

_____

6. The bank on Main Street has an automatic teller machine with a Braille keypad. (Change to future.)

_____

7. The class talked about a special show featuring sea turtles at the museum. (Change to past perfect progressive.)

_____

8. By the end of her trip to Germany, Eliza will travel to Berlin and several other cities. (Change to future perfect.)

_____

9. I read about a small, powerful microscope for examining objects indoors and outdoors. (Change to past progressive.)

_____

10. London, England, plans to hold the Summer Olympic Games in 2012. (Change to present progressive.)

_____

SPECIAL PROBLEMS IN THE USE OF TENSES

17h When describing events that occur at the same time, use verbs in the same tense.

EXAMPLE The leaves fall and the air **grows** cold.
The leaves fell and the air **grew** cold.

17i When describing events that occur at different times, use verbs in different tenses to show the order of events.

EXAMPLE At present I **own** a Ford; my old car **was** a Honda. [I have a Ford now, so *own* is in the present tense. I used to own but no longer have a Honda, so *was* is in the past tense.]

17j Avoid the use of *would have* in "if clauses" that express the earlier of two past actions. Use the past perfect tense.

NONSTANDARD If you would have called the museum first, you would have known their hours.

STANDARD If you **had called** the museum first, you would have known their hours.

EXERCISE 9 Using Tenses Correctly

In each of the following sentences, draw a line through the incorrect verb form. Write the correct verb form on the line before each sentence.

EX. _____*flew*_____ 1. In 1927, Charles Lindbergh flies across the Atlantic in thirty-three hours, but now the same trip takes about six hours.

_____ 1. Today, people watch television regularly, but before 1925, television does not exist.

_____ 2. The first musical Mickey Mouse films are released in 1929, the same year Herbert Hoover was inaugurated.

_____ 3. In October, 1929, the stock market crashed and an international economic crisis begins.

_____ 4. Paavo Nurmi sets a world record for running the mile in 1923, then won four gold medals in the 1924 Olympics.

_____ 5. If New York would have scored two more runs in the 1926 World Series, they would have been champions.

_____ 6. Calvin Coolidge was elected in 1924 and serves for four years as president.

_____ 7. *The Great Gatsby* was published in 1925 and had become a famous book since then.

_____ 8. In the 1920s, a new refrigerator costs less than ninety dollars; today, a new refrigerator costs hundreds of dollars.

_____ 9. Duke Ellington releases his first record in 1926 but did not gain fame as a jazz musician until the early Forties.

_____ 10. Argentinian Enrique Tiriboschi swam across the English Channel in 1923; then Gertrude Ederle had crossed the Channel in 1926.

_____ 11. If President Harding would not have died in 1923, he might have been impeached for the Teapot Dome Scandal later that year.

_____ 12. A. A. Milne writes *Winnie-the-Pooh* in 1926, and it is still enjoyed today.

_____ 13. Emanuel Lasker has been the world chess champion since 1894; but in 1921, José Raoul Capablanca, a Cuban, won the title.

_____ 14. People ride street cars often during the 1920s but have lost interest over the years.

_____ 15. If you would have lived in 1928, you could have paid less than seven hundred dollars for a new car.

_____ 16. Born in 1924, William Rehnquist was forty-eight years old when he first sits on the Supreme Court.

_____ 17. The Harlem Globetrotters is organized in 1927 and still plays around the world.

_____ 18. Juan de la Cierva developed the autogiro in 1923, but now the helicopter had replaced it for the most part.

_____ 19. William Butler Yeats wins the 1923 Nobel Prize for literature; he had been writing poetry for many years.

_____ 20. Construction of the Cascade Tunnel began in 1926 and had ended in 1929.

17k   The *present infinitive* is used to express an action or a state of being that occurs after another action or state of being.

EXAMPLE   Pepita had wanted **to catch** the four o'clock bus. [The action expressed by *to catch* follows the action expressed by *had wanted*.]

17l The *present perfect infinitive* is used to express an action or a state of being that occurs before another action or state of being.

EXAMPLE   The women had expected **to have moved** to Santa Fe by now.

17m The *present participle* is used to express an action or a state of being that occurs at the same time as another action or state of being.

EXAMPLE   **Reading** the map, Mosi gave us a choice between two routes.

17n The *present perfect participle* is used to express an action or a state of being that comes before another action or state of being.

EXAMPLE   **Having finished** in good time, we took the rest of the afternoon off.

EXERCISE 10   Correcting Verb Tense

On your own paper, rewrite the incorrect verb forms in the following sentences, using the correct verb forms.

EX.   1. Recycling most containers, they felt they had contributed to a cleaner and healthier environment.

    1. Having recycled

1. Arriving early, Daniel decided to walk around the yard before he went in.

2. Ponchitta plans to have read the chapter notes while she eats lunch.

3. I should have known better than to underestimate your ability to finish on time.

4. Explaining how she calms herself before a piano recital, the young musician then moved around nervously.

5. Vincent saved for six months to have bought a replica of a historic fire truck.

6. Inheriting the trunk from her grandfather, Barbara Testa was shocked to find half of the original copy of Mark Twain's *Huckleberry Finn* inside.

7. Having served in France during World War I, the members of the 369th Infantry Regiment, a famous African American regiment, displayed great courage in battle.

8. The prime minister crushed the rebellion in order to have established a democracy.

9. Astronauts practice maneuvers in huge tanks of water to have prepared for performing the same tasks while in space.

10. Listening to the recorded bird sounds for fifteen minutes, the male robin finally attacked the tape deck.

11. Having begun her essay with a startling question, Anita quickly grabbed the reader's attention.

12. Lee would like to buy that blouse, but she didn't get back to the store before it closed.

13. The police chief said that the only way people will improve the quality of city life is for them to have gotten personally involved.

14. Being in Kaohsiung, Taiwan, the photographer knew that motorcycles outnumber cars and trucks there.

15. Having quietly closed the door behind her, Roberta didn't know everyone was still up.

16. Tsai learned to have danced by watching dance instruction videos.

17. Participating in such an obvious act of treason, the king's guards will be punished severely.

18. Losing my notebook with my homework assignments, I called Linda.

19. Your brother must be really talented for him to sing with the Boys Choir of Harlem for four years.

20. When Italian film director Federico Fellini was asked to have identified his all-time-favorite films, he included *8 1/2*, one of his own films.

21. I would give anything to be at my cousin's first concert.

22. Having compared the two kinds of bears, Vida explained how they are similar.

23. Discovering that computers can help some students learn faster, many schools have tried to find extra funds needed to purchase computers.

24. Keiko's mother was so nice to cook an authentic Japanese meal for us when we visited them last week.

25. In his autobiography, he claimed to be lost in the Amazon rain forest for ten years.

FRANK & ERNEST® by Bob Thaves

Frank & Ernest reprinted by permission of NEA, Inc.

ACTIVE VOICE AND PASSIVE VOICE

Voice is the form a transitive verb takes to indicate whether the subject of the verb performs or receives the action.

17o   When the subject of a verb performs the action, the verb is in the *active voice*. When the subject receives the action, the verb is in the *passive voice*.

ACTIVE VOICE   We **threw** stones across the water. [*We* performed the action; *stones* is the direct object.]

PASSIVE VOICE   The stones **were thrown** across the water. [The subject, *stones*, received the action.]

A verb in the active voice often has an indirect object as well as a direct object. When such a verb is put into the passive voice, either object can become the subject. The other subject then serves as a complement called a *retained object*.

S	V	I	DO

ACTIVE VOICE   Our teacher gave the class a tour of the new school.

PASSIVE VOICE   The class was given a tour of the new school (by our teacher). [The indirect object *class* becomes the subject, and the direct object *tour* becomes the retained object.]

PASSIVE VOICE   A tour of the new school was given the class (by our teacher). [The direct object *tour* becomes the subject, and the indirect object *class* becomes the retained object.]

17p   Use the passive voice sparingly.

(1)   Use the passive voice when you do not know who or what performed the action.

EXAMPLE   **Had** all the books on China **been checked** out of the library?

(2)   Use the passive voice when you do not want to reveal who or what performed the action.

EXAMPLE   The only copy of my term paper **was destroyed** last night.

(3)   Use the passive voice when you want to emphasize the receiver of the action rather than the performer.

EXAMPLE   **Was** Tina's favorite teddy bear **found** by her brother?

EXERCISE 11   Identifying Voice in Sentences

Identify the verbs in each of the following sentences as active or passive. Write *act.* for *active* or *pass.* for *passive* on the line before each sentence.

EX.   <u>act.</u>   1.   We read about some unusual injuries.

_____   1.   A worker in Beijing, China, was rushed to the hospital.

_____ 2. He suffered from severe pain in the area of the intestines.

_____ 3. The doctors had seen the problem two previous times in recent weeks.

_____ 4. In all cases, the patients had been afflicted with pain after playing with a plastic hoop.

_____ 5. Their intestines had been twisted by the repeated rotation of their hips.

_____ 6. The hoops, light plastic rings, are spun around a person's body by the movement of the person's hips.

_____ 7. The hoop-spinning fad spread throughout China in 1992.

_____ 8. Youths in the United States were introduced to the joys of hoop-spinning decades earlier.

_____ 9. To prevent further incidence of intestinal injuries, doctors in China cautioned patients against using the hoops right after eating.

_____ 10. Proper warm-up techniques were also advised.

EXERCISE 12   Revising Sentences in the Passive Voice

On your own paper, rewrite each sentence below, using the active voice.

EX.   1. During World War I, a serious concussion was suffered by Bela Lugosi, the star of *Dracula*.

1. During World War I, Bela Lugosi, the star of <u>Dracula</u>, suffered a serious concussion.

1. An injured soldier was being saved by Lugosi; but during the rescue mission, Lugosi was hurled into the air by an explosion.

2. The concussion was caused by his head hitting a rock on the ground.

3. Serious wounds were suffered by other famous men on the battlefield.

4. Twelve operations were endured by Ernest Hemingway after serious wounds were caused to him by bullets and shell fragments.

5. An ambulance was being driven by the famous author in Italy during World War I when the injuries were received by him.

6. In a 1571 battle against the Turks, the left hand of Miguel de Cervantes, the author of *Don Quixote*, was permanently disabled by a cannon ball.

7. During World War II, the chest of François Mitterrand, a future president of France, was hit by shrapnel.

8. His wounds were barely recovered from when Mitterrand was taken prisoner by enemy forces.

9. Doctors were convinced by Jean Renoir's mother not to amputate her son's leg.

10. The French artist's leg had been broken by a bullet in a World War I battle.

MOOD

Mood is the form a verb takes to indicate the attitude of the person using the verb. Verbs may be in one of three moods: the *indicative*, the *imperative*, or the *subjunctive*.

17q   The *indicative mood* expresses a fact, an opinion, or a question.

EXAMPLES   Liliuokalani **was** queen of the Hawaiian Islands.
Shana **believes** that her school is the best.
Does Yuen Hui **have** a sister?

17r   The *imperative mood* expresses a direct command or request.

EXAMPLES   **Bring** me the gauze and scissors quickly!
Please **adopt** one of the puppies.

17s   The *subjunctive mood* expresses a suggestion, a necessity, a condition contrary to fact, or a wish.

EXAMPLES   Mom suggested that Aunt Latoya **read** a poem.
If you **were** on a safari, would you use a different camera?

(1) The *present subjunctive* expresses a suggestion or a necessity.

EXAMPLES   The waiter recommended that Pedro **try** the cold soup.
It is essential that Camilla **find** a safer apartment.

(2) The *past subjunctive* expresses a wish or a condition contrary to fact.

EXAMPLES   If Ben Franklin **were** alive today, would he be a politician?
I wish I **were relaxing** in a hammock.

EXERCISE 13   Using Subjunctive Mood Correctly

Most of the following sentences contain errors in the use of the subjunctive mood. If a sentence is incorrect, write the correct form of the verb on the line before the sentence. If a sentence is correct, write *C*.

EX.   _____*be*_____   1. Anna recommended that Alexis is in charge of refreshments for the party.

_____   1. If dogs are allowed on the beach, then I would bring my German shepherd.

_____   2. Tedra wishes that Peter was more agreeable to making changes in the organization's constitution.

_____ 3. She slept for only fifteen minutes, but when she opened her eyes, she felt as though it was the next day.

_____ 4. The bird squawked as if someone or something was about to disturb its nest.

_____ 5. Darihuu Undarmaa, a professional contortionist from Mongolia, twists her body as if it were made of rubber.

_____ 6. It is essential that Cory locks her bike on the bike rack in front of school.

_____ 7. The class has recommended that Tom and Pearl are co-presidents.

_____ 8. Mr. Finkel has proposed that all members of the science club are tutors for students in lower grades.

_____ 9. I wish I wasn't so nervous about flying; it takes some of the fun out of traveling.

_____ 10. It is important that Karina mails this package to her brother in Finland by express mail.

_____ 11. We had had so much rain that it seemed as though the sun was never going to shine again.

_____ 12. Mom suggested that Winona considers other people's feelings before speaking out.

_____ 13. It is urgent that he be allowed to talk to the officer in charge.

_____ 14. If he was around when we arrived, he could have explained what he wanted us to do.

_____ 15. The people had demanded that a mayor is elected who would work for a cleaner, safer city environment.

_____ 16. Mo acts as if Joey was his best friend, although they just met two days ago.

_____ 17. Falling down for the tenth time, Shari said, "I wish I was as good on in-line skates as Kimmy Navarro."

_____ 18. The sales clerk recommended that *Selected Poems* by Rita Dove, this country's first African American Poet Laureate, be included on our reading list.

_____ 19. "I wish Coach was here to see this," Benny whispered as the crowd went wild.

_____ 20. If I was she, I wouldn't worry about anything.

CHAPTER REVIEW

A. Proofreading Sentences for Correct Verb Usage

Identify the errors in verb usage in each of the sentences below. Draw a line through each incorrect verb form, and write the correct form of the verb above it. Some sentences may require no change.

EX.   1. Cammie wishes that her brother ~~was~~ *were* coming home for Thanksgiving.

1. If we had paid attention, we would have knowed that the quiz was today.

2. "I wish that this photograph of the Grand Canyon were clearer," Dave said.

3. If I were Tony, I wouldn't have wrote about such a confusing topic.

4. Violetta regretted the angry words she said to her parents the night before.

5. I didn't know that your friend Sue Ellen and my friend Lynda were sisters.

6. When the actor playing Grandfather walks on stage, the other actor is setting on the sofa.

7. The teacher asked Boris and Yoko to raise and tell the class about their cooperative assignment for English.

8. Having graduated from Harvard in 1890, W. E. B. Du Bois gave a graduation speech about Confederate President Jefferson Davis.

9. By the time our food gets here, we will be sitting at this table for an hour.

10. Miss Marotta had wanted to set and read to us about Chief Passaconaway, but she ran out of time.

B. Proofreading a Paragraph for Correct Verb Usage

Identify the errors in verb usage in the following paragraph. Draw a line through each incorrect verb form, and write the correct form of the verb above it. Be sure all verbs are in the active voice. Some sentences may be correct.

EX.   [1] Penguins have intrigued me since I ~~have watched~~ *watched* a special about them on television several years ago.

[1] Having lived in Antarctica, penguins face many challenges as they attempt to travel from place to place. [2] These flightless birds spent more than half of their lives in the water, and they swim like fish. [3] They use their

251

feet and tails to have steered themselves in the water and their strong flippers to push themselves forward. [4] I wish I was as fast a swimmer as a penguin, which can go up to fifteen miles an hour! [5] Emperor penguins are incredible divers and have been knowed to go down a thousand feet. [6] No other bird has ever dive that deep. [7] Sometimes a penguin acts as if it was a porpoise and propels itself up and out of the water. [8] This ability helps penguins to have escaped predators when they're being chased. [9] By the time a predator is ready to strike, the penguin will leap out of the water and onto the ice. [10] Have you ever seen a penguin walking quickly across an icy, snowy surface, and think it looked as if it were about to fall over? [11] On land, a penguin has taken short steps and sways from side to side. [12] Their sharp claws are used by them to grip the icy surface as they hop from one block of ice to another. [13] When it has been necessary for them to move extremely fast, penguins resort to their specialty, belly tobogganing. [14] Penguins appear comical and clumsy as they slide across slippery surfaces on their fat bellies. [15] This method of travel is called tobogganing, and it's how penguins get around when they have wanted to travel fast.

C.   Writing a Postcard

While you are on vacation, you decide to send a postcard to your friend back home. Use maps, encyclopedias, and magazines to make a list of parks, towns, local attractions, and highways that will help you describe your trip. Use five past forms and five past participle forms of the irregular verbs in the chart on pages 231–233. In your message, underline the verbs you use.

EX.

> June 23, 2008
>
> Dear Ramona,
>
> This has been the trip of a lifetime. New Mexico is amazing! We had driven for two hours yesterday when we finally arrived at the Carlsbad Caverns. What an incredible place that was! I took some great photographs. Today we headed southwest on Route 180, toward the Rio Grande.
>
> Brenda

USES OF MODIFIERS

18a   Use an adjective to modify the subject of a linking verb.

The most common linking verbs are the forms of *be: am, is, are, was, were, be, been,* and *being.* A linking verb is often followed by a *predicate adjective*—a word that modifies the subject.

EXAMPLES   That exam question is **complicated.**
            Tuesday will be **fair** and **sunny.**

18b   Use an adverb to modify an action verb.

An action verb is often modified by an *adverb*—a word that explains *how, when, where,* or *to what extent* the action is performed.

EXAMPLES   Miguel **cleverly** avoided hitting the dock.
            In the end, those who worked **conscientiously** were rewarded.

Some verbs may be used as linking verbs or action verbs.

EXAMPLES   Greta **looked** serious. [*Looked* is a linking verb, followed by *serious,* an adjective.]
            Greta **looked** seriously at the lock. [*Looked* is an action verb, followed by *seriously,* an adverb.]

To determine whether to use an adjective or an adverb after a verb, replace the verb with a form of the linking verb *seem.* If *seem* makes sense in the sentence, the original verb is being used as a linking verb. If *seem* is absurd in the sentence, the original verb is being used as an action verb. Once you have determined whether the verb is an action verb or a linking verb, apply rule 18a or 18b.

EXAMPLES   Greta looked serious. [Since *Greta seemed serious* makes sense, *looked* is being used as a linking verb and calls for the adjective *serious.*]
            Greta looked seriously at the lock. [Since *Greta seemed seriously at the lock* is absurd, *looked* is being used as an action verb and calls for the adverb *seriously.*]

EXERCISE 1   Selecting Modifiers to Complete Sentences

In the following sentences, underline the correct modifier in parentheses.

EX.   1. Joshua played the piano (*wonderful*, <u>*wonderfully*</u>).

1. She walked (*confident*, *confidently*) onstage.

2. Guido grew (*proud*, *proudly*) at hearing his name called.

3. They asked us to send the flowers (*prompt, promptly*) to 10 Richardson Avenue.

4. Roberta always speaks so (*sincere, sincerely*).

5. The snowfall yesterday was (*light, lightly*).

6. Mandy seemed (*curious, curiously*) about astronomy.

7. Thousands of people (*enthusiastic, enthusiastically*) voted today.

8. The tired pitcher walked (*grumpy, grumpily*) to the dugout.

9. Those cards and letters made her feel (*cheerful, cheerfully*).

10. We liked the film because it presented the subject (*realistic, realistically*).

11. Please reach into that basket and (*careful, carefully*) pull out the plates.

12. Vanya (*desperate, desperately*) waited for the messenger.

13. After receiving the call, Sam left the theater (*immediate, immediately*).

14. We gazed as the clouds moved (*brisk, briskly*) overhead.

15. Right before the storm, the horses were acting (*restless, restlessly*).

16. The audience laughed (*loud, loudly*) at the comedian's joke.

17. The lost patrol stumbled (*blind, blindly*) through the dark woods.

18. The new teacher seemed (*efficient, efficiently*).

19. Everyone in the class was working (*diligent, diligently*) on the project.

20. Is it necessary to shout so (*loud, loudly*)?

21. Do you students have to be so (*noisy, noisily*)?

22. I have never seen anyone eat as (*hungry, hungrily*) as Paulina did tonight after the tournament.

23. How (*quick, quickly*) do you think you can finish herding those horses?

24. The first-time soloist (*nervous, nervously*) waited for her cue.

25. The dentist's drill sounded (*harsh, harshly*) on the old filling.

SIX TROUBLESOME MODIFIERS

Bad and *Badly*

18c *Bad* **is an adjective.** *Badly* **is an adverb. In standard English, only the adjective form should follow a sense verb, such as** *feel, see, hear, taste,* **or** *smell,* **or other linking verb.**

NONSTANDARD   Too much salt made the soup taste badly.
STANDARD   Too much salt made the soup taste **bad**.

 NOTE   The expression *feel badly* has become acceptable in informal situations, but use *feel bad* in formal speaking and writing.

18d *Good* **is an adjective.** *Well* **may be used as an adjective or an adverb. Avoid using** *good* **to modify an action verb. Instead, use** *well* **as an adverb meaning "capably" or "satisfactorily."**

NONSTANDARD   Molly writes short stories good.
STANDARD   Molly writes short stories **well**.

NONSTANDARD   You did good to tell the truth.
STANDARD   You did **well** to tell the truth.

As an adjective, *well* means "in good health" or "satisfactory in appearance or condition."

EXAMPLES   I saw Bill and he looked **well**.
Last week, Rhonda had the flu, but she feels **well** now.
All's **well** that ends **well**.

Slow and *Slowly*

18e *Slow* **is an adjective.** *Slowly* **is an adverb. Although** *slow* **is also labeled an adverb in many dictionaries, this usage applies only to informal situations and colloquial expressions, such as** *drive slow* **and** *go slow*.

INFORMAL   Walk **slow** and wave.
FORMAL   Walk **slowly** and wave.

EXERCISE 2   Proofreading for Correct Modifiers

For each of the following sentences, underline the correct modifier in parentheses.

EX.   1. I hope my little sister did not behave (*bad, badly*).

1. As the museum director advised us, we moved (*slow, slowly*) through the exhibits.

2. Sabrena was determined to show them she could play (*good, well*).

3. Avoid eating fish if it smells (*bad, badly*).

4. The once fertile fields along the Nile have been (*bad, badly*) served by the Aswan Dam.

5. Jasper steered the boat pretty (*good, well*), considering the high winds.

6. "Take your partner's hand and lead her (*slow, slowly*) down the middle of the stage," the director explained.

7. "How (*good, well*) do you know him?" Martha asked.

8. That hot dog tasted so (*bad, badly*) that Jiro didn't eat another one for a month.

9. The (*good, well*) woman returned the wallet I'd dropped at the movies.

10. The face of the Sphinx in Gîza is crumbling (*slow, slowly*).

EXERCISE 3   Proofreading for Correct Modifiers

For each of the following sentences, draw a line through the incorrect modifier and give the correct form in the space provided. If the sentence is correct, write C.

EX. __well__ 1. Two days after taking the doctor's advice, she felt good.

_____ 1. He would have done good if he'd practiced a little harder.

_____ 2. The bumps on this road are bad.

_____ 3. Some Easter Island statues are damaged bad.

_____ 4. The instruction manual said, "Breathe slow and count to three."

_____ 5. Considering all the survivors had been through, they didn't look so badly.

_____ 6. How good do you know this subject?

_____ 7. My uncle told me I shouldn't feel too badly about what happened.

_____ 8. The Inca raised the alpaca for its fur, which feels well.

_____ 9. We never liked it when our aunt Tilly told us in a very angry voice, "Chew your food slow!"

_____ 10. You'll have to speak up when talking to our dog Mortimer because his hearing is bad.

COMPARISON OF MODIFIERS

18f *Comparison* **refers to the change in the form of an adjective or an adverb to show increasing or decreasing degrees in the quality that the modifier expresses.**

There are three degrees of comparison: *positive, comparative,* and *superlative.*

ADJECTIVES	tall	taller	tallest
	hopeful	more hopeful	most hopeful
	good	better	best
ADVERBS	soon	sooner	soonest
	urgently	less urgently	least urgently
	well	better	best

(1) Most one-syllable modifiers form the comparative and superlative degrees by adding *–er* **and** *–est.*

EXAMPLES	small	small**er**	small**est**
	near	near**er**	near**est**
	late	lat**er**	lat**est**

(2) Some two-syllable modifiers form the comparative and superlative degrees by adding *–er* **or** *–est.* **Other two-syllable modifiers form the comparative and superlative degrees by using** *more* **and** *most.*

EXAMPLES	healthy	healthier	healthiest
	simple	simpler	simplest
	gladly	more gladly	most gladly

NOTE   If you are not sure how a two-syllable modifier is compared, look in a dictionary.

(3) Modifiers of more than two syllables form the comparative and superlative degrees by using *more* **and** *most.*

EXAMPLES	considerate	more considerate	most considerate
	reluctantly	more reluctantly	most reluctantly

(4) To show a decrease in the qualities they express, all modifiers form the comparative and superlative degrees by using *less* **and** *least.*

EXAMPLES	full	less full	least full
	visible	less visible	least visible
	calmly	less calmly	least calmly
	thoroughly	less thoroughly	least thoroughly

(5) Some modifiers do not follow the regular methods of forming the comparative and superlative degrees.

EXAMPLES	good	better	best		well	better	best
	bad	worse	worst		many	more	most
	little	less	least		much	more	most

EXERCISE 4   Writing the Comparative and Superlative Forms of Modifiers

On the lines provided, write the comparative form and the superlative form of each of the modifiers below. Use a dictionary to check any words you are not sure about.

EX.   1.   near
nearer, nearest

1. thick

2. clearly

3. thankful

4. gray

5. little

6. silently

7. rapid

8. elegant

9. dramatically

10. long

11. elaborate

12. much

13. narrow

14. green

15. fully

16. precious

17. successful

18. happy

19. likely

20. warmly

21. bad

22. ill

23. tiny

24. completely

25. good

USES OF COMPARATIVE AND SUPERLATIVE FORMS

18g **Use the comparative degree when comparing two things. Use the superlative degree when comparing more than two things.**

COMPARATIVE   Yesterday we walked to the park, because it was **nearer** our house than the lake was. [comparison of two distances]
It was difficult to tell which joke was **more humorous**, Millie's or Juanita's. [comparison of two jokes]

SUPERLATIVE   Of the three trees in our back yard, that old oak is definitely the **largest**. [comparison of three trees]
Hui Chun was a big tennis fan and enjoyed **most** of the matches. [comparison of many matches]

NOTE   In informal situations, the superlative degree is sometimes used to emphasize the comparison of only two things. Avoid such use of the superlative degree in formal speaking and writing.

INFORMAL   Ethel didn't know which she liked least, cold mornings or humid nights.

FORMAL   Ethel didn't know which she liked **less**, cold mornings or humid nights.

The superlative degree is also used to compare two things in some idiomatic expressions.

EXAMPLE   Put your best foot forward.

18h **Include the word *other* or *else* when comparing one member or a group with the rest of the members.**

NONSTANDARD   We went to Switzerland to film the Matterhorn, which is more photogenic than any mountain in Europe. [The Matterhorn is one of the mountains in Europe; it cannot be more photogenic than itself.]

STANDARD   We went to Switzerland to film the Matterhorn, which is more photogenic than any **other** mountain in Europe.

NONSTANDARD   Phoebe, who is secretary of the senior class, has a bigger stamp collection than anyone in the senior class. [Phoebe is in the senior class; she cannot have a bigger stamp collection than herself.]

STANDARD   Phoebe has a bigger stamp collection than anyone **else** in the senior class.

18i   Avoid double comparisons.

A *double comparison* is the result of using two comparative forms (usually *-er* and *more*) or using the two superlative forms (usually *-est* and *most*) to modify the same word.

NONSTANDARD   Nora picked out the wristwatch with the more smaller face.
STANDARD   Nora picked out the wristwatch with the **smaller** face.

NONSTANDARD   Often, the first climber to the top was the most strongest.
STANDARD   Often, the first climber to the top was the **strongest**.

EXERCISE 5   Using the Comparative and Superlative Forms of Modifiers

In each sentence below, draw a line through the incorrect modifier. Write the correct form of the modifer above it.

EX.   1. Do you think Yuri will get there *sooner* ~~more sooner~~ than Lita?

1. Vincent studies harder than anyone in that class.

2. Which of the three books did you enjoy reading more?

3. Which is the least able to withstand the cold, an alligator or a lizard?

4. Will Rogers was one of the better-known American humorists of his day.

5. My dog Bowser was the most calmest of us all during the storm.

6. I've heard that Hercules was supposed to be stronger than anyone in the world.

7. Cristina ran quick, quicker than Ryan, and quickest of all the students.

8. Apples and oranges are both sweet, but oranges are usually more juicier.

9. Suzette, Fredo, and Rick saw the exhibit; Fredo was the more interested.

10. Which of the ten largest cities has the worse pollution?

11. Yori's eyesight is rather bad, but his right eye is the least bad.

12. Often, it is the most well publicized of the two candidates who wins.

13. He was sure Judy Collins could sing that song better than anyone.

14. The first act was bad enough, but the second was more worser.

15. My best friend asked me which I liked least, *Star Wars* or *E.T.*

CHAPTER REVIEW

A. Using Modifiers Correctly

The sentences below contain errors in the use of modifiers. Underline each error, and write the correct form on the line before the sentence.

EX. _____easier_____ 1. We could never find directions <u>more easy</u> to follow than the ones in that manual.

_____ 1. Marty could run more quickly than any member of the team.

_____ 2. Our captain guided the ship steady toward the harbor.

_____ 3. Of all the singers who auditioned, Sondra was the more extraordinary.

_____ 4. Tai Kwong usually approaches his homework quite thoughtful.

_____ 5. When I came to a fork in the path, I chose the easiest way.

_____ 6. Rocky later admitted he should have known not to eat it because it tasted so badly.

_____ 7. Neil's garden contains the lovelier flowers on the block.

_____ 8. Do you think people go to movies more than anywhere?

_____ 9. On our way to Colorado, we saw the more wonderful scenery.

_____ 10. My friend Leti draws better pictures than anyone I know.

_____ 11. In geography class today, some students were arguing about which had the hottest climate, Uruguay or Paraguay.

_____ 12. The team would have played better, but the quarterback had a cold and felt badly that day.

_____ 13. Mother likes table tennis and square-dancing but still thinks that long walks are the more fun.

_____ 14. If you're just learning to dive, make sure you avoid the most deepest parts of the lake.

_____ 15. While following the suspect, the detective looked careful at everything around him.

B.   Proofreading a Paragraph for Correct Use of Modifiers

In the paragraph below, draw a line through each incorrect modifier, and write
the correct form on your own paper. If a sentence is correct, write C.

EX.   [1] Alexander Pushkin is often considered to be Russia's ~~most greatest~~ poet.
         1. greatest

[1] Pushkin's grandfather was Abram Hannibal, a transplanted African who
became famouser in his own right as a soldier fighting for the Russian czars.
[2] Pushkin wrote during the early 1800s and is still wide read by his modern
countrymen. [3] Some Russians, if they must choose among Pushkin, Tolstoy,
or Dostoyevsky, will say Pushkin is the better of the three. [4] He was short and
had a flat nose and a roughly complexion. [5] Some people have said that you
could tell he was a poet because of how bright his eyes shone. [6] Pushkin
attended school, but afterward, he quick entered the foreign ministry. [7] His
early poems, "Ode to Freedom" and "Noel," were not received too good by the
czar. [8] Because he spoke bad about the government in these poems, Pushkin
was exiled to a place far away from the center of political influence. [9] But,
because he loved writing poetry more than anything he had ever done, Pushkin
used the time there to create his epic, "Ruslan and Ludmila." [10] Eventually, he
was discharged from his government job and returned home. [11] From that
time on, he did nothing but what he was better at, which of course was writing
poetry. [12] Of all his later works, "Boris Godonuv" and "Eugene Onegin" are
the more popular. [13] Both poems became well known part because they were
later made into operas. [14] Pushkin made it clear in his work that he felt
individual rights were no least important than those of the state. [15] A man
whose life was often as dramatically as his poetry, he died fighting a duel at the
age of thirty-eight.

C.   Writing Sentences Using the Comparative
and Superlative Forms of Modifiers

Modern three-ring circuses present their audiences with a wonderful selection of
entertainment. Think of two different acts that you might see performed at the
circus, and write five sentences using adverbs and adjectives to compare them. Then
add a third act, and write five more sentences comparing all three. In your sentences,
use ten or more modifiers from below. Underline the modifiers in your sentences.

funny	heartwarming	incredible	well	silly
clever	loud	intelligent	dazzling	bad
little	colorful	sad	death-defying	suspenseful
ridiculous	good	strong	charming	beautiful

MISPLACED MODIFIERS

A modifying phrase or clause that is placed too far from the word it sensibly modifies is called a *misplaced modifier*.

19a   Avoid using a misplaced modifier.

To correct a misplaced modifier, place the phrase or clause as close as possible to the word you intend it to modify.

MISPLACED	Filling the air with thick smoke, we watched the garage burn.
CLEAR	We watched the garage burn, **filling the air with thick smoke.**
MISPLACED	Jovita bought a new CD player for the family which never worked well.
CLEAR	Jovita bought the family a new CD player, **which never worked well.**

19b   Avoid placing a phrase or clause so that it seems to modify either of two words. Such a misplaced modifier is often called a *two-way*, or *squinting, modifier.*

MISPLACED	Tell Gwen between acts I would like to see her.
CLEAR	**Between acts,** tell Gwen I would like to see her.
CLEAR	Tell Gwen I would like to see her **between acts.**

EXERCISE 1   Revising Sentences by Correcting Misplaced Modifiers

Revise each of the following sentences by moving the misplaced phrase or clause as close as possible to the word it modifies. Write your revised sentences on the line provided.

EX.   1.   Plants are sold by florists that grow in the tropics.

        Plants that grow in the tropics are sold by florists.

1.   Fran talked about the illness she had had on the way home from the

     hospital. _____

     _____

2.   Digging a hole with his front paws, Harold saw your dog Spike. _____

     _____

3.   My neighbor has a parakeet who writes children's books. _____

     _____

4. We watched the clouds drift by eating our picnic lunch. _____

    _____

5. I remember during a hurricane in Florida I was involved in
    the recovery effort. _____

    _____

6. Please put this vase near the piano on the table. _____

    _____

7. He made a loaf of bread for his family that has raisins in it. _____

    _____

8. The teacher asked the two students after class to report to the office. _____

    _____

9. Lori said after Hanukkah we would go to Santa Fe. _____

    _____

10. We found a veterinarian for my cat who specializes in skin diseases. _____

    _____

11. Please tell the man on Monday I need the firewood. _____

    _____

12. Hidden under the table, I can see your shoes. _____

    _____

13. They learned at the museum she was a tour guide. _____

    _____

14. A woodchuck dug a hole in the garden that is unbelievably deep. _____

    _____

15. We hired for my sister a tutor who needs extra help in math. _____

    _____

DANGLING MODIFIERS

A modifying phrase or clause that does not sensibly modify any word or group of words in the sentence is called a *dangling modifier*.

19c   Avoid using a dangling modifier.

You may correct a dangling modifier in several ways.

(1) Add a word that the phrase or clause can sensibly modify.

(2) Add, change, or delete words in the phrase or clause so that your meaning is clear.

(3) Reword the sentence.

DANGLING	The car went off the road while trying to read the map.
CLEAR	The car went off the road **while I was trying to read the map.**
CLEAR	I drove the car off the road **while trying to read the map.**
DANGLING	Talking about the game, dinner was forgotten entirely.
CLEAR	**Talking about the game,** Claudia and Shane forgot dinner entirely.
CLEAR	**Because Claudia and Shane were talking about the game,** dinner was forgotten entirely.

NOTE   A few dangling modifiers have become standard idiomatic expressions.

EXAMPLES   **Generally speaking,** the Japanese *ryokan* is the place to choose if you want to stay at a peaceful inn.
To be perfectly frank, that writer's only good book was her first one.

REFERENCE NOTE: For more about using commas after introductory words, phrases, and clauses, see page 303.

EXERCISE 2   Revising Sentences by Eliminating Dangling Modifiers

On the lines provided, revise each sentence to eliminate the dangling modifier.

EX.   1. To win the championship, an undefeated season is necessary.
To win the championship, our team needs an undefeated season.

1. While fishing, these trout were caught. _____

_____

2. Flying out of Cuba, the coast of Florida could be seen. _____
_____

3. Performing beautifully, her reward was loud applause. _____
_____

4. Extremely talented, singing and dancing are her strengths. _____
_____

5. The movie version seemed dull after reading the book. _____
_____

6. Missing Tanya, sadness filled the neighborhood. _____
_____

7. To do well in school, hard work is often necessary. _____
_____

8. Looking for our friends, the concert began. _____
_____

9. My travel plans were made having read about Samoa. _____
_____

10. Watching the children play, the afternoon slipped by. _____
_____

11. When training for a race, sturdy shoes are helpful. _____
_____

12. To learn about current events, newspapers should be read. _____
_____

13. While hiking in the mountains, a storm began suddenly. _____
_____

14. Telling jokes and funny stories, their laughter could be heard. _____
_____

15. Built of bricks, strength is guaranteed. _____
_____

CHAPTER REVIEW

A. Revising Sentences by Correcting Misplaced Modifiers

On the lines provided, rewrite each sentence below, correcting the misplaced and squinting modifiers.

EX.   1. Blowing in the wind, we saw the red-and-white flag of Indonesia.
          We saw the red-and-white flag of Indonesia blowing in the wind.

1. In one legend, gray birds that arrive within forty days at that mosque turn white. _____

_____

2. Gwen made a costume for her brother covered with stars and stripes. ____

_____

3. Please give the woman a program in the blue dress. _____

_____

4. Painted by Alicia, Roberto hung the picture above the sofa. _____

_____

5. The firefighters spoke about the need for courage at a school assembly. ___

_____

6. Paolo cheered when Claudio crossed the finish line, also an Italian bicycle racer. _____

_____

7. These vases will hold several flowers that are made of marble. _____

8. He built a boat for his cousin made from recycled materials. _____

_____

9. Gerry bought stamps that show rock-and-roll musicians performing at the post office. _____

_____

10. I want to ask Rosemary when she finishes her work to have lunch with me.

_____

B.   Revising Sentences by Correcting Dangling Modifiers

On your own paper, rewrite each sentence below, correcting the dangling modifiers.

EX.   1.   Standing on the riverbank, a large snapping turtle was seen.
      1.   While Emma was standing on the riverbank, she saw a large snapping turtle.

1.   While watching the movie, my brother came home.

2.   Begun as an experiment, Joe's dad is now a successful businessman.

3.   Looking at old photographs, memories came back.

4.   To find the meanings of words, a dictionary should be used.

5.   Having chopped the vegetables, the meal was ready to serve.

6.   Listening to Erik's description, vivid pictures came to mind.

7.   Anxious to begin the play, the stage was filled with tension.

8.   Taking another helping of salad, his plate was full.

9.   His pride became stronger, thinking about past victories.

10.   My face turned bright red, forgetting the poem I had memorized.

C.   Writing a Story Starter

You are writing a science fiction story. To help you get started, you have jotted down the following prewriting list of phrases and clauses. On your own paper, write at least ten sentences to begin your story. Use at least five of the phrases and clauses listed below. Make sure that you don't have any dangling or misplaced modifiers. In your story starter, underline the phrases and clauses you use from the list.

from outer space	without any engine
that made strange noises	hidden behind a grove of trees
flashing its lights	scattering birds and small animals
having spotted it in the night sky	that really startled me
to try to describe what I saw	feeling curious and adventurous
cruising over the treetops	because it hovered in one spot

EX.   feeling curious and adventurous
      1.   Feeling curious and adventurous, I decided to walk toward the meadow.

ADAPT, ADOPT / BEING AS, BEING THAT

This chapter contains a *glossary,* or alphabetical list, of common problems in English usage. Many examples are labeled *standard* or *nonstandard*. *Standard English* is the most widely accepted form of English. *Nonstandard English* is language that does not follow the rules and guidelines of standard English.

adapt, adopt   *Adapt* means "to change or adjust something in order to make it fit or to make it suitable." *Adopt* means "to take something (someone) and make it (him or her) one's own."

EXAMPLES   We **adapted** the old clothes to make our costumes.
The Percys have **adopted** three children.

all the farther, all the faster   These expressions are used informally in some parts of the United States. In formal situations, use *as far as* and *as fast as.*

NONSTANDARD   Ten miles was all the farther the group could walk.
STANDARD   Ten miles was **as far as** the group could walk.

allusion, illusion   An *allusion* is an indirect reference to something. An *illusion* is a mistaken idea or a misleading appearance.

EXAMPLES   Her speech contained **allusions** to the legends of King Arthur.
The door really was a window, a cleverly painted **illusion.**

alumni, alumnae   *Alumni* is the plural of *alumnus* (a male graduate). *Alumnae* is the plural of *alumna* (a female graduate). As a group, the graduates of a coeducational school are usually called *alumni.*

EXAMPLES   Because he is an **alumnus** of that university, he supports the scholarship fund.
The two women are **alumnae** of the same college.
The **alumni** gather every five years for a reunion.

amount, number   Use *amount* to refer to a single word. Use *number* to refer to a plural word.

EXAMPLES   The **amount** of food at the feast was astonishing.
The **number** of donations this year has increased.

as   See **like, as.**

as, as if   See **like, as, as if.**

> **at**   Avoid using *at* after a construction beginning with *where.*
>
> NONSTANDARD   Where are the newspapers at?
>   STANDARD   **Where** are the newspapers?
>
> **being as, being that**   Avoid using these expressions for *since* or *because.*
>
> NONSTANDARD   My grandmother walks every day being as walking is good exercise.
>   STANDARD   My grandmother walks every day **because** walking is good exercise.

EXERCISE 1   Identifying Standard Usage

For each sentence below, underline the correct word or expression in parentheses.

EX.   1.   (*Being as, Because*) a storm is predicted, the parade has been cancelled.

1.   When the paved road ended, Rob said, "I think that this is (*all the farther, as far as*) as we can go."

2.   The glittering decorations created an (*allusion, illusion*) of a starry night.

3.   Nina is an (*alumna, alumnus*) of a women's college in Vermont.

4.   We saw an enormous (*number, amount*) of geese flying south today.

5.   We couldn't find the stray kitten's owners, so we decided to (*adapt, adopt*) her.

6.   For the second time that day, he could not remember where his glasses (*were, were at*).

7.   Twenty-five miles an hour is (*all the faster, as fast as*) you can drive near the school.

8.   The (*alumni, alumnae*), who were all members of the Men's Chorus, keep in touch through a newsletter.

9.   Gladys has a large (*number, amount*) of foreign coins.

10.   In her poems Kyra made (*allusions, illusions*) to her childhood.

11.   The music was (*adapted, adopted*) from a classical piece by Beethoven.

12.   He was late (*because, being as*) the rain had closed the roads.

13.   Where should we (*meet, meet at*)?

14.   It was hard to believe that the magician's tricks were just (*illusions, allusions*).

15.   (*Being that, Because*) Anna's grandparents live in Denmark, she does not see them often.

CREDIBLE / LIKE, AS, AS IF

credible, creditable, credulous *Credible* means "believable." *Creditable* means "praiseworthy." *Credulous* means "inclined to believe too readily."

EXAMPLES   The teacher agreed that their reasons for being late were **credible.**
He gave a **creditable** performance in *Hamlet*.
The **credulous** audience believed that the magician could bend spoons using his mental powers.

data *Data* is the plural form of the Latin *datum.* In informal English, *data* is frequently used like a collective noun, with singular pronouns and verbs. In formal usage, *data* is used with plural nouns, verbs, and pronouns.

INFORMAL   The new **data is** here, and **it seems** to be accurate.
FORMAL   The new **data are** here, and **they seem** to be accurate.

emigrate, immigrate *Emigrate* means "to leave a country or region to settle elsewhere." *Immigrate* means "to come into a country or region to settle there."

EXAMPLES   Poverty has caused some people to **emigrate** from other countries to the United States.
My grandparents were among the Ellis Island **immigrants.**

famous, notorious *Famous* means "widely known." *Notorious* means "widely but unfavorably known."

EXAMPLES   The speaker is **famous** for her work among the poor.
One **notorious** figure from the West was Jesse James.

illusion See **allusion, illusion.**

immigrate See **emigrate, immigrate.**

imply, infer *Imply* means "to suggest something indirectly." *Infer* means "to interpret" or "to get a certain meaning from a remark or action."

EXAMPLES   In her remarks, the judge **implied** that it had been a complicated case.
From her remarks, I **inferred** that she had made a difficult decision.

like, as, as if *Like* is a preposition. In formal situations, do not use *like* for the conjunctions *as, as if,* or *as though* to introduce a subordinate clause.

INFORMAL   It looks **like** it is going to rain.
FORMAL   The computer screen shines **like** a mirror.
FORMAL   It looks **as if** it is going to rain.

EXERCISE 2   Identifying Correct Usage

For each of the sentences below, underline the correct word in parentheses.

EX.   1. Myron seemed like a (<u>credible</u>, *credulous*) witness when the lawyers cross-examined him.

1. Genghis Khan was a Mongol chief who was (*famous, notorious*) for his cruelty.

2. The speaker (*implied, inferred*) that she hadn't understood the question.

3. I would like to be (*famous, notorious*) for my writing one day.

4. The data (*suggest, suggests*) that her theory about comets may be correct.

5. Many Russian (*immigrants, emigrants*) have settled in this area.

6. In his article, the reporter revealed that the person selling stocks at low rates was a (*famous, notorious*) swindler.

7. Wars and revolutions have caused many people to (*emigrate, immigrate*) to neighboring countries.

8. To our delight, the experiment worked (*as, like*) we had hoped it would.

9. I (*implied, inferred*) from the hastily scribbled message that Yoshi was worried about being late.

10. No one was (*creditable, credulous*) enough to believe Tony when he said that the Martians had landed.

EXERCISE 3   Proofreading Sentences to Correct Usage Errors

For each sentence below, draw a line through the error in usage. Then write the correct usage in the space above each word. Some sentences may be correct.

EX.   1. Noni's family ~~immigrated~~ *emigrated* from Italy during the war.

1. At the meeting, Loni will present data that shows that the new traffic plan is working.

2. We can't prove our point without credulous evidence.

3. Mrs. Ramirez is becoming notorious for her beautiful photographs of the mountains.

4. The newspaper article implied that the mayor was on vacation at that time.

5. I cleaned my room just like I said I would.

NAUSEATED, NAUSEOUS / WHO, WHICH, THAT

nauseated, nauseous *Nauseated* means "sick." *Nauseous* means "disgusting" or "sickening."

EXAMPLES   The doctor asked if I was feeling **nauseated**.
               The factory was ordered to stop emitting the **nauseous** fumes.

notorious See **famous, notorious.**

number See **amount, number.**

of   *Of* is a preposition. Do not use *of* in place of *have* after verbs such as *could, should, would, might, must,* and *ought [to].* Also, do not use *had of* for *had.*

NONSTANDARD   I should of bought my tickets right away.
   STANDARD   I **should have** bought tickets right away.

off, off of   Do not use *off* or *off of* for *from.*

NONSTANDARD   I bought some apples off that stand by the farm.
   STANDARD   I bought some apples **from** that stand by the farm.

or, nor   Use *or* with *either.* Use *nor* with *neither.*

EXAMPLES   We need **either** red **or** green paint to finish the poster.
              Neither Andrea **nor** Morgan had the right answer.

persecute, prosecute *Persecute* means "to attack or annoy someone constantly." *Prosecute* means "to bring legal action against someone for unlawful behavior."

EXAMPLES   They were **persecuted** for their religious beliefs.
              The district attorney arrested and **prosecuted** the suspect.

some, somewhat In formal situations, avoid using *some* to mean "to some extent." Use *somewhat.*

INFORMAL   After the holiday, the workers' spirits improved **some.**
  FORMAL   After the holiday, the workers' spirits improved **somewhat.**

than, then   *Than* is a conjunction used in comparisons. *Then* is an adverb telling *when.*

EXAMPLES   Lillian is taller **than** both of her sisters.
              First we ate lunch; **then** we went to the show.

this here, that there   Avoid using *here* or *there* after *this* or *that*.

NONSTANDARD   This here map is hard to read.
  STANDARD   **This** map is hard to read.

who, which, that   *Who* refers to persons only. *Which* refers to things only. *That* may refer to persons or things.

EXAMPLES   Marcia is the one **who** has the key to the gym.
            The teacher loaned her the key, **which** is the only copy.
            It's also the key **that** opens the storage room.

EXERCISE 4   Identifying Correct Usage

For each sentence below, underline the correct word or words in parentheses.

  EX.   1. The photographer (*which*, <u>*who*</u>) took this photo has an eye for detail.

1. Myra should (*have*, *of*) told us she needed a ride to school.

2. Neither Carmen (*nor*, *or*) Jenna has seen that play yet.

3. We planned to try every ride at the carnival, but after a few rides I began to feel (*nauseous*, *nauseated*).

4. The heavy winds eased (*some*, *somewhat*) by morning.

5. You could (*of*, *have*) told me you had no free time.

6. Mika got some good advice (*from*, *off of*) the veterinarian about how to care for her new dog.

7. Have you ever seen a robot (*that*, *who*) solves math problems?

8. Our new car certainly runs better (*than*, *then*) our old one did.

9. (*That*, *That there*) magazine article described yesterday's earthquake.

10. First choose your topic; (*than*, *then*) write an outline.

11. Because they felt they were being (*persecuted*, *prosecuted*) by the newspaper's reporters, the two executives filed a lawsuit.

12. A (*nauseated*, *nauseous*) smell rose from the compost heap.

13. The attorney did not have enough evidence to (*persecute*, *prosecute*).

14. We can use (*that*, *that there*) bouquet of flowers for a centerpiece.

15. Ramona wants to prepare either chimichangas (*or*, *nor*) enchiladas for the potluck dinner.

THE DOUBLE NEGATIVE

A *double negative* is a construction in which two negative words are used where one is enough.

NONSTANDARD	We did not meet no people on the trail.
STANDARD	We did **not** meet **any** people on the trail.
STANDARD	We met **no** people on the trail.

barely, hardly, scarcely   Do not use *barely, hardly,* or *scarcely* with another negative word.

| NONSTANDARD | There wasn't scarcely any rain this summer. |
| STANDARD | There was **scarcely any** rain this summer. |

the contraction *n't*   Do not use the contraction *n't*, meaning *not*, with another negative word.

NONSTANDARD	I couldn't find no change for the parking meter.
STANDARD	I could**n't** find **any** change for the parking meter.
STANDARD	I could find **no** change for the parking meter.

no, none, not, nothing   Do not use any of these negative words with another negative word.

NONSTANDARD	Amy said she didn't have no more stamps.
STANDARD	Amy said she did**n't** have **any** more stamps.
STANDARD	Amy said she had **no** more stamps.
NONSTANDARD	Although we didn't hear nothing, the dog sensed the stranger at the door.
STANDARD	Although we did**n't** hear **anything,** the dog sensed the stranger at the door.
STANDARD	Although we heard **nothing,** the dog sensed the stranger at the door.

EXERCISE 5   Identifying Correct Usage

In each of the following sentences, underline the correct word or words in parentheses.

EX.   1. Because of her allergies, Layla can't eat (<u>*any*</u>, *no*) dairy products.

1. We heard fire engines, but we couldn't see (*any, no*) smoke.

2. There are hardly (*no, any*) fish in the pond.

3. Now that she has a part-time job, Zina (*has, hasn't*) scarcely any time.

4. Before he moved to Canada, Peter hadn't (*ever, never*) seen snow.

5. They ordered borscht, but the server said there wasn't (*any, none*) left.

6. Our seats were so far from the stage that we (*could, couldn't*) barely hear the music.

7. They searched where the map said the treasure was buried, but they didn't find (*nothing, anything*).

8. I hadn't (*ever, never*) heard of Kwanzaa until Tanya told me about it.

9. Julian said he had not told (*no one, anyone*) about the secret entrance to the cave.

10. Because of the blizzard, there isn't (*any, no*) school today.

EXERCISE 6   Correcting Errors in Usage

In each sentence below, draw a line through the error in usage. Write the correct form above the error.

EX.   1. I have seen scarcely no cardinals this year.

1. We couldn't wait no longer for the latecomers.

2. Mirette wanted to buy mangoes, but the store didn't have none.

3. Do not pay no attention to what your opponent says; instead, watch what he or she does.

4. I haven't never seen a tornado, but I'm not complaining!

5. Tena said that when they moved to the city, they couldn't hardly see any stars at night.

6. Don't never touch a live electrical wire.

7. Zuri tried to find the door, but in the dark she couldn't see nothing.

8. The salesperson says that there aren't no more copies of that video.

9. Leo could not barely wait to read the next chapter in the mystery.

10. Because of the landslide, we cannot use that route no more.

CHAPTER REVIEW

A. Correcting Errors in Usage

In each of the following sentences, draw a line through the error in usage. Write the correct usage in the space above the word.

EX. 1. ~~Being as~~ Akio knows Japanese, we asked him to translate the poem. *(Because)*

1. Professor Plissas often uses historical illusions in her lectures.

2. Where do most of your relatives live at?

3. Lani didn't have no idea the paper was due today.

4. Gary borrowed skates and a hockey stick off Tony.

5. The polenta tastes like it needs some seasoning.

6. Did you know that this movie was adopted from a Broadway play?

7. The police warned the townspeople to be on the lookout for the famous con artist.

8. "Trespassers will be persecuted," the sign said.

9. Shing reads much faster then I do.

10. The senator's speech inferred that the problem would be solved soon.

11. Neither the television or the radio worked when the power failed.

12. We had not scarcely arrived when the performance began.

13. That there building has been vacant for three years.

14. Cheryl feels like she needs warmer clothes.

15. The detective which solved the mystery was promoted.

16. According to reviews, her performance as Juliet is credulous.

17. Every year the alumnae, both male and female, sponsor a rally before the big game.

18. If I had known that the stores were closing early, I would of done my shopping yesterday.

19. After Gloria took the medicine, her headache eased some.

20. Anoki likes roller coaster rides, although they sometimes make him feel nauseous.

21. When we came to the fork in the trail, Geoff said, "This is all the farther I can go."

22. I couldn't find nothing to read while I waited for the plane to arrive.

23. Have you checked to make sure that all the data is correct?

24. When the car's engine overheated, we got some help off of the mechanic.

25. The amount of computers in our school has doubled.

B.   Proofreading a Paragraph for Errors in Usage

In the paragraph below, draw a line through the errors in usage. Write the correct usage in the space above the word. Some sentences may be correct.

EX.   [1] Sook ~~emigrated~~ *immigrated* to the United States when she was eight years old.

[1] Her parents left their country because of political prosecution by the dictatorship in power. [2] In a dictatorship, the political power is either in the hands of one person nor in the hands of just a few people. [3] Under this type of government, people feel as if they have few rights. [4] Life must of been quite difficult for Sook and her family before they emigrated. [5] From what Sook has told me, I've implied that her family is very happy with their new life in this country.

C.   Writing a Newspaper Article

A well-known scientist who graduated from your school is making a return visit to unveil a new invention. No one knows exactly what it is. The scientist, who moved from Russia to the United States when she was quite young, has said only that the invention will greatly change daily life for the average person. You have been chosen to meet the scientist and to get a sneak preview of the product that she will unveil to the public later in the day. Your assignment is to write about your meeting for a local newspaper. The editor wants a description of the invention, along with some background information on the scientist. On your own paper, write a brief article using at least ten of the following words correctly.

from	famous	nothing	amount
illusion	somewhat	adapt	number
emigrant	that	any	as fast as
either . . . or	as if	credulous	alumna
could have	then	creditable	alumni
prosecute	who	imply	data

EX.   *data*
        *After all the data have been studied, scientists believe that Protopov's
        invention is outstanding.*

PLACES AND PEOPLE

21a Capitalize geographical names.

Type of Name	Examples
towns, cities	Rockport, San Juan, Tokyo, Bakersfield, Milan
counties, states	Riverside County, Essex County, North Carolina
countries	Taiwan, Bolivia, Saudi Arabia, Holland, Russia
islands	Tonga Islands, Anguilla, the Cyclades, St. Thomas
bodies of water	Lake Huron, Hudson River, Atlantic Ocean
forests, parks	Muir Woods, National Park, Lincoln Park, Yosemite
streets, highways	Madison Avenue, U.S. Route 66, Interstate 80
mountains	the Sierra Nevada, Mount Fuji, the Catskills
continents	Antarctica, Australia, Europe, North America
regions	the Northwest, the East, East Africa, Southeast Asia

 NOTE Do not capitalize words such as *east, west, north,* or *south* when they indicate direction.

EXAMPLES Maggie's poem was about the hills north of Boston.
The Salinases traveled west on Interstate 80.

 NOTE Do not capitalize the second part of a hyphenated street number.

EXAMPLE West Forty-second Street

21b Capitalize the names of persons.

EXAMPLES Mr. Starbuck, Ms. Hiro, Sasha, Jeannette Rankin, Raoul

Some names contain more than one capital letter. Usage varies in the capitalization of *van, von, du, de la,* and other parts of many multiword names. Always verify the spelling of a name with the person, or check the name in a reference source.

EXAMPLES Mcknight   von Rosenvinge   de la Scale
McKnight   Von Rosenvinge   De La Scale

EXERCISE 1   Correcting Errors in Capitalization

For each sentence below, correct the errors in capitalization by drawing a line through each error and writing the correct form in the space above it.

EX.   1.   Toni Ramírez lives on ~~b~~each ~~s~~treet.   [corrections above: B S]

1.   The irish sea lies between ireland and england.

2.   According to the encyclopedia, mount kilimanjaro is over nineteen thousand feet high.

3.   The cities of Vienna, budapest, and Belgrade lie on the danube river.

4.   The dead sea is very salty.

5.   The fifth largest island in the world is baffin island.

6.   Have you visited mesa verde national park in colorado?

7.   The country of portugal is in the southern part of Europe.

8.   Mr. and Ms. suzuki will be traveling through the west.

9.   The largest county in the United States is los angeles county.

10.   The directions say to turn north on langley road.

EXERCISE 2   Proofreading Sentences for Correct Capitalization

In the sentences below, correct the errors in capitalization by drawing a line through each error and writing the correct form in the space above it. Some sentences may be correct.

EX.   1.   Ms. ~~s~~ilva drove down ~~i~~nterstate 93 to ~~b~~oston.   [corrections above: S I B]

1.   Writer kurt vonnegut was born in indianapolis, indiana.

2.   Gretchen has an apartment on Fifty-Eighth street.

3.   California's mount whitney is almost fifteen thousand feet high.

4.   The oil tanker moved slowly through the persian gulf.

5.   Is big bend national park in texas or alabama?

6.   Hartford, albany, and providence are small cities in the northeast.

7.   The colorado river empties into the gulf of california.

8.   Enormous evergreen trees grow in sequoia national park.

9.   The Southwest is known for its deserts and its big blue skies.

10.   Thailand, vietnam, and laos are all in southeast asia.

SCHOOL SUBJECTS, FIRST WORDS, PROPER ADJECTIVES

21c Do *not* capitalize the names of school subjects, except for names of languages and course names followed by a number.

EXAMPLES   geography   biology   orchestra   government
English   French   Algebra II   Science III

21d Capitalize the first word in every sentence.

EXAMPLE   The famous scientist, Ms. Chien-Shiung Wu, is our neighbor.

The first word of a sentence that is a direct quotation is capitalized even if the quotation begins within a sentence.

EXAMPLE   Tara said, "Some of these Irish songs are really beautiful."

Traditionally, the first word in a line of poetry is capitalized.

EXAMPLES   A white moth circled the bright chandelier
And danced around the flames without any fear.

The pronoun *I* and the interjection *O* are capitalized whether or not they are the first words of sentences. The common interjection *oh* is capitalized only when it begins a sentence or is part of a title.

EXAMPLES   "When can I schedule this work?" asked the dentist.
The folk song began, "Oh, sing me a song of the seafaring life."

21e Capitalize proper nouns and proper adjectives.

A ***common noun*** names any one of a group of people, places, or things. A ***proper noun*** names a particular person, place, or thing. A ***proper adjective*** is formed from a proper noun.

Proper Nouns	Proper Adjectives
Rome	Roman toga
William Shakespeare	Shakespearean drama
Christian Doppler	Doppler principle

NOTE   Proper nouns and proper adjectives may lose their capitals after many years of use.

EXAMPLES   watt   boycott   puritan

EXERCISE 3   Using Capital Letters Correctly

For each sentence below, correct the errors in capitalization by drawing a line through each error and writing the correct form in the space above it.

EX.   1.   Kimberly said, "I just love writing these verses!"

1.   Nico taught us some lovely brazilian folk songs.

2.   The team song began, "o victory, sweet victory."

3.   Will you be taking geometry or algebra I this year?

4.   The first two lines of the poem read

> if you were I and I were you,
>
> what silly things we two might do!

5.   Pauline asked, "just how tall is an alaskan brown bear?"

6.   Marieke wrote a paper about the Aztecs for her Social Studies class.

7.   the balalaika is a russian instrument that is like a mandolin.

8.   This lamp takes three 100-Watt bulbs.

9.   We needed furniture for the set of our play, so i rented some from a local antique store.

10.   We learned some italian art songs in our music class.

11.   oh, what a perfect day for a swim.

12.   My sister Aretha is studying ukrainian in college.

13.   "I have studied latin, but I still can't speak it," said Mr. Robb.

14.   The first line of julia's poem was "at sixteen I learned to speak in confidences and dark allusions."

15.   "Do you want some belgian waffles or some swedish potato pancakes?" asked the waiter.

16.   In english class we studied the poetry of Countee Cullen.

17.   What do you know about roman holidays?

18.   Adrian said, "have you met my girlfriend, Pandora?"

19.   In the mexican restaurant, spanish guitar music played in the background.

20.   have you ever been to Hawaii?

GROUPS, ORGANIZATIONS, AND RELIGIONS

21f **Capitalize the names of teams, organizations, businesses, institutions, buildings, and government bodies.**

Type of Name	Examples
teams	Oakland Athletics Minnesota North Stars
organizations	Oxfam America Buffalo Consumers' League
businesses	Riggs National Bank Seaside Cycle
institutions	Yale University Smithsonian Institution
government bodies	Government Printing Office Cherokee Nation

 NOTE The names of organizations, business, and government bodies are often abbreviated as a series of capital letters. If you are not sure whether to use periods with the abbreviations, look in a dictionary.

EXAMPLES Federal Communications Commission   **FCC**
American Red Cross   **ARC**
United Nations Children's Fund   **UNICEF**
(originally United Nations International Children's Emergency Fund)

 REFERENCE NOTE: Do not capitalize words such as *building, hotel, theater, college, high school, post office*, and *courthouse* unless they are part of a proper name. For more discussion about the differences between common and proper nouns, see page 125.

21 g **Capitalize the names of specific nationalities and peoples.**

EXAMPLES Arab, Portuguese, Latin, American, Caucasian, Asian, Highlander, Iroquois, Shawnee

21h **Capitalize the names of religions and their followers, holy days, sacred writings, and specific deities.**

EXAMPLES Catholicism, Judaism, Muslim, Episcopalian, Rosh Hashana, Easter, Koran, New Testament, Psalms, Dead Sea Scrolls, Bhagavad-Gita, Heavenly Father, Allah, Christ, Shiva

EXERCISE 4   Identifying Correct Capitalization

Write the letter *C* on the line before each phrase that is capitalized correctly.

EX.   _____ 1. a. denver broncos
       __C__   b. Denver Broncos

_____ 1. a. Japanese American   _____ 6. a. Trans World Airlines

_____   b. japanese american   _____   b. Trans World airlines

_____ 2. a. House of Representatives   _____ 7. a. Harvard university

_____   b. House of representatives   _____   b. Harvard University

_____ 3. a. Philadelphia Flyers   _____ 8. a. attending high school

_____   b. Philadelphia flyers   _____   b. attending High School

_____ 4. a. U. S. Coast Guard   _____ 9. a. the Old Testament

_____   b. U. S. coast guard   _____   b. the old testament

_____ 5. a. buddhism   _____ 10. a. jewish scholars

_____   b. Buddhism   _____   b. Jewish scholars

EXERCISE 5   Proofreading Sentences for Correct Capitalization

For each sentence below, correct the errors in capitalization by drawing a line through each error and writing the correct form above it. Some sentences may contain no errors.

EX.   1. There are over two million ɱuslims in the United States.
                                    M

1. Darryl is a troop leader for the boy scouts of america.

2. My sister Estelle now works for the bureau of the census.

3. Yolanda joined the Peace Corps to work in a third-world country.

4. The debate was sponsored by the league of women voters.

5. Is Allan Bristow still coach of the charlotte hornets basketball team?

6. We bought some bleeding hearts and forget-me-nots at silva brothers florists.

7. Does Rico really play tuba with the new york philharmonic?

8. Marc took us to an authentic Sicilian restaurant called leonardo's.

9. On christmas eve we read passages from the new testament.

10. Who founded the hudson's bay company?

REVIEW EXERCISE

A. Identifying Correct Use of Capitalization

For each item below, write the letter of the correct form (a or b) on the line provided.

EX. __a__ 1. a. Colorado River
     b. Colorado river

_____ 1. a. travel east on highway 8
           b. travel east on Highway 8

_____ 2. a. taking Algebra and English
           b. taking algebra and English

_____ 3. a. He said, "Please wait!"
           b. He said, "please wait!"

_____ 4. a. eating Japanese Food
           b. eating Japanese food

_____ 5. a. Oh, I wish I could go!
           b. oh, I wish I could go!

_____ 6. a. attending Westridge high school
           b. attending Westridge High School

_____ 7. a. living on East Twenty-third Street
           b. living on East Twenty-Third Street

_____ 8. a. buy it at Travel Bags to Go
           b. buy it at Travel Bags to go

_____ 9. a. reading about catholicism
           b. reading about Catholicism

_____ 10. a. coach of the Atlanta Falcons
            b. coach of the Atlanta falcons

B. Writing Sentences with Correct Capitalization

On the lines after each of the following items, write a brief sentence using a specific noun for each general noun given (and not at the beginning of the sentence).

EX. 1. team ____My favorite team is the Dallas Cowboys.____

1. aunt _____

   _____

2. business _____

   _____

3. institution _____

   _____

4. religion _____

_____

5. nationality _____

_____

6. town or city _____

_____

7. country _____

_____

8. street _____

_____

9. region _____

_____

10. island _____

_____

11. forest or park _____

_____

12. mountains _____

_____

13. school subject _____

_____

14. a food modified with a proper adjective _____

_____

15. a body of water _____

_____

OBJECTS, EVENTS, AND AWARDS

21i Capitalize the brand names of business products.

The names of the types of products are not capitalized.

EXAMPLES Ritz crackers, Post-It flags, Kleenex tissues

21j Capitalize the names of historical events and periods, special events, and calendar items.

EXAMPLES Great Depression, Fall of Rome, Restoration, Dark Ages, Roaring Twenties, Kentucky Derby, Valentine's Day, Tuesday

21k Capitalize the names of ships, monuments, awards, planets, and any other particular places, things, or events.

Type of Name	Examples
ships, trains	**HMS** *Frolic, Broadway Limited*
aircraft, spacecraft, missiles	*Spitfire, Mariner 4*, **T**itan rocket
monuments, memorials	the **S**phinx, **J**efferson **M**emorial
awards	**E**mmy, **G**uggenheim **F**ellowship
planets, stars, constellations	**S**aturn, **P**hobos, **P**ole **S**tar, **S**corpius

EXERCISE 6 Proofreading Sentences for Correct Capitalization

For each of the following sentences, draw a line through each incorrectly capitalized word, and write the word correctly on the line below the sentence.

EX. 1. How many moons does the planet ~~jupiter~~ have?

  Jupiter

1. Have you ever visited the Washington monument?

  _____

2. The ferry *salem express* rammed a coral reef near Safaga, Egypt, in 1991.

  _____

3. Lupe's computer is a macintosh.

  _____

4. What events led up to the boston tea party?

  _____

5. Mom has both memorial day and veterans day off from work.

_____

6. Someday your reporting work might earn you a pulitzer prize.

_____

7. People often play harmless pranks on april fools' day.

_____

8. F. Scott Fitzgerald was one of the famous writers of the jazz age.

_____

9. The planet venus has a surface temperature of about 887° F.

_____

10. In December of 1987, the Philippine ferry *dona paz* and the oil tanker *victor* collided, killing more than three thousand people.

_____

11. For heroism on the battlefield, my uncle was awarded the medal of honor.

_____

12. Which occurred first, the french revolution or the american revolution?

_____

13. "You will be flying on a boeing 727," the pilot said.

_____

14. In what year was the new york world's fair held?

_____

15. The closest star to our own sun is alpha centauri.

_____

16. The enlightenment was a period of scientific discovery and invention.

_____

17. Last wednesday we viewed the rings of saturn through a telescope at a local observatory.

_____

18. Would you like to contribute money to support the special olympics?

_____

19. Margorie uses only verbatim brand computer diskettes.

_____

20. The constellation pegasus is named for a mythological horse with wings.

_____

TITLES

21l   Capitalize titles.

(1) Capitalize the title of a person when it comes before the person's name.

EXAMPLES   **D**r. Carter G. Woodson founded the Association for the Study of Negro Life and History in 1915.
Did **S**enator Howard Metzenbaum serve on the committee?

(2) Capitalize a word showing a family relationship when the word is used before or in place of a person's name but not when it is preceded by a possessive form.

EXAMPLES   **G**randpa and **A**unt Gwendolyn both play tennis.
Have I introduced you to my cousin Rigoberta?

(3) Capitalize the first and last words and all important words in titles of books, periodicals, poems, short stories, historical documents, movies, television programs, and works of art and music.

Unimportant words in titles include articles (*a, an, the*), coordinating conjunctions (*and, but, for, nor, or, so, yet*), or prepositions of fewer than five letters (*at, for, from, with*).

 NOTE   An article (*a, an,* or *the*) in a title is not capitalized unless it is the first word of the title.

Type of Title	Examples
books	*The Kitchen God's Wife, Searoad*
periodicals	*New York Times, Motor Trend*
poems	"Snake," "Not Waving but Drowning"
short stories	"Araby," "B. Wordsworth"
historical documents	Treaty of Versailles, Mayflower Compact
movies	*Miracle on 34th Street, Hotel Rwanda*
television programs	*Good Morning America, Jeopardy*
works of art	*The Blue Boy, American Gothic*
works of music	"Go Down, Moses," Sonata in E-flat

EXERCISE 7   Proofreading for Correct Capitalization

For each sentence below, correct the errors in capitalization by drawing a line through each error and writing the correct form in the space above it. Some sentences may be correct.

EX.   1. Jaime did a report on the career of ~~a~~dmiral Chester W. Nimitz. *(A)*

1. Financial expert Charles J. Givens wrote *Wealth without risk.*

2. I read an article about Montreal in *national geographic.*

3. My Mom asked Aunt Consuelo to edit the newsletter for her.

4. Langston Hughes wrote the poem "blues at dawn."

5. *The wall street journal* is a popular newspaper among business people.

6. The television series *everybody loves raymond* won Emmy Awards in 2003 and 2005.

7. Have you read Uri Orlev's book *the man from the other side*?

8. Dwight, you can see Dr. Sanchez now.

9. Paulo loves to watch the television show *entertainment tonight.*

10. We heard a moving performance of Brahms's piano concerto no. 2.

11. How many people signed the declaration of independence?

12. Have you seen *star wars, return of the jedi,* or *the empire strikes back*?

13. Thomas Friedman wrote the book *from Beirut to Jerusalem.*

14. The lecture on Indian women writers will be given by Professor Zenobia Battacherya.

15. "The *des moines register* is an excellent newspaper," said Maria.

16. The strategic arms reduction treaty was signed by George Bush and Mikhail Gorbachev.

17. Did uncle Toshiro actually cook dinner for you?

18. Isaac Bashevis Singer wrote a fine short story called "the fatalist."

19. On September 29, 2005, chief justice John G. Roberts, Jr., took his place on the Supreme Court.

20. Carmen Lomas Garza's painting *birthday party for lala and tudi* shows children gathered around a piñata.

CHAPTER REVIEW

A. Correcting Errors in Capitalization

For each sentence below, correct the errors in capitalization by drawing a line through the error and writing the correct form in the space above it.

EX. 1. The ~~p~~etrified ~~f~~orest ~~n~~ational ~~p~~ark is in ~~a~~rizona.
          P   F   N   P   A

1. While in italy, we visited mount etna, an active volcano.

2. Did you say eddie was a cashier at rosie's fajitas?

3. There are two houses in parliament, the governing body of great britain.

4. My Father asked, "did you send that form to the irs?"

5. I would love to see rodin's *the thinker* at a museum.

6. I got information for that report from *the norton anthology of american literature.*

7. My brother Jeremiah bought tylenol at the new stop & shop last saturday.

8. Our neighbors are saving money to visit the great wall of china after thanksgiving.

9. uncle virgil's favorite collection of poems, *the rubáiyát,* was written by omar khayyám.

10. My spanish class meets every friday afternoon at 148 beacon street.

B. Proofreading for Correct Capitalization

Rewrite the paragraph below on your own paper. Correct the errors in capitalization. Some sentences may be correct.

EX. [1] My best friend emilio is from honduras.
    1. My best friend Emilio is from Honduras.

[1] Emilio showed me a photograph of the caribbean sea, which

borders Honduras to the North. [2] His family moved to the united states

two years ago on september 15, which is also independence day in

Honduras. [3] Honduras got its independence from spain in 1821.

[4] among the largest cities in Honduras is Tegucigalpa, which is the

capital. [5] The area where this country lies was first inhabited by the

Mayan civilization. [6] Native people, the lenca, also made homes in this territory. [7] Today Honduras is mainly made up of mestizos and indian people. [8] The country is a republic led by president rafael leonardo callejas romero. [9] The country is governed by the national congress, which has 128 members. [10] Honduras does most of its trading with the United States and is a member of the central american common market.

C.   Writing a Guidebook

You've been asked to write a guidebook for a group of visitors from your town's sister city in Russia. Write an informative booklet of at least fifteen sentences that helps your visitors take a brief walking or driving tour through your town. Include sights and historical points of interest. In your booklet, use at least ten proper nouns and five proper adjectives. Pay special attention to the correct use of capital letters.

EX.   Welcome to Haddington! As you enter this exciting city, you will first want to drive by Haddington City Hall to see the interesting architecture. If you are hungry for a snack, be sure to stop at Guipetto's, the Italian bakery right next door to City Hall. In the bakery you can get Sicilian pizza slices, warm rolls, or sandwiches. After you've had your snack, you can take a drive down Route 83 to Rainbow Lake.

END MARKS

End marks—periods, question marks, and exclamation points—are used to indicate the purpose of a sentence.

22a   A statement (or declarative sentence) ends with a period.

EXAMPLE   Zena is waxing the car**.**

When an abbreviation with a period is written at the end of a sentence, another period is not used as an end mark. However, a question mark or an exclamation point is used as needed.

EXAMPLES   The Méndezes are moving to Broken Arrow, Okla**.**
Are the Méndezes moving to Broken Arrow, Okla**.?**

22b   A question (or interrogative sentence) ends with a question mark.

EXAMPLES   Did you ask for an application**?**
Whose lunch is this**?**

(1) Do not use a question mark after a declarative sentence containing an indirect question.

EXAMPLES   Mara wondered why elephants have tusks.
Billy Ray asked me if I knew how to play chess.

(2) A polite request in question form may be followed by either a period or a question mark.

EXAMPLES   Will you please complete this form**?**
or
Will you please complete this form**.**

(3) If a quotation is a question, place the question mark inside the closing quotation marks. Otherwise, place it outside the closing quotation marks.

EXAMPLES   Mara asked, "Why do elephants have tusks**?"** [The quotation is a question.]
Did you hear me say "I don't know**"?** [The quotation is not a question.]

22c   An *exclamation* ends with an exclamation point.

EXAMPLES   How incredible that game was**!**   Oh my**!**   Wow**!**

(1) An interjection at the beginning of a sentence is usually followed by a comma. It may be followed by an exclamation point for greater emphasis.

EXAMPLES   Hey**,** quiet down**!**   or   Hey**!** Quiet down**!**

(2) If a quotation is an exclamation, place the exclamation mark inside the closing quotation marks. Otherwise, place it outside the closing quotation marks.

EXAMPLES   Della exclaimed, "Ahah**!**" [The quotation is an exclamation.]
I can't believe you said "OK"**!** [The quotation is not an exclamation.]

22d   An imperative sentence may end with either a period or an exclamation point.

EXAMPLES   Please listen to what I have to say**.** [a request]
Be quiet**!** [a command]

Sometimes a command is stated in question form. However, since its purpose is to give a command, it should be followed by an exclamation point.

EXAMPLE   Will you just wait a minute**!**

EXERCISE 1   Correcting Sentences by Adding End Marks

Add the proper end mark to each of the sentences below.

EX.   1. Are we there yet**?**

1. That's amazing

2. Frank asked, "What's for dinner"

3. Whose pile of laundry is this

4. Sarah asked why we don't visit her more often

5. Last night Herb balanced his checkbook

6. Are you going to Yolanda's graduation party

7. This town enforces its speed limits

8. Run, Chester, run

9. Nancy put on her jacket and sped away

10. How is Mr. Joseph's condition today

11. Don't you dare tell

12. Did you hear Laura say, "Thank you"

13. Miriam yelled, "Yikes"

14. Will you just forget it

15. We asked Rudy about his job interview

ABBREVIATIONS

22e   An abbreviation is usually followed by a period.

Abbreviations with Periods	
Personal Names	E. L. Doctorow, Sally K. Ride
Titles Used with Names	Dr., Jr., Sr., Mr., Mrs., Ms.
States	La., Ind., Tenn., Colo.
Organizations and Companies	Co., Inc., Corp., Assn.
Addresses	St., Rd., Ave., P.O. Box, Blvd.
Times	A.M., P.M., A.D., B.C.
Abbreviations Without Periods	
Government Agencies	FBI, CIA, FDA, NASA
State Abbreviations Followed by Zip Code	Ashland, OH 44805 Charlotte, NC 28212
Units of Measure	cm, kg, ml, oz, ft, yd, mi, lb
Widely Used Abbreviations	VCR, PBS, PTA, NAACP, UNICEF

NOTE   Inch(es) is abbreviated *in.* to avoid confusing it with *in,* the preposition. Two-letter state codes are used only when the ZIP Code is included. These state codes are not followed by periods.

EXAMPLES   That board is 22 **in.** long.
Kansas City, **MO** 64131

EXERCISE 2   Proofreading for Correct Punctuation of Abbreviations

In the items below, add or delete periods where needed. Some items may be correct.

EX.   1. 6:45 A.M.

1. Eugene, OR 97404
2. Dr Ivan Ivanovich
3. 12 oz
4. 2 kg.
5. NBA
6. Luisa Gutierrez, DDS
7. SPCA
8. AD 1237
9. Little Rock, Ark
10. State Police Assn

REVIEW EXERCISE

A. Correcting Punctuation in Sentences

In the sentences below, add periods, question marks, and exclamation points where needed.

EX. 1. She addressed the invitation to Dr. Ruth B. Epstein.

1. The 10-lb package was mistakenly shipped to Fargo, N Dak

2. Could you see the lunar eclipse after 10:00 PM

3. After programming the DVR, we recorded our favorite PBS program

4. You should talk to J B Lancer, Jr

5. Why do we have to leave so early for the Howard St station

6. Ace Co, Bravo Assn, and Competent Corp were cited as up-and-coming U S businesses

7. Did Mr Elliott really have an interview with the FBI at 8 A M

8. According to the story I heard, Constance caught a 6-lb trout

9. B J Chee ran the 50-yd dash in under six seconds

10. The letter was addressed to Ms Sally V Shelton

11. We've recently moved to 138 Ash St, Portland, Oreg

12. The FCC issued new rules for cell phones.

13. Dr Fisk said the baby weighed exactly 8 lb at birth

14. The tournament was in Madison, Wis, at the university

15. No Come back later

B. Writing Notes

Suddenly this morning, thousands and thousands of letters, postcards, and packages started falling from the sky! Burying entire streets, houses, and buildings, the mail storm is causing general confusion and panic. You grab your coat and bike helmet and go outside to investigate. You have a notebook and pen in your pocket. Write fifteen sentences about what is happening. Use all three types of end marks in your sentences.

EX. 1. A mail storm is paralyzing the town of Greenville, S.C.

2. Whom is all of this mail for?

COMMAS IN A SERIES

22f   Use commas to separate items in a series.

WORDS   I am going to the lecture with Maurice, Loretta, Candace, and Mauricio.

PHRASES   We put up campaign posters in the main hall, in the cafeteria, in the gym, and near the concession stand.

CLAUSES   The counselor said that I had worked hard, that I had completed all the make-up assignments, and that I could play with the team again.

Some paired words—such as *macaroni and cheese*, or *peanut butter and jelly*—may be considered a single item.

EXAMPLE   Sally had milk, peanut butter and jelly, and carrots for lunch.

(1) When *and, or,* or *nor* joins the last two items in a series, you may omit the comma before the conjunction. Never omit the final comma when doing so may make the sentence unclear.

CORRECT   Computer programming, surfing and croquet are my favorite activities. [The sentence is clear without the final comma.]

INCORRECT   Larissa, Hoy and Warren are my lab partners. [The sentence is unclear without the final comma. It appears as if Larissa is being spoken to.]

CORRECT   Larissa, Hoy, and Warren are my lab partners. [The sentence states clearly that all three are the speaker's lab partners.]

Some writers recommend always using a comma before the conjunction in a series. Follow your teacher's instructions.

(2) If all items in a series are joined by *and, or,* or *nor*, do not separate them with commas.

EXAMPLES   This tablet contains vitamin E **and** vitamin K **and** folic acid.
Would you prefer to ride along the eastern shore **or** the western shore **or** over the hill into Owl Valley?

22g   Use commas to separate two or more adjectives preceding a noun.

EXAMPLES   Luke had a stimulating, eventful, tiring day with his tutor.
Heidi is a steady, experienced, highly skilled golfer.

Proofreading Sentences for the Correct Use of Commas

Insert commas where needed in the sentences below. If a sentence is correct, write C on the line before the sentence.

EX. _____ 1. Green orange and purple are the secondary colors.

_____ 1. On Tuesday, Martin misplaced his books his wallet and his watch.

_____ 2. Every morning, Darren enjoys oatmeal wheat toast with peanut butter and juice.

_____ 3. Before chewing the couch, the puppy ate my slippers my gloves and my brother's hat.

_____ 4. The leaves on the tree are orange and maroon and red.

_____ 5. Marco and Marie named their four children Martha Mary Marsha and Sam.

_____ 6. I'm hungry for breakfast, but I can't decide whether to eat yogurt or eggs and toast.

_____ 7. The decorations committee hung balloons in the cafeteria in the gymnasium and above the lockers in the hall.

_____ 8. Franklin, Yoshi and James are my three best friends.

_____ 9. I'm not sure if we're going to a movie or to a play this Saturday night.

_____ 10. Many of the plays performed at this theater were written by well-known playwrights such as Wasserstein Shepard Stoppard and Mamet.

_____ 11. Exercising three times a week eating a balanced diet and drinking water will bring you good health and well-being.

_____ 12. They say she is a dedicated experienced and energetic leader.

_____ 13. Gary and Ricardo and Che visited Lionel over the weekend.

_____ 14. Nobody knew who the contest winners were when they had been selected or when they would be announced.

_____ 15. My little brother's favorite foods are rice macaroni and cheese and bananas.

_____ 16. The critic hailed the author's latest mystery novel as "Cunning suspenseful wicked and wonderful!"

_____ 17. Go to the corner of West End and 76th Street turn right onto 76th and walk three blocks to our apartment.

_____ 18. Carmen enjoys her classes in history, math, and science.

_____ 19. Thank you for the lovely evening the delicious dinner and the exquisite dessert.

_____ 20. Choose any of these colors: green yellow blue red.

COMMAS WITH COMPOUND INDEPENDENT CLAUSES

22h Use commas before *and, but, for, nor, or, so,* and *yet* when they join independent clauses.

EXAMPLE   Prajit said he enjoyed the book**, but** Adelita said she thought the writing was awkward.

 NOTE   Before *for, so,* and *yet* joining independent clauses, always use a comma. However, before *and, but, nor,* and *or,* the comma may be omitted if the clauses are very short and if there is no possibility of misunderstanding their meanings.

CORRECT   I waited **but** nobody else showed up.
INCORRECT I waited with Clara and Lars and Yoko searched.
CORRECT   I waited with Clara**, and** Lars and Yoko searched.

Do not confuse a compound sentence with a simple sentence that has a compound verb.

SIMPLE SENTENCE   I raked the leaves **and** loaded them into the barrel.
[one independent clause with a compound verb]
COMPOUND SENTENCE   I raked the leaves**, and** I loaded them into the barrel.
[two independent clauses]

 Independent clauses in a series are usually separated by a semicolon. For more about this use of the semicolon, see page 311.

EXERCISE 4   Correcting Compound Sentences by Adding Commas

For each of the following sentences, insert commas where needed. If a sentence is correct, write *C* on the line before the sentence.

EX. _____ 1. Mara folded the towels, and her brother ironed the shirts.

_____ 1. Yukio explained her reasoning but Charles wasn't listening.

_____ 2. The oranges were large and plump yet the apples looked more refreshing.

_____ 3. I called the box office but the concert was already sold-out.

_____ 4. For Thanksgiving we placed extra chairs around the table and everyone felt too crowded.

_____ 5. Una smiled and held out two invitations.

_____ 6. The sculptor did not want the clay to dry so he covered it with a damp cloth.

_____ 7. Everyone was offered a choice of rice or potatoes yet many people asked for couscous.

_____ 8. In the attic, Emily found old letters stored in shoeboxes and she didn't know what to do with them.

_____ 9. Jack usually enjoys ice skating or skiing but the weather is too warm this winter.

_____ 10. Jamal studied the photographer's technique for he wanted to learn the process.

_____ 11. Bob suggests that I plant marigolds around the garden or pests will invade the tomatoes again.

_____ 12. The sky darkened and everyone knew a storm or tornado was approaching.

_____ 13. I baked the potatoes and served them with cottage cheese.

_____ 14. Adele and Ted enjoyed the book but they didn't want to see the film adaptation.

_____ 15. Chad was so tired after two hours of shoveling yet he cleared his neighbor's sidewalk, too.

_____ 16. Juanita read the letter that night and wrote her sister a reply the next morning.

_____ 17. Odessa is a person's name and it is also the name of a place.

_____ 18. Is the Coliseum in Paris or is it in Rome?

_____ 19. Only yesterday Tamisha left on the train yet Phoebe says it feels like weeks have passed since her visit.

_____ 20. The tutor says my work is improving but she thinks I need better study habits.

_____ 21. We looked at the Roman drawings and sculptures and then we stood in line to see the Hermitage collection.

_____ 22. Finally, the children took a nap but they didn't stay asleep for long.

_____ 23. Vanya completed the experiment and developed her notes into a lab report.

_____ 24. The store is only open Monday through Friday but the owner will schedule special appointments for Saturday.

_____ 25. Ivan and Ben spoke different languages yet that was not a barrier to their friendship.

COMMAS WITH NONESSENTIAL ELEMENTS

22i Use commas to set off nonessential participial phrases and nonessential clauses.

A *nonessential* (or *nonrestrictive*) participial phrase or clause is one containing information that is not needed to understand the main idea of the sentence.

NONESSENTIAL PHRASES	The runner**, hampered by the injury,** did not do as well as expected.
	Aretha Cao**, having passed the bar examination,** is now an attorney.
NONESSENTIAL CLAUSES	Joey Fox**, who completed his lap in the relay,** passed the baton beautifully.
	My cousin's farm**, which is in eastern Washington,** is a great place to visit.

Each nonessential clause or phrase in the examples above could be omitted without changing the main idea of the sentence.

EXAMPLES	The runner did not do as well as expected.
	Aretha Cao is now an attorney.
	Joey Fox passed the baton beautifully.
	My cousin's farm is a great place to visit.

An *essential* (or *restrictive*) clause or phrase is not set off by commas because it contains information that is necessary to the meaning of the sentence.

ESSENTIAL PHRASES	The man **feeding the pigeons** did not notice us.
	The film **scheduled for Friday** has been cancelled.
ESSENTIAL CLAUSES	We hired a lawyer **who is named Al Hopkins.**
	Anyone **who solves the puzzle** will win a prize.

Notice how omitting the essential phrase or clause changes the main idea of the sentence.

EXAMPLES	The man did not notice us.
	The film has been cancelled.
	We hired a lawyer.
	Anyone will win a prize.

NOTE   Adjective clauses beginning with *that* are nearly always essential.

       EXAMPLE   Please return the CD **that I lent you last month.**

EXERCISE 5   Correcting Sentences by Adding Commas

For each of the sentences below, identify the italicized phrase or clause by writing *e.* for *essential* or *n.e.* for *nonessential* on the line before the sentence. Insert commas where needed.

EX. __n.e.__ 1. The finch, *watched by the cat* flew to a higher branch.

_____ 1. Monday *which is my sister's birthday* is the first day of school.

_____ 2. The dog *covered with fleas* would not stop scratching.

_____ 3. Alice Munro *who is my favorite author* lives in Canada.

_____ 4. I enjoy a tomato sauce *that tastes fresh and tangy.*

_____ 5. The trout *which had been caught by Uncle Bob* was served for dinner.

_____ 6. After Alisha meets with her accountant *who is our neighbor* she'll file her income taxes.

_____ 7. This park *known for its orchid hybrids* has a new groundskeeper.

_____ 8. I gave Jennie the birthday gift *that her father suggested.*

_____ 9. Any photographs *needing to be framed* must be turned in this morning.

_____ 10. Amanda was determined to learn Spanish, a language *that had always interested her.*

_____ 11. Hector washed his little brother's face *which was covered with peanut butter.*

_____ 12. The staff *excited by the promise of a holiday* worked even harder.

_____ 13. Tell Maxine *that the new movie has a thrilling and complex plot.*

_____ 14. Jasmine *who had excelled in science* has been nominated for a Pulitzer Prize.

_____ 15. Brussels sprouts *which look like tiny cabbages* flourish in cool weather.

_____ 16. The writer *frustrated by the neighbor's loud stereo* did not complete the manuscript on time.

_____ 17. Any detective *who solves the mystery* will be promoted.

_____ 18. My older brother's children *who are named Stefan and Tasha* make me feel young and energetic.

_____ 19. Natalie Beltoya *whose parents are from Belorussia* fluently speaks three languages.

_____ 20. We were amazed that the architect *pressured by construction deadlines* completed the building on schedule.

COMMAS WITH INTRODUCTORY ELEMENTS

22j **Use a comma after certain introductory elements.**

(1) Use a comma after mild exclamations, such as *well* or *why*, and after other introductory words such as *yes* and *no*.

EXAMPLES   **Oh,** didn't you know anyone else was here?
Why, I think I'll just go for a walk.
Yes, you may accompany me if you prefer.

(2) Use a comma after an introductory participial phrase.

EXAMPLES   **Peeking around the corner,** she spied the woman with the briefcase.
Buried in the yard, the iron post began to rust.

(3) Use a comma after two or more introductory prepositional phrases.

EXAMPLES   **In the morning before school,** I practice for my piano lessons.
In the watering can on the shelf beneath the stairs, I've hidden my diary.

 NOTE   A single introductory prepositional phrase does not require a comma unless the phrase is parenthetical or unless the sentence is confusing without the comma.

EXAMPLES   **By Saturday** we will have finished the report. [clear without comma]
By the way, I need to borrow your notes. [The comma is needed because the phrase is parenthetical.]

(4) Use a comma after an introductory adverb clause.

An introductory adverb clause may appear at the beginning of a sentence or before any independent clause in the sentence.

EXAMPLES   **As I look back,** I can see that I made a few mistakes.
I only hope that **when we finally get there,** there will still be some watermelon left.

EXERCISE 6   Proofreading Sentences for Correct Use of Commas

For each of the following sentences, insert commas where needed. If a sentence is correct, write *C* on the line before the sentence.

EX.   _____ 1. On the shelf in the back entry, a clutter of dog leashes, sticks, and frisbees is assembled.

_____ 1. No we do not wish to order dinner yet.

303

_____ 2. Covered completely with dust the bookshelves, cabinets, and chairs revealed neglect.

_____ 3. Hey did you hear Juanita's good news?

_____ 4. Scratching at the carpet the old dog tried to bury an imaginary bone.

_____ 5. On the shelf behind the tureen I've hidden Hank's birthday gift.

_____ 6. When they called I met them at the airport.

_____ 7. After her morning shower Alisha feels alert, awake, and ready to go.

_____ 8. Holding the model in her hands Maxine dreamed about planes she'd fly someday.

_____ 9. Until the rooster crowed not even the cows mooed.

_____ 10. Maybe but let's see what happens next.

_____ 11. In a low valley under a pine tree they finally pitched their tent for the night.

_____ 12. Swinging their arms they happily walked along the beach.

_____ 13. After the first phone call the office jumps to life.

_____ 14. Quick as ever the juggler tossed a dozen tomatoes into the air and caught them.

_____ 15. Dressed in brightly colored costumes we danced in the streets at Mardi Gras.

_____ 16. Yes I got your message.

_____ 17. Anxious that David was late Luis called David's parents.

_____ 18. After the guests had left and throughout the rest of the night they washed dishes.

_____ 19. Well I don't really know what to think.

_____ 20. Having sung the aria the diva left the stage.

_____ 21. At the base of the mountain in a cave a reclusive miner keeps his home.

_____ 22. Thanking all of the volunteers the radio announcer finally ended the fund drive.

_____ 23. Man is it ever cold out here!

_____ 24. Okay but let's meet at the movies anyway.

_____ 25. After she found her tickets Amelia put on her coat, locked the door, and hurried to the airport.

COMMAS WITH OTHER SENTENCE INTERRUPTERS

22k   Use commas to set off elements that interrupt the sentence.

(1) Use commas to set off appositives and appositive phrases.

An *appositive* is a noun or pronoun that follows another noun or pronoun to identify or explain it. An *appositive phrase* consists of an appositive and its modifiers.

EXAMPLES   Young at Heart, **a toy store,** has some part-time openings.
             Both of them, **he and his brother,** helped me fix my ten-speed.

Sometimes an appositive is so closely related to the word preceding it that it should not be set off by commas. Such an appositive is called a *restrictive appositive*.

EXAMPLES   Howie's cat **Arnie** ate all of its supper.
             My partner **Chim** did most of the work.

(2) Use commas to set off words used in direct address.

EXAMPLES   **Ilya,** have you seen my gloves?
             Your car, **Shing,** has the largest bumpers I've ever seen.
             Is there no end to your surprises, **Di?**

(3) Use commas to set off parenthetical expressions.

Parenthetical expressions are remarks that add incidental information or relate ideas to each other.

Commonly Used Parenthetical Expressions		
after all	I believe (hope, etc.)	naturally
at any rate	incidentally	nevertheless
by the way	in fact	of course
consequently	in general	on the contrary
for example	in the first place	on the other hand
for instance	meanwhile	that is
however	morever	therefore

EXAMPLES   **After all,** you did say to make the banner large.
             I did not, **however,** give you permission to use the living room.
             It was the only room large enough for our meeting, **of course.**

Some of these expressions are not always parenthetical. When not used parenthetically, they should not be set off by commas.

EXAMPLES   **In the first place,** we already have a car. [used parenthetically]
He found the ring **in the first place** he looked. [not parenthetical]

 NOTE   A contrasting expression introduced by *not* or *yet* is parenthetical and must be set off by commas.

EXAMPLES   It was at Tammy's birthday party**, not mine,** that you sang for the group.
These boots are tight**, yet not too tight.**

EXERCISE 7   Correcting Sentences by Adding Commas

For each of the sentences below, insert commas where needed. If a sentence is correct, write *C* on the line before the sentence.

EX. _____ 1. In general**,** we try to go to sleep before midnight.

_____ 1. Your cat by the way seems quite friendly.

_____ 2. In fact Victor flew to Moscow last week.

_____ 3. Carole have you seen the book that I was reading?

_____ 4. Frank's mother an engineer likes the household to run smoothly.

_____ 5. Haley's lab partner Terry wrote the conclusion to their report.

_____ 6. Parsley the best-growing plant in our garden is often nibbled to its roots by birds.

_____ 7. Our parakeet Hubert is named after one of our friends.

_____ 8. I wonder Tom when you'll bring us good news.

_____ 9. That shade of purple looks terrific on you Latisha.

_____ 10. Nevertheless Jeff Brown the class president asked for a vote recount.

_____ 11. For example I study after school with Jamal a math tutor.

_____ 12. Naturally our Labrador Chester didn't feel well after eating that many treats.

_____ 13. Marjoram tastes sweet yet slightly pungent when simmered with tomatoes.

_____ 14. My brother said, "Nick you need a haircut."

_____ 15. I framed the photo I took of my mother's cat Gertrude.

OTHER USES OF COMMAS

22l Use a comma to separate items in dates and addresses.

EXAMPLES I was born on Friday, **July 1, 1990,** in this small hospital. Write to me at 109 Sun St., **Oak Creek, WI 53154,** after the first of March.

Notice that commas are not placed between the month and the day, between the house number and the street name, or between the two-letter state code and the ZIP Code. Notice also that a comma separates the final item in a date and in an address from the words that follow it.

22m Use a comma after the salutation of a friendly letter and after the closing of any letter.

EXAMPLES Dear Moira,   Yours sincerely,

22n Use a comma before an abbreviation such as *Jr., Sr.,* or *M.D.* following a name and also after the abbreviation when the name and the abbreviation are used together in a sentence.

EXAMPLES Reynard Lincoln, **M.D.**
Albert Smith, **Jr.,** has the same birthday as my dad.

22o Do not use unnecessary commas.

Use a comma only when a rule requires one or if the meaning is unclear without one.

INCORRECT The movie camera that takes 16mm film and needs no batteries, is the one I used. [*Camera* is the subject; it must not be separated from its verb *is*.]

CORRECT The movie camera that takes 16mm film and needs no batteries is the one I used.

EXERCISE 8 Correcting Sentences by Adding Commas

For each of the following sentences, insert commas where needed. If a sentence is correct, write *C* on the line before the sentence.

EX. _____ 1. He addressed the invitation to Harry Gillespie Jr.

_____ 1. After writing the letter, she signed it, "Sincerely yours Odessa."

_____ 2. Isn't that Frank Sinatra Jr. singing that song?

_____ 3. My dental appointment is on Monday February 13 2008.

_____ 4. He lived at 110 Cactus Court Albuquerque New Mexico for ten years.

_____ 5. Louis Sr. visited Louis Jr. in Farmington last week.

_____ 6. Someone that you haven't heard from in a while called today.

_____ 7. The invitation read, "Dear Alani Please join us for dinner on Saturday."

_____ 8. The socks that you gave me for my birthday are warm and soft.

_____ 9. Arthur Lewitt Jr. has the same birthday as I do.

_____ 10. A young researcher made the discovery at the University of Rochester in Rochester New York.

_____ 11. Seattle Washington is still considered a desirable place to live.

_____ 12. I heard that Sharon arrives next Saturday March 14.

_____ 13. Her business cards read, "Tina Nakai J.D."

_____ 14. He wrote a letter of complaint to 22 Stratosphere Lane, Jupiter.

_____ 15. We arrived late at the graduation of Helen Carter M.D. Ph.D.

_____ 16. On August 21 2008 we had a wonderful picnic.

_____ 17. Our son Victor Reynosa Jr was born on March 17 1977.

_____ 18. The sign above the doorbell read, "Janet Washington M.D."

_____ 19. The nearest fruit market is located at Highway 30 Racine Wisconsin.

_____ 20. Put the bill and your check in an envelope, and mail them to the electric company.

_____ 21. The boy in our class named Ivan is from Moscow.

_____ 22. Our next meeting will be at 30 Cedar Street Davenport IA 52803.

_____ 23. Did you know that Derek Maddox Jr. made the varsity team?

_____ 24. The store no longer stocks the shampoo that I usually buy.

_____ 25. After turning right at the corner, you'll find 500 Main Street Eugene Oregon on your left.

CHAPTER REVIEW

A. Proofreading Sentences for Correct Punctuation

For each of the following sentences, insert commas and end marks where needed. Draw a line through any commas or periods that are unnecessary. If a sentence is correct, write C on the line before the sentence.

EX. __C__ 1. Wide-eyed, eager, and alert, we began our great adventure.

_____ 1. Quick throw the ball to Hank

_____ 2. Una played the flute and the violin and the drums.

_____ 3. Charles Washington Jr my neighbor lives down the block at 7500 Paulina Street

_____ 4. She signed the letter, "Yours truly Veronica I Smith."

_____ 5. Was she born on March 1 2007 or March 7 2001

_____ 6. The talk show guest who was a famous athlete announced his retirement, and spoke of his future plans.

_____ 7. Karen ironed her shirts pants and skirts; and Misha her husband folded the last load of clothes from the dryer.

_____ 8. Hot, and sweaty, and tired they pulled dozens of weeds from the garden

_____ 9. Taking the bench the judge looked at the jury cleared his throat and asked if they had reached a decision yet.

_____ 10. Do you know if F.B.I. stands for Federal Bureau of Investigation

_____ 11. She wondered if Stefan heard her but he didn't.

_____ 12. After our visit to Grandma's farm, the city's smog seemed thicker.

_____ 13. Ms Schumann a promising scientist prefers to spend her holidays reading adventure novels

_____ 14. Running ahead of the other dogs the boxer caught the stick that I threw

_____ 15. Well you could have fooled me

_____ 16. Eager to be at sea the young men volunteered their services aboard the steamer *Argos* and they leave tomorrow.

_____ 17. For example if Jim Jr comes home early you can bet soccer practice will be cancelled

_____ 18. Energetic and strong the gymnast who was last year's silver medalist won the gold

_____ 19. Henry before those muffins burn take the pan out of the oven

_____ 20. The sweater that I bought yesterday is too large.

B. Proofreading a Paragraph for Correct Punctuation

In the paragraph below, add end marks and commas where needed. Draw a line through any punctuation marks that are misplaced. If a sentence is correct, write C on the line before the sentence.

EX. _____ [1] What is so unusual about bonsai those small trees**?**

_____ [1] Bonsai small ornamental trees, are grown in low shallow pots.

_____ [2] Very slow growers they are shaped over a long period of time

_____ [3] For example one of the bonsai a dwarf maple is over fifty years

old. ___.___ [4] Some bonsai if cared for tenderly, and properly live to be

hundreds of years old _____ [5] These bonsai, passed down from one

generation to another, are rare and valuable.

C. Working Cooperatively to Write a Report

You are a copywriter for Educational Toys, Inc. You have been asked to create a game based on a school subject. Work with a partner to write a brief report of at least ten sentences to explain your ideas. Use a variety of end marks, and include commas where needed. If you use abbreviations, punctuate them correctly.

Use the answers to the questions below in your report.

    —What school subject is the game based on?
    —What is the name of the game?
    —What is the object of the game?
    —What are the rules?
    —What, if any, playing pieces, boards, cards, or other materials or equipment is used?

EX. Our game, called "Socko Science!", is based, obviously, on the subject of science. In this game, for both lovers and nonlovers of science, players form teams and search the rain forest for the cure to the common cold.

SEMICOLONS AND COLONS

23a **Use a semicolon between closely related independent clauses if they are not joined by *and, but, for, nor, or, so,* or *yet.***

EXAMPLE   Bill had won his heat; he caught his breath and drank some water before the finals.

23b **Use a semicolon between independent clauses joined by a conjunctive adverb or transitional expression which is followed by a comma.**

EXAMPLE   Hannah decided not to braid her hair; **instead,** she wore a bun.
Gene tuned his car's engine; **as a result,** his gas mileage is better.

23c **Use a semicolon (rather than a comma) between independent clauses joined by a coordinating conjunction when the clauses contain commas.**

EXAMPLE   To prepare for the meeting, Andy arranged the chairs around the conference table; he laid a fresh notepad, a pencil, and a cup of water at each place; and then he set up a microphone for the speaker, Mr. Foster Kern of the Tennessee Industrial Council.

23d **Use a colon before a list of items, especially after such expressions as *as follows* and *the following.***

EXAMPLES   For her talk to the class, Rebecca planned to use several visual props: the chalkboard, two posters, and a short video.
Those applying for the trade school scholarship must submit **the following:** a completed application form, two letters of reference, and photographs or samples of their best work.

23e **Use a colon before a long, formal statement or quotation.**

EXAMPLE   Although Mom was so surprised that she could hardly speak, she finally said: "Thank you all for coming and making my fortieth birthday so special. I love you all. And thank you, whoever planned this surprise party for me. I am just so touched by all of this."

23f **Use a colon between independent clauses when the second clause explains or restates the idea of the first, or between a title and its subtitle.**

EXAMPLES   Davie and many of his friends were late for school: They were on their way when the school bus's transmission seized up, and then they had to wait for another bus to pick them up.
Genealogy: A Practical Research Guide [book title]

EXERCISE 1   Proofreading Sentences for Correct Use of Semicolons and Colons

The sentences below are missing semicolons and colons. In each sentence, write the missing punctuation mark where it is needed. Some sentences may be correct.

EX.   1. Terence said nothing; he didn't want to give any hints about the surprise party.

1. Sandi decided to cut her hair it had started to hang over her eyes.

2. The coach called a time out, and he told the team which play to run then he sent in a substitute for Kramer.

3. Donna is no longer on the cheerleading squad instead, she stays after school to catch up on her classwork.

4. We rarely buy bread anymore we have been making it ourselves at home.

5. Paquito put on an apron, hot mitt, and chef's hat then he asked us if we wanted red, orange, or green peppers in our omelettes.

6. Their book was titled *Dimensions of Tolerance: What Americans Believe About Civil Liberties.*

7. When you arrive at Camp Winnebago, be sure you have brought the following items towels, shampoo, insect repellent, rain gear.

8. The burglar seemed to know exactly where the alarm system was how he knew is still a mystery.

9. Feeling tired, I took a hot bath I had a light snack and I went to bed early.

10. Dorotea was staying up all night her government term paper was due the next day, and she had barely begun to work on it.

11. I am certainly much too clumsy to perform in public nevertheless, I enjoy dancing so much that I had to audition.

12. "Your oral reports will be graded on the following points organization, clarity, completeness, and audience interest," the teacher informed us.

13. Mr. Mori said "Ladies and gentlemen, we are here tonight to honor a distinguished co-worker and longtime friend."

14. Mario invited me to his house he's got a new math game for his computer.

15. Kibbe loved his home however, he also wanted to visit new places.

OTHER MARKS OF PUNCTUATION

23g Use a dash to indicate an abrupt break in thought.

EXAMPLES   She said we were going to a tea party—a tea party!
            Now Stephan, you know—and we've been over this before—
            that your homework is your responsibility.

23h Use a dash to mean *namely*, *in other words*, *that is*, and similar expressions that come before an explanation.

EXAMPLE   I made this cake for the reason I told you—tomorrow is Katrina's
           birthday.

23i Use parentheses to enclose informative or explanatory material of minor importance.

EXAMPLES   We drove to the beach (it was the first sunny day in weeks) with
            high hopes.
            As we passed through the valley (formed eons ago by a long-
            dead river), we were still playing "Twenty Questions."

23j Use ellipsis points (. . .) to mark omissions from quoted material and pauses in a written passage.

(1) If the quoted material that comes before the omission is not a complete sentence, use three ellipsis points with a space before the first point.

EXAMPLE   De Luca writes, "I never felt threatened . . . when confronted by
           a great white shark."

(2) If the quoted material that comes before the omission is a complete sentence, keep the end mark and add the ellipsis points.

EXAMPLE   De Luca writes, "I never felt threatened . . . when confronted by
           a great white shark. . . . It could have been fatal. But I was
           careful."

(3) If one or more than one sentence is omitted, the ellipsis points follow the end mark that precedes the omission.

EXAMPLE   De Luca writes, "I never felt threatened . . . when confronted by
           a great white shark. . . . But I was careful."

(4) To indicate a pause in a written passage, use three ellipsis points with a space before the first point.

EXAMPLE   "Well, . . . I guess I could try," Marc replied.

NOTE You may use other punctuation on either side of the ellipsis points if it helps to make sense of what has been omitted.

EXAMPLES   For example, . . . do not fold the cover.
Joel wrote . . . "we should all be proud."

(5) To show that a full line or more of poetry has been omitted, use an entire line of spaced periods.

EXAMPLE   A lupine, strong and tall
Stands proudly by the wall
. . . .
never could I pluck it

Note that the line of periods is as long as the line of poetry above it.

EXERCISE 2   Correcting Sentences with Dashes, Parentheses, and Ellipsis Points

In the sentences below, correct each error in punctuation by marking a caret (∧) and writing the missing punctuation mark above it.   (   )

EX.   1. Be sure to use the proper form for your letter. ∧See page 27.∧

1. Vincente considered. "Well, . . I'm not so sure about that."

2. I said that what was mine was hers not that I had much to give.

3. The author made one character say, "Yipes . . . Now I have nowhere to go!"

4. The first people in North America the people Columbus called "Indians" lived on both coasts and everywhere in between.

5. The new rule is you probably already heard this everyone has to wear a white shirt.

6. Dr. Seuss his real name was Theodor Geisel also wrote under the pseudonym Theo. LeSieg.

7. The quarterback I can't think of his name threw six touchdown passes.

8. Former senator John Glenn Ohio first gained fame as an astronaut.

9. "I think I hear . . something in the basement," Tal whispered.

10. Some of the other students Lula and Esteban, for example have already begun their third project.

UNDERLINING (ITALICS)

Italics are printed characters that slant to the right. To indicate italics in handwritten or typewritten work, use underlining.

23k **Underline (italicize) titles of books, plays, periodicals (magazines and newspapers), films, television programs, works of art, long musical compositions, trains, ships, aircraft, and spacecraft.**

Type of Name	Examples
Books	*The Fixer, Rabbit at Rest*
Plays	*Driving Miss Daisy, The Piano Lesson*
Periodicals	*Sacramento Bee, New Republic*
Films	*Iron Will, Beauty and the Beast*
Television Programs	*The Today Show, The Tonight Show*
Works of Art	*No. 1: The Artist's Mother, The Storm*
Long Musical Compositions	*Third Symphony, Pagliacci*
Trains	*Century Limited, City of New Orleans*
Ships	USS *Lexington, Lusitania*
Aircraft	*Graf Zeppelin, Enola Gay*
Spacecraft	*Odyssey, Voyager 2*

NOTE Italicize the title of a poem only if the poem is long enough to be published in a separate volume. Such long poems are usually divided into titled or numbered sections. The titles of these sections are enclosed in quotation marks.

23l **Underline (italicize) foreign words as well as words, letters, and figures referred to as such.**

EXAMPLES   There are two *a*'s and two *e*'s in *separate*.
I can't tell whether this is an *a* or an *e*.
The abbreviation *etc.* stands for the Latin words *et cetera*, which mean "and so on."

EXERCISE 3   Correcting Sentences with Underlining (Italics)

In the sentences below, underline each word or item that should be italicized.

    EX.   1. I guess Chaucer's <u>Canterbury Tales</u> is the longest poem I've ever read.

1. It's rare for a motion picture to win the Academy Awards for Best Actor, Best Director, and Best Picture, as Ben-Hur did, isn't it?

2. My favorite Frank Sinatra album is Strangers in the Night. What's yours?

3. When I want to watch reruns of old television shows, I always look for Bewitched.

4. The musical play The Wiz was based on the film The Wizard of Oz.

5. My neighbor Bill Neibergall is a photographer for the Des Moines Register.

6. The first steam-powered ship to cross the Atlantic was the Savannah in 1818.

7. Fraktur is the German name for the fancy typeface that somewhat resembles Gothic script.

8. My dad and I watch 60 Minutes together, but we skip the commercials.

9. I plan to read The Age of Innocence before I see the film version.

10. There's a reproduction of Trumbull's painting The Declaration of Independence in my civics book.

11. The world's largest submarine, the USS Triton, is over thirty years old.

12. What have you learned about Michael Collins, one of the astronauts on Apollo 11?

13. Can you tell me the difference between whoever and whomever?

14. This book, What Color is Your Parachute, is about getting a job, but it also helps you learn about yourself.

15. The movie Beethoven's 2nd uses a 2, not two, in the title.

16. If you were famous, would you rather have your picture on the cover of Life or the National Enquirer?

17. If you think the play Cats is popular, you should know that A Chorus Line had more than six thousand performances on Broadway.

18. I heard someone joke, "Either you liked the movie Wayne's World, or you're an adult."

19. Although it has no rhyme, Homer's epic Iliad is written in verse.

20. My three-year-old sister Uma called her clay blob Penguins at School.

APOSTROPHES

23m Use an apostrophe to form the possessive of nouns and some pronouns.

(1) To form the possessive of a singular noun, add an apostrophe and an *s*.

EXAMPLES   the teacher**'s** pencil   Franklin**'s** clarinet
           the desk**'s** surface   love**'s** simplicity

NOTE   To form the possessive of a singular noun ending in an *s* sound, add only an apostrophe if the noun has two or more syllables and if adding '*s* will make the word awkward to pronounce. Otherwise, add '*s*.

     EXAMPLES   Mars**'s** atmosphere   Thomas**'s** vest
                amaryllis**'** scent   for goodness**'** sake
                Odysseus**'** travels   Paris**'** museums

(2) To form the possessive of a plural noun ending in *s*, add only the apostrophe.

EXAMPLES   the planets**'** orbits   the Mosses**'** house
           maple trees**'** roots   the Wildcats**'** locker room

The few plural nouns that do not end in *s* form the possessive by adding '*s*.

EXAMPLES   teeth**'s** enamel   children**'s** story hour

NOTE   Do not use an apostrophe to form the plural of a noun.

     INCORRECT   Some of these nail's are bent.
      CORRECT   Some of these **nails** are bent.

(3) Do not use an apostrophe with possessive personal pronouns or with the possessive pronoun *whose*.

INCORRECT   Do you know it's weight?   That pen is her's.
 CORRECT   Do you know **its** weight?   That pen is **hers**.

(4) To form the possessive of an indefinite pronoun, add an apostrophe and an *s*.

EXAMPLES   **Everyone's** dog must be leashed.
            I want to see **everybody's** essay on time.

Form the possessive of such forms as *anyone else* and *somebody else* by adding an apostrophe and an *s*.

EXAMPLES   anyone else**'s**   anybody else**'s**   someone else**'s**

☞   **REFERENCE NOTE:**   For more information about pronouns, see page 127.

(5) To form the possessive of a hyphenated word, the name of an organization or a business firm, or a word in a group showing joint possession, add 's or an apostrophe only to the last word.

EXAMPLES   mother-in-law**'s** apartment   Acme Hardware**'s** sale
            Lewis and Clark**'s** expedition   Jagger and Richard**'s** song

(6) To show individual possession of similar items by each noun in a word group, add 's or an apostrophe only to each noun in the group.

EXAMPLE   Jared**'s**, Dalila**'s**, Jewel**'s**, and Paco**'s** campaign posters were all convincing.

(7) Use an apostrophe to form the possessive of words that indicate time or that indicate an amount in cents or dollars.

EXAMPLES   five **minutes'** rest   a full **day's** work
            a **year's** time   a **dollar's** worth

EXERCISE 4   Forming Possessive Nouns and Pronouns

Each group of words below expresses possession by means of a prepositional phrase. On your own paper, rewrite each word group to express the same possession using a possessive noun or pronoun instead of a preposition.

EX.   1. blare of the trumpets
       1. *trumpets' blare*

1. march of the toy soldiers
2. the hat of Charles
3. the lunch box of whom
4. the house of them
5. the office of Stone & Rock Co.

6. a guess of someone
7. the drawings of Sheila and Bill
8. food for the cats
9. plans of someone else
10. honks of the geese

QUOTATION MARKS

23n **Use quotation marks to enclose a *direct quotation*—a person's exact words. A direct quotation always begins with a capital letter.**

EXAMPLES   Sal said, **"**Help me carry these books, guys.**"**
The president began, **"**My fellow Americans . . .**"**

Do not use quotation marks for an ***indirect quotation.***

DIRECT QUOTATION   Nellie asked, **"**May I go?**"** [Nellie's exact words]
INDIRECT QUOTATION   Nellie asked if she could go. [not Nellie's exact words]

23o **When an expression such as *he said* divides a quoted sentence into two parts, the second part begins with a small letter.**

EXAMPLE   "I hope," Maria said, **"**that you remembered the binoculars."

If the second part of a divided quotation is a new sentence, a period (not a comma) follows the interrupting expression. The second part then begins with a capital letter.

EXAMPLE   "Tranh will come tomorrow," Hale said**.** **"**He's taking his father to the airport."

NOTE   An interrupting expression is not part of a quotation, so it should never be located inside the quotation marks.

INCORRECT   "Kayla, Mom called, have you done your chores?"
CORRECT   "Kayla,**"** Mom called, **"**have you done your chores?"

23p **Separate a direct quotation from the rest of a sentence with a comma, a question mark, or an exclamation point, but not with a period.**

EXAMPLES   "If you want to help**,"** Chika said, "you'll have to be quieter."
"Will you join me at the show**?"** Willis asked.
"Hold on**!"** Juana exclaimed.

23q **Always place commas and periods inside the closing quotation marks.**

EXAMPLE   "No**,"** Nori said, "I've never acted before. But I know I'll be a good performer**."**

23r **Always place colons and semicolons outside the closing quotation marks.**

EXAMPLE   Tai Kwong said, "We are really desperate**";** they still hadn't found enough workers for the science fair.

23s **Place question marks and exclamation points inside the closing quotation marks only if the quotation is a question or an exclamation. Otherwise, place them outside the closing quotation marks.**

EXAMPLES   "Who is the current prime minister of Canada**?**"
            Sarah yelled, "Out**!**"
            Did I hear you say, "Cab Calloway"**?**
            Don't you tell me, "No"**!**

Notice in the last two examples given above that the end mark belonging with each quotation has been omitted. In a question or an exclamation that ends with a quotation, only the question mark or exclamation point is necessary, and it is placed outside the closing quotation marks.

23t **When writing *dialogue* (a conversation), begin a new paragraph each time the speaker changes, and enclose each speaker's words in quotation marks.**

EXAMPLE   "Hey!" Paula said. "This ad in the paper says that there is going to be a sale at all the stores in the mall."
           "Oh my gosh!" exclaimed Fay. "I have to go."
           "You are always so interested in shopping," scolded Paula. "Why do you love shopping so much?"
           Fay answered, "Paula, you love it as much as I do."

23u **Use single quotation marks to enclose a quotation within a quotation.**

EXAMPLES   Leonard said, "Don't forget. You said, 'Leonard, I promise to take you to the library when we're finished here.'" [Notice that the period is placed inside the single quotation mark.]
            "What does he mean by saying, 'Last name first, first name, middle initial'?" Nadia asked. [Notice that the question mark is placed inside the double quotation marks, not the single quotation marks, because the words in the single quotation marks do not ask a question.]

23v **Use quotation marks to enclose titles of short works, such as short stories, short poems, essays, articles, songs, episodes of television series, and chapters and other parts of books.**

Type of Title	Examples
Short Stories	"Mother and Daughter"
Short Poems	"The Highwayman"
Essays	"Dream Children"
Articles	"Driver's Ed"
Songs	"Unforgettable"
TV Episodes	"The Confidence Mystery"
Parts of Books	"Speaking and Listening Workshop"

EXERCISE 5   Correcting Sentences with Quotation Marks and Other Punctuation

In the sentences below, correct each error in punctuation by marking a caret ( ) and writing the missing punctuation mark above it. Some sentences may require no change.

EX.   1. I have trouble understanding geometry, Ralph said.

1. Our teacher read us Bacon's essay entitled Gardens.

2. Coach, said Adrian please explain your strategy once more

3. The referee yelled Break it up

4. The firefighter came on the radio and asked Where's the fire

5. Did Luna really say The dog ate my homework

6. Stop asking questions yelled Ms. Stamos, exasperated.

7. The artist said, The sunshine is beautiful; it is reflecting magically off the water.

8. Let me come begged Joe, and I will help with the work—and the food!

9. Surely you are joking said the principal sternly

10. Kichi said, My favorite poem is My Mother Pieced Quilts.

EXERCISE 6   Proofreading Sentences

In the sentences below, correct each error in punctuation by marking a caret ( ) and writing the missing punctuation mark above it. Some sentences may require no change.

EX.   1. "Let me practice my speech for you," she said

1. The announcer said I asked Nancy Kerrigan What's the most important skill for a skater

2. The title of this story, The Moustache, really interests me.

3. Bill, come here quickly yelled Magda. The birds are building a nest.

4. The pirate growled Tell me the secret

5. Did your grandmother always say to you, Eat your vegetables!

6. Buying a lottery ticket, Ken said Sometimes you win; but I say, "not very often.

7. Tammy's best friend Hilda asked her What did you mean when you told Guido Hilda's getting to be a pest

8. This is serious said our mother, and I will not tolerate any joking.

9. The census taker inquired, What's your name

10. Who's your daddy asked the little girl

11. Was it James Hurst asked Matti who wrote The Scarlet Ibis?

12. What would you think about a song called Don't Worry. Be Happy?

13. Julio declared that lacrosse was his game.

14. Well drawled the impersonator, who do you think I'm supposed to be

15. Excuse me she said, clearing her throat. Is there any chance you could supply us with menus?

CHAPTER REVIEW

A. Correcting Sentences by Adding Punctuation Marks

In each of the sentences below, add the correct punctuation where needed. Some sentences may require no change.

EX. 1. "The parade is rescheduled for next Saturday," said the mayor

1. Is that James' or the Joneses rake?
2. I think this is its best machine yet.
3. Does everyones lunch have a raw vegetable and a piece of fruit?
4. The Bureau of Indian Affairs news release was important.
5. I'd say that's a good weeks work" she estimated.
6. "So . . ," the questioner began, "you say you did not arrive until 7:12 P.M.
7. To decide whether to write a or an, think about the way in which the next word is spelled and pronounced.
8. The artistry of The Persistence of Memory is not only in the painting but also in the name.
9. At a museum we saw a life-size replica of the Spirit of St. Louis, Charles nicknamed "Lucky" Lindbergh's famous airplane.
10. I always fall asleep just before Entertainment Tonight comes on the television.
11. How many u's are in vacuum?
12. I'm sure you've heard the overture to Rossini's opera William Tell.
13. My stepbrothers car needs new upholstery and new tires.
14. The womens locker room looks just like the mens.
15. Hey Corinne asked Why did that man name his boat Elvis

B. Proofreading a Paragraph for Errors in Punctuation

Working with a partner, use proofreading marks to correct the punctuation errors in the following paragraph.

EX. [1] The book <u>Youth: Transition to Adulthood</u> was published in 1974.

[1] James S Coleman, a sociologist from the University of Chicago, chaired

the Panel on Youth, which wrote this book. [2] The panel asked itself an

enormous question How are young people brought into adulthood in the U S

[3] In an agricultural society, children work with adults one can see examples

in Little House on the Prairie and many other books. [4] With industrialization, children have become more isolated from family for work, being done mostly in the city, is isolated from family life. [5] Children do not learn as often the work of their parents childrens futures are no longer determined by their parents occupations. [6] A striking fact of modern times is that, besides their parents and teachers, children have less contact with adults. [7] The group feels age segregation had its benefits it freed adults to work more efficiently and protected children from dangerous workplaces.

[8] However, children now have less opportunity to learn what adult life is like adults have less opportunity to enjoy being with children there is less sharing of activities less discussion and consequently less understanding between generations. [9] The panel suggested that the costs of age segregation see chart are higher than the benefits. [10] They suggest we ask if schools are the only places in which young people can learn to work their answer is No

C. Writing an Announcement

Your class is sponsoring a used-book sale. You have been chosen by the class president to write an announcement about the sale, to be published in a community newsletter. Decide what information to include in your announcement by answering the *5W-How?* questions. (See page 8 for more information about these prewriting questions.) Then write an announcement ten sentences long. Use at least three types of punctuation marks discussed in this chapter.

EX.   Announcing a Bargain Book Sale!

Come to Fulton High School cafeteria on Saturday, May 10, at 10:00 A.M.

THE DICTIONARY

A dictionary entry is divided into several parts. Study the parts of the following sample dictionary entry.

cop•y (käp´ē), *n., pl.* cop'ies [Middle English < *copie;* Medieval Latin < *copia;* Latin *copia,* plenty] **1.** a thing made just like another; an imitation; a reproduction [a *copy* of the original] **2.** [Now Rare] a model to be imitated, as of penmanship **3.** any of a number of items, e.g. books or magazines, printed from identical plates [a *copy* of the March issue] —*vt., vi.* cop'ied, cop'y•ing **1.** to make one or more copies of; reproduce; transcribe [*copy* a page] **2.** to imitate [*copy* his gestures] —copy•ist, *n.*

SYN. reproduction, duplicate *ANT.* original

1. **Entry word.** The entry word shows the correct spelling of a word. An alternate spelling may also be shown. The entry word shows how the word should be divided into syllables and may also show whether the word should be capitalized.
2. **Pronunciation.** The pronunciation is shown using accent marks, phonetic symbols, and diacritical marks. Each *phonetic symbol* represents a specific sound. *Diacritical marks* are special symbols placed above letters to show how those letters sound.
3. **Part-of-speech labels.** These labels are usually abbreviated and show how the entry word should be used in a sentence. A word may be used as more than one part of speech. In such cases, a part-of-speech label is given before the set of definitions that matches each label.
4. **Other forms.** Sometimes a dictionary shows principal parts of verbs, spellings of plural forms of nouns, or the comparative forms of adjectives and adverbs.

5. **Etymology.** The *etymology* tells how a word or its parts entered the English language. It also shows how the word has changed over time.
6. **Definitions.** If the word has more than one meaning, its definitions are numbered or lettered.
7. **Sample usage.** Some dictionaries include sample phrases to illustrate particular meanings of words.
8. **Special usage labels.** These labels identify how a word is used (*Slang*), how common a word is (*Rare*), or how a word is used in a special field, such as botany (*Bot.*).
9. **Related word forms.** These are forms of the entry word created by adding suffixes or prefixes. Sometimes dictionaries also list common phrases in which the word appears.
10. **Synonyms and antonyms.** Words similar in meaning are *synonyms*. Words opposite in meaning are *antonyms*. Many dictionaries list synonyms and antonyms at the end of some word entries.

EXERCISE 1   Using a Dictionary

Use a dictionary to answer the questions below.

EX.   1. How many syllables are in the word *provincial*? _____three_____

1. How is the word *momentarily* divided into syllables? _____

2. What is the spelling for the plural form of *potato*? _____

3. What are three different meanings for the word *pound*? _____

    _____

4. What is the past tense of *defy*? _____

5. What is the etymology of the word *muckraker*? _____

    _____

EXERCISE 2   Writing Words with Alternate Spellings

For each of the words below, write the alternate spelling on the line after the word.

EX. 1. disc ___disk___

1. theater   _____   4. encyclopedia _____

2. valor   _____   5. synagogue   _____

3. blamable   _____

SPELLING RULES

---

ie and *ei*

24a   Write *ie* when the sound is long *e*, except after *c*.

EXAMPLES   believe, piece, field, receive, conceit, perceive
EXCEPTIONS   weird, either, seize, leisure, neither, species

24b   Write *ei* when the sound is not long *e*, especially when the sound is long *a*.

EXAMPLES   freight, weigh, veil, heir, forfeit
EXCEPTIONS   mischief, conscience, view, friend, science, pie

–cede, *–ceed*, and *–sede*

24c   The only word ending in *–sede* is *supersede*. The only words ending in *–ceed* are *exceed*, *proceed*, and *succeed*. All other words with this sound end in *–cede*.

EXAMPLES   accede, concede, recede, precede, intercede, secede

---

EXERCISE 3   Writing Words with *ie* and *ei*

Fill in the blank in each word below with the letters *ie* or *ei* to spell the word correctly. Use a dictionary as needed.

EX.   1. ach _ie_ ve

1. rec _____ pt
2. p _____ ce
3. gr _____ f
4. handkerch _____ f
5. n _____ ce
6. p _____ r
7. f _____ ld
8. s _____ zed
9. br _____ f

10. th _____ r
11. f _____ rce
12. fr _____ nd
13. f _____ gn
14. ch _____ f
15. b _____ ge
16. c _____ ling
17. n _____ ther
18. sl _____ gh

19. bel _____ f
20. pr _____ st
21. counterf _____ t
22. w _____ rd
23. sh _____ ld
24. r _____ ndeer
25. y _____ ld

EXERCISE 4   Proofreading a Paragraph to Correct Spelling Errors

The paragraphs below contain ten spelling errors. Underline the misspelled words, and write the correct spelling above each misspelled word. Some sentences may contain no errors.

EX.   [1] For first prize in the science fair, I recieved tickets to go whale

watching.

received

[1] Whale watching is something my freind Jake and I had always wanted to do, so I proceded to sign us up for the first available trip. [2] As we left the harbor and the land receeded from veiw, all the passengers on the whale-watching boat grew excited. [3] Two sceintists who study whales were on board. [4] They provided interesting information, and they also interceeded in discussions. [5] For example, two people got into an argument about which were larger, modern whales or the anceint dinosaurs.

[6] The scientists said that this year they were seeing fewer whales. [7] The preceeding day, they had spotted only one humpback whale, but this day they were hoping to see more. [8] The passengers acceeded to the scientists' request that we scan the horizon for whales. [9] After only ten minutes, something happened that I could not beleive. [10] The water rippled, and a giant humpback leaped out of the water.

Cartoon by Jim Willoughby, in *The Rotarian*, August 1969, p. 16. Reprinted by permission of *The Rotarian*.

"IS IT ⊙ BEFORE ⨆, EXCEPT AFTER 𝍥, OR..."

PREFIXES AND SUFFIXES

A *prefix* is a letter or a group of letters added to the beginning of a word to change its meaning.

24d   When adding a prefix to a word, do not change the spelling of the word itself.

EXAMPLES   re + assure = **re**assure   super + human = **super**human
            un + tie = **un**tie   under + sea = **under**sea
            il + legal = **il**legal   over + rate = **over**rate

A *suffix* is a letter or a group of letters added to the end of a word to change its meaning.

24e   When adding the suffix –*ness* or –*ly* to a word, do not change the spelling of the word itself.

EXAMPLES   lean + ness = lean**ness**   great + ness = great**ness**
            glad + ly = glad**ly**   habitual + ly = habitual**ly**

NOTE   For most words that end in *y*, change the *y* to *i* before adding –*ly* or –*ness*. One-syllable adjectives ending in *y* usually follow rule 24e.

> EXAMPLES   ordinary + ly = ordinar**ily**   dry + ly = dry**ly**
>   empty + ness = empt**iness**   shy + ness = shy**ness**

24f   Drop the final silent *e* before a suffix beginning with a vowel.

Vowels are the letters *a, e, i, o, u,* and sometimes *y.* All other letters of the alphabet are *consonants.*

> EXAMPLES   use + able = us**able**   create + ive = creat**ive**
>   write + er = writ**er**   amaze + ing = amaz**ing**

EXCEPTIONS   Keep the final silent *e*
• in words ending in *ce* or *ge* before a suffix beginning with *a* or *o*: *peaceable, courageous*
• in *dye* and in *singe* before –*ing*: *dyeing, singeing*
• in *mile* before –*age*: *mileage*

24g   Keep the final silent *e* before a suffix beginning with a consonant.

> EXAMPLES   fate + ful = fate**ful**   noise + less = noise**less**
>   late +ly = late**ly**   awe + some + awe**some**

EXCEPTIONS   argue + ment = argu**ment**   true + ly = tru**ly**
              judge + ment = judg**ment**   nine+ th = nin**th**

EXERCISE 5   Spelling Words with Prefixes and Suffixes

On the lines below, complete the word problem by adding the given prefix or suffix to the word. Use a dictionary as needed.

EX.   1. re + arrange   _rearrange_

1. un + do   _____   11. open + ness   _____
2. kind + ness   _____   12. notice + able   _____
3. re + make   _____   13. merry + ly   _____
4. become + ing   _____   14. re + discover   _____
5. un + intentional _____   15. advantage + ous _____
6. wise + ly   _____   16. dis + appoint   _____
7. mile + age   _____   17. final + ly   _____
8. im + mortal   _____   18. store + ed   _____
9. sure + ly   _____   19. im + material   _____
10. il + logical   _____   20. dense + ly   _____

EXERCISE 6   Spelling Words with Suffixes

On the lines below, complete the word problem by adding the given suffix to the word. Use a dictionary as needed.

EX.   1. silly + ness   _silliness_

1. mediate + or   _____   11. dose + age   _____
2. judge + ment   _____   12. busy + ly   _____
3. brave + ly   _____   13. cleanly + ness   _____
4. care + ful   _____   14. continue + ous   _____
5. active + ity   _____   15. happy + ly   _____
6. practical + ly   _____   16. moderate + ion   _____
7. outrage + ous   _____   17. interesting + ly _____
8. heavy + ness   _____   18. note + able   _____
9. time + less   _____   19. hopeful + ly   _____
10. real + ly   _____   20. fascinate + ion _____

24h   For words ending in *y* preceded by a consonant, change the *y* to *i* before any suffix that does not begin with *i*.

EXAMPLES   forty + eth = fort**ieth**   glory + ous = glor**ious**
             reply + ed = repl**ied**   rely + able = rel**iable**
EXCEPTIONS   shy + ly = shy**ly**   sly + ness = sly**ness**

24i   For words ending in *y* preceded by a vowel, keep the *y* when adding a suffix.

EXAMPLES   play + ful = play**ful**   array + ed = array**ed**
EXCEPTIONS   lay + ed = la**id**   gay + ly = ga**ily**

24j   Double the final consonant before adding a suffix that begins with a vowel if the word (1) has only one syllable or has the accent on the final syllable and (2) ends in a single consonant preceded by a single vowel.

EXAMPLES   run + er = run**ner**   grab + ed = grab**bed**
             sit + ing = sit**ting**   big + est = big**gest**

Do not double the final consonant unless the word satisfies both of the conditions.

EXAMPLES   near + est = near**est**   feel + ing = feel**ing**
             clean + er = clean**er**   fear + ed = fear**ed**

For some words, the final consonant may or may not be doubled. Either spelling is acceptable.

EXAMPLES   cancel + ed = cance**led** *or* cancel**led**
             program + er = progra**mer** *or* program**mer**

EXERCISE 7   Spelling Words with Suffixes

On your own paper, complete the word problem by adding the given suffix to the word.

EX.   1. fly + ing
       1. flying

1. cook + ing
2. funny + er
3. bat + ed
4. marry + ing
5. treat + ed
6. near + est
7. joy + ful
8. fair + est
9. ship + ed
10. put + ing
11. smart + er
12. coy + ness
13. sunny + er
14. sail + ing
15. wary + ly
16. hop + ing
17. pair + ed
18. red + est
19. sled + ing
20. carry + ed

EXERCISE 8   Proofreading to Correct Spelling in a Composition

In the paragraphs below, underline the twenty spelling errors. Write the correct
spelling above each misspelled word. Some sentences may contain no errors.

EX.   [1] We have been <u>studiing</u> the legend of Atlantis, the lost continent.
studying (written above "studiing")

[1] Ordinaryly, I am not very interested in science fiction or mythology, but
this story fascinates me. [2] Atlantis, some people believe, was a mysteryous
continent that existed thousands of years ago. [3] No one is exactly sure of the
beginings of the Atlantis story. [4] However, varyous ancient accounts
describe Atlantis and how it vanished. [5] The Greek philosopher Plato told a
story about a beautyful island that existed in the Atlantic Ocean long before
his time. [6] He described great cities and people living in prosperity and
happyness on this island. [7] Then an earthquake occured. [8] The earthquake
destroied the island, and it sank beneath the sea.

[9] An extraordinaryly popular account of the Atlantis story was written
by Ignatius Donnelly and published in 1882. [10] He believed that the first
people in Europe, Asia, and the Americas were colonists who had sailled
from Atlantis. [11] Donnelly portraied their gloryous, lost civilization.

[12] Jules Verne creatted his own version of Atlantis in his novel *Twenty
Thousand Leagues Under the Sea*. [13] The novel tells of the adventures of Captain
Nemo and his submarine. One scene describes a visit to Atlantis.

[14] Other writers have called the lost continent Lemuria and have located
it nearrer to Asia than to Europe. [15] A retired British army officer wrote four
books in which he tryed to persuade people that there had been a lost
civilization called Lemuria, or Mu. [16] He claimmed he had seen tablets
written by the people of Mu. [17] According to his story, the tablets were kept
in monasterys in India.

[18] Did the lost continent really exist, and is it today traped beneath the
ocean? [19] You might think that this idea is terrifiing or impossible.
[20] There is no deniing, however, that the idea is intriguing.

PLURALS OF NOUNS

24k Form the plurals of most nouns by adding –s.

SINGULAR	car	tree	radio	tent	president
PLURAL	cars	trees	radios	tents	presidents

24l Form the plurals of nouns ending in s, x, z, ch, or sh by adding –es.

SINGULAR	beach	blintz	fox	bush	mess
PLURAL	beaches	blintzes	foxes	bushes	messes

NOTE Proper nouns usually follow these rules, too.

EXAMPLES Ericksons   Navarros
          Davises   Lopezes

EXERCISE 9   Spelling the Plurals of Nouns

On the line after each noun, write the correct plural form.

EX. 1. stitch _stitches_

1. waltz _____
2. valley _____
3. dime _____
4. Forster _____
5. mountain _____
6. song _____
7. radish _____
8. glass _____
9. Martinez _____
10. turtle _____
11. lunch _____
12. wish _____
13. idea _____

14. box _____
15. Katz _____
16. dancer _____
17. Morrison _____
18. watch _____
19. inventor _____
20. dish _____
21. dress _____
22. Ross _____
23. fez _____
24. benefit _____
25. march _____

24m Form the plurals of nouns ending in *y* preceded by a consonant by changing the *y* to *i* and adding *–es.*

SINGULAR   story   sky   theory   city   party
           stor**ies**   sk**ies**   theor**ies**   cit**ies**   part**ies**

EXCEPTION   With proper nouns, simply add *–s.*

       EXAMPLES   the Chomskys, the Kerrys

24n Form the plurals of nouns ending in *y* preceded by a vowel by adding *–s.*

SINGULAR   boy   tray   turkey   Monday   convoy
   PLURAL   boys   trays   turkeys   Mondays   convoys

24o Form the plurals of most nouns ending in *f* by adding *–s.* The plurals of some nouns ending in *f* or *–fe* are formed by changing the *f* to *v* and adding *–es.*

SINGULAR   staff   roof   cliff   leaf   elf   wife
   PLURAL   staffs   roofs   cliffs   lea**ves**   el**ves**   wi**ves**

NOTE   When you are not sure how to spell the plural of a noun ending in *f* or *fe*, check the spelling in a dictionary.

EXERCISE 10   Spelling the Plurals of Nouns

On the line after each noun, write the correct plural form. Use a dictionary as needed.

EX.   1. belief   _beliefs_

1. wolf _____
2. Tuesday _____
3. essay _____
4. carafe _____
5. trophy _____
6. Kelly _____
7. enemy _____
8. knife _____
9. life _____
10. penny _____

11. laundry _____
12. lamp _____
13. wharf _____
14. monkey _____
15. chief _____
16. Hardy _____
17. baby _____
18. reef _____
19. journey _____
20. folly _____

24p   Form the plurals of nouns ending in *o* preceded by a vowel by adding *–s*. Form the plurals of many nouns ending in *o* preceded by a consonant by adding *–es*.

SINGULAR	patio	stereo	veto	potato	tomato
PLURAL	patios	stereos	vetoes	potatoes	tomatoes

EXCEPTIONS	silos	photos	burritos

Form the plurals of most musical terms ending in *o* by adding *–s*.

SINGULAR	piano	concerto	solo	oratorio
PLURAL	pianos	concertos	solos	oratorios

NOTE   To form the plurals of some nouns ending in *o* preceded by a consonant, you may add either *–s* or *–es*.

SINGULAR	grotto	mosquito	cargo
PLURAL	grottos	mosquitos	cargos
	or	*or*	*or*
	grottoes	mosquitoes	cargoes

NOTE   When you are not sure how to spell the plural of a noun ending in *o*, check the spelling in a dictionary.

24q   The plurals of a few nouns are formed in an irregular manner.

SINGULAR	mouse	ox	man	goose	foot
PLURAL	mice	oxen	men	geese	feet

24r   Form the plural of a compound noun consisting of a noun plus a modifier by making the modified noun plural.

SINGULAR	attorney-at-law	passerby	editor in chief	blueprint
PLURAL	attorneys-at-law	passersby	editors in chief	blueprints

EXERCISE 11   Spelling the Plurals of Nouns

On the line after each noun, write its correct plural form. Use a dictionary as needed.

EX.   1. solo   _solos_

1. igloo   _____
2. lasso   _____
3. soprano   _____
4. radio   _____
5. cello   _____

6. louse   _____
7. child   _____
8. father-in-law   _____
9. hairdo   _____
10. runner-up   _____

EXERCISE 12   Proofreading to Correct Spelling Errors in Sentences

In the sentences below, underline the spelling errors. Write the correct spelling above each misspelled word. Some sentences may contain no errors.

EX.   1.   All the <u>childs</u> in the Kelly family are musical.
children

1. Two rooms in their house are used as music studioes.

2. Passerbys often pause to listen to Cara and her brother when they play their pianos.

3. Cara has played concertoes and other symphonic pieces with the local symphony orchestra.

4. Cara says that most of her heros are musicians.

5. I have seen photoes in the newspaper of Cara's sister and mother, who perform together.

6. They are both sopranoes and love to sing opera.

7. Both of Cara's sisters-in-laws have become interested in music.

8. The family made a recording, and discs jockeys in our town often play selections from it.

9. Each year the Kellys perform soloes at a concert in our town.

10. This concert is so popular that even the threat of tornadoes wouldn't keep people from coming to it.

EXERCISE 13   Using Plurals Correctly

On your own paper, write a sentence for each word below, using that word's plural form. Use a dictionary as needed.

EX.   1.   notary public
     1.   All three notaries public will certify documents for free.

1. looker-on
2. foot
3. piano
4. mosquito
5. echo
6. burrito
7. pueblo
8. goose
9. halo
10. two-year-old
11. cameo
12. tooth
13. tomato
14. brother-in-law
15. alto
16. barrio
17. torpedo
18. firefighter
19. woman
20. veto
21. soprano
22. hero
23. runner-up
24. bookshelf
25. zero

CHAPTER REVIEW

A. Correcting Spelling Errors in Sentences

Underline all misspelled words in each sentence below. Then write the words correctly on your own paper.

EX. 1. This recipe calls for green <u>tomatos</u>.
    1. *tomatoes*

1. Volunteers worked all day preparing releif packages for the victims of the storm.

2. Every year my nephew waits to see Santa Claus and his riendeer.

3. My mother is always saying, "If at first you don't sucede, try again."

4. After the second-string quarterback scored three touchdowns, the announcers agreed that they had underated his abilities.

5. The pharmacist wrote down the correct doseage for the medicine.

6. Although it was late and they were tired, the campers sat around their campfire, singing merrily.

7. Do you know which states seceded from the Union?

8. Cho Yia's couragous act was highly praised.

9. My favorite poems have a timless quality to them.

10. Fortunately, Lian had remembered to bring along a magnifiing glass.

11. I find my new daily planner very usful.

12. The coollest spot in the yard was under the old oak tree.

13. When the famous bater stepped up to the plate, the crowd roared in anticipation.

14. In this area of South America, the visitors found many ranchs and farms.

15. Rosa dropped her keyes in the snow, and it took quite a while to find them.

16. Joe Santiago is new to my school, and the Santiagoes have invited several families in the neighborhood to a block party this Saturday.

17. The class made a study of the varieties of fish found in corals reefs.

18. Andrea is doing a report about the lifes of women politicians.

19. The ceremonys have been repeated every year.

20. As we called from the rim of the canyon, our echos filled the air.

B. Proofreading a Paragraph to Correct Spelling Errors

Underline the misspelled words in paragraph below, and write the correct spelling above each misspelled word. Some sentences may contain more than one error.

EX.   [1] The history of mountaineering is filled with *stories* ~~storys~~ of adventure.

[1] Some people beleive that mountaineering began in 218 B.C. when Hannibal crossed the Alps with nine thousand mans and thirty-seven elephants. [2] Another early mountain-climbing feat occured in 126 A.D., when Emperor Hadrian scalled Mt. Etna, in Italy, to see a sunrise. [3] The sport of mountaineering really had its begining, however, in the 1800s, when people tryed to climb the great peaks of the Alps. [4] Between 1854 and 1865, climbers suceded in reaching the summits of 180 previously unclimbed Alpine mountains. [5] Another range of mountains that began to recieve attention from mountaineers at this time was the Himalayas, the tallest mountains in the world. [6] One of the great mysterys of mountaineering is the story of George Mallory and Andrew Irvine, who tried to climb the world's highest mountain, Mt. Everest, in 1924. [7] They disappeared as they were nearring the summit, and no one knows if they actually reached the top. [8] That acheivement was accomplished officially in 1953 by Edmund Hillary and Sherpa Tenzing Norgay. [9] No matter how carefully climbers plan their ascent, they are still at the mercy of sudden changes in the weather. [10] But the thrill of reaching one of the highest places in the world seems to make up for the riskes these climbers take.

C. Creating a Spelling Lesson

You have volunteered to teach English to newly arrived immigrants. Your task is to help them understand the rules of English spelling. Choose two of the spelling rules from this chapter to present to your students. On your own paper, write each rule and provide examples. Then, for each rule, make up an exercise that contains at least five items. List the answers on a separate piece of paper.

EX.   1.   RULE: Write *ie* when the sound is long *e*, except after *c*.
EXAMPLES: achieve, receive, brief, ceiling
EXERCISE 1 Spelling Words with *ie* and *ei*
On the line in each word, write *ie* or *ei* to spell the word correctly.
EX. s *ei* ze